Sociological Inquiry
and
Legal Phenomena

CLIVE GRACE AND
PHILIP WILKINSON

COLLIER MACMILLAN·LONDON

COLLIER MACMILLAN LIMITED
Stockley Close, West Drayton,
Middlesex UB7 9BE
and at Sydney, Auckland, Toronto, Johannesburg,

an affiliate of Macmillan Publishing Co. Inc.,
New York

First published 1978

ISBN 0 02 977310 5

Filmset in 'Monophoto' Baskerville 10 on 12 pt. and
printed in Great Britain by
Richard Clay (The Chaucer Press), Ltd.,
Bungay, Suffolk

To Madge, Wass and Lesley Grace, and Margaret, Ernest and Ray Wilkinson, and to our wider families and friends.
And to Murph.

ACKNOWLEDGEMENTS

This book was conceived, and many of the ideas developed, during a period of doctoral research at the Centre for Socio-legal Studies, Oxford. Our time there was funded by the S.S.R.C. under the auspices of the Sociology and Law Sub-Committee. We would like to acknowledge their support and that of the staff at the Centre, and to express our thanks for the opportunity to think through the issues we have addressed.

Work for the Nuffield Foundation under the direction of Pauline Morris enabled us further to test some of the ideas expressed in Chapter Six and facilitated their refinement, and at various stages of preparation Ross Cranston and Martin Albrow provided helpful criticism.

Finally, and in lighter vein, we would like to thank the anonymous law student who, reading an early draft being used by the authors to teach the sociology of law, was prompted to insert the following message between the poorly photocopied pages:

'H.M. Govt. warning:
  This document liable to fuddle the brain and ruin the eyes.
                                 D.P.P.'

We hope that the substantial changes made following this and other student comments will have resulted in a presentation which remains true to sociology but which avoids gratuitous sociological mystification.

Clive Grace and Philip Wilkinson
Oxford, 1977

CONTENTS

Weber on Methodology—the scheme of ideal types—the typology of action—problems in Weber's methodology.

Weber on Law:—Weber's definition of law—ideal types of legitimate orders—the nature of legal rationality—the importance of subjective rights—the relationship between law and capitalism.

Conclusion to Durkheim and Weber—the relationship of their sociologies to the sociology of law—Durkheim and normative, and Weber and interpretive, sociology.

Part Two

Parsons—the nature of Parsonian functionalism—law as a normative phenomena—law as an instrument of social control—the conditions of law's effectiveness—the problems of legitimacy, sanctions, jurisdiction and interpretation.

Bredemeier—law as an integrative mechanism—his relationship to Parson's analysis—the adaptive, goal pursuance and pattern maintenance processes in relation to law.

Renner—Marx's analysis of law—legal positivism and Marx's economic theory—the functions of law—the changing functions of the institutions of property.

Chambliss and Seidman—the conflict perspective—conflict and functionalist views of law and society—the conflict analysis of law creation and adjudication.

Selznick—the relationship of law to society—sociology and the quest for legality—'responsive' law.

Law and Society: Commentary—the subject-matter addressed by the work—law as law—law as a species of social norm. The thwarting of the dialectic—the parallels between functionalist and conflict perspectives on law.

Conclusion—the convergence of opposing accounts of law—Renner and Durkheim.

The nature of the work—the themes identified by Treves and Schur.

Law and Social Change—terminological difficulties—normative and structural change—conditions for the legal promotion of social change—avenues of investigation.

Social Stratification—law, stratification and power—lawyers as an elite group.

Studies of Legislation—analytic schemes for study of the emergence and implementation of legislation—the conflict/power model—the work of Aubert, Carson and Lukes.

The Legal Profession—professions and the wider society—trait and functionalist theories—the client in theories of the profession—the ethnography of the profession.

Interpretive sociology and the study of law—temptations to be avoided in the sociological study of law.

INTRODUCTION

Aspiring sociologists of law, as well as that greater profusion of students seeking a limited understanding of the sociological approach to law for examination or other purposes, both encounter a paternal intransigence amongst the authors who compete for their attention. For whilst numerous publications attempt a sociological account of the legal aspects of society, there has been little preparedness to detail fully the sociological bases on which those accounts have been generated and according to which their validity must be assessed. Sociology is an unknown quantity in much of the contemporary sociology of law. In a very general sense it is the purpose of this book to supply the missing sociological dimension.

In pursuing this task we have taken a hard line against the sociological pretensions of much contemporary work and have tried to understand why the founding fathers of sociology failed to create a bedrock for the sub-discipline on which an unfolding development could have been based. We take issue not only with the parameters of the sociology of law as presently constituted and as envisioned by its many sponsors but also with the limitations of functionalism, conflict theory and behaviourism, which remain the major avenues pursued by those practitioners determined to lift the sub-discipline from its retreat into a branch of eclectic social policy. The infusion of sociology into the sub-discipline along these avenues could only lead to an over muscular normative sociology: perhaps a fitting end to a discipline which has constantly taken law to be the social norm par excellence.

In our view the critical problem for the sociology of law is to escape from the prevailing emphasis on normative analysis and conceptions. By stressing the sociological core of social action we are able not only to show the limitations of normative sociology and the research to which it has given rise, but also to generate an alternative programme of work. The alternative sociology of law accepts itself for what it is— simply the study of *social action* as it pertains to legal events and arenas; and it also accepts that the study of social action can only be pursued through the means furnished by interpretive sociological approaches.

This task of redirecting the sociology of law has been accomplished within the framework of a general textbook on the subject. There is little programmatics to be found within the following pages, and the criticisms we make provide a unifying theme rather than a cathartic experience for the authors' or readers' benefit. Further, the book had to become a basic text in sociological theory. An appreciation of sociological perspectives as they have, or have not, informed the sociology of law shows that development can proceed without losing the benefit of studies of sociological value already undertaken.

We have allowed the purposes of a general text to dictate not only the content of this work, but also its format; the extent to which arguments develop through the pages provides the unifying theme which we regard as essential.

In Chapter I we review contemporary proponents of the sociology of law and show how they operate under a faulty conception of the nature and capacity of social science research. We then relate our own view of the sub-discipline as 'fragmented' and lay out the structure of this fragmentation around both empirical and methodological issues. Such issues are drawn together and the sociology of law placed in the framework of ongoing debates within sociology itself. Partly as a corrective to this initial emphasis on contemporary work, but, more importantly, as a recognition of their sociological stature, Chapter II reviews the sociologies of law of Durkheim and Weber. The review covers their methodological treatises as well as their empirical work.

In Chapters III and IV we provide a commentary on contemporary work. The reviews aim to give the student a broad knowledge of the field and its sociological components. We have endeavoured to limit the number of authors and works reviewed in order that comment can be both full and understandable. At the same time the chapters are more than a collation of work done. Each chapter organizes the work around those issues raised in Chapter I in order that our own arguments and criticism can be clearly developed.

These four chapters comprise the first two parts of the book and for them we would claim only limited originality. We have laid out the components of the sociology of law in a fashion not previously available and have marked the areas where criticism is most to be applied.

In Part Three we begin more strongly to advocate and develop an alternative approach. Chapter V analyses the basic sociological perspectives most often encountered in, or lying behind, the sub-discipline; these are the perspectives of positivism, behaviourism and functionalism. Further, it contains an analysis of perspectives which have not as yet informed the sociology of law; these are the perspectives of symbolic interactionism, phenomenological sociology and ethnomethodology. We have been concerned, not to synthesize these three latter perspectives but to display a potential within their basic tenets to answer the problems inhering within the sociology of law. Having identified this potential we then conclude the chapter with an appraisal of both normative and interpretive sociology on those issues most pertinent to the future development of the sub-discipline. In Chapter VI we continue the argument by indicating the properties of a concept of law informed by interpretive approaches. We build up from a concept of law as a 'categorization of experience' into a piece of empirical work guided by this concept.

The reorientation offered, then, is neither tentative nor speculative. It is argued for from an understanding of how interpretive analysis departs from those analyses conventionally undertaken. By marking the differences with reference to a piece of empirical work we can also show the capacity of interpretive analysis to survive the exigencies of actual research situations.

We should also say a word on what we have *not* done. This book does not offer any discussion of jurisprudence, criminology or anthropology of law. The reason is in part one of space; to make the book possible we had to draw boundaries which are in a sense artificial. Equally, there is such a range of literature on those subjects that we would not have been able to do justice to their wealth of ideas and materials. But there are more than purely pragmatic reasons. Our purpose was to highlight the sociological as the reference point and related areas must in a sense take care of themselves. They would only serve to distract attention from our main concern.

Finally, we have recognised in writing the text that it will be used by students of varying backgrounds and experience. In particular it may be used by students of both sociology and of law. To those who come to the book with little or no sociological background we suggest a second reading of certain chapters, especially One, Five and Six, at a point when the substantive work of the middle sections has been digested.

PART I
CHAPTER I

Discovering the Sociology of Law

Observers of the sociology of law might be forgiven for imagining that the discipline has much in common with a shy débutante. Eligible practitioners wait for her to shed all philosophic garb and accept the mantle of sociological propriety. For several decades the air has been punctuated by calls for a sociology of law, but to the extent that such calls continue we can only assume that the sub-discipline lingers in the shadows at a time when it should be bathing in the limelight of concentrated sociological attention.

That the field has yet to come of age is reflected in the programmatic statements for development still appearing in the literature. We are asked to accept that insufficient development has taken place for sponsorship to be replaced by the implementation of the project. Whereas Pound could write in 1907 of the 'need of sociological jurisprudence',[1] Timasheff in 1937 that 'there is room for a sociology of law'[2] and Gurvitch in 1947 that 'the sociology of law is still in full course of formulation',[3] it was possible for Schwarz to introduce a series of essays in the sociology of law in 1965 as 'the birth of a new sub-discipline within American sociology'[4] and in 1972 it was still being said, this time by Morris,[5] that 'the sociological perspective has so far been ignored: the sociologists have made only a belated appearance on the scene'.

The more recent callers do appreciate that the absence of development should occasion surprise.[6] Given the prominence of law as a social phenomenon and the desire of many practitioners for its inclusion in the sociological prospectus, underdevelopment is regarded with academic concern. There is a keen sense that the multiplicity of institutions, personnel and activities which constitute and surround the legal system should have provided almost unlimited opportunities for sociological research. Quite apart from the areas of inquiry which the law may afford as a result of its peculiar character, it appears to be thought that a mere transfer of existing sociological questions from traditional substantive areas to that of law would create sufficient research projects to engage the sociological beavers for all time.

Such engagement is a possibility, but not one to be viewed with professional pride. It would simply reproduce the many problems of sociology as presently undertaken. Sociology is a contested, we would say fragmented, discipline. It is contested at the levels of theory, method, technique and epistemology. Asserting the need for application of sociology to the phenomena of law does not provide a firm base for development of the sub-discipline. Disagreements are no more likely to be settled by virtue of being transferred to a new venue.

The availability of multiple sociologies, then, militates against simple endorsement of the call. Sociologists of law dupe themselves and their audience if they represent sociology as an unproblematic tool for the study of law. Moreover, the deception is compounded if law is taken as an unproblematic object of study. Law is often taken as the subject-matter of the sociology of law. To deny this may seem an outrage, but it will be denied here. The assumed eminence of law for study, given its concrete existence, permanence and facticity, has contributed an unreflective attitude towards the sociological enterprise, particularly on matters pertaining to the nature of social phenomena. Obviously a sociology is always of something (education, organizations, family, deviance, etc.) but the sub-disciplines must in some way remain a common enterprise. It is only by reference to a common subject-matter that we can provide criteria for identifying work undertaken from a sociological perspective. The breakdown of sociology into sub-disciplines is a matter of convenience, the subject-matter remains the same.

What we will argue in the present chapter is that if the sociology of law has not developed, immaturity should be located in the failure both to appreciate the importance of competing sociologies and to approach law in a sociological manner. The chapter discusses the nature of the sociological enterprise, the subject-matter of sociology and the relation between sociology and its sub-disciplines. We address our conception of the present state of the sociology of law as 'fragmented' and review debates on competing approaches within sociology.

These are for us the major lines of inquiry fundamental to any appraisal, be it critical or appreciative, of work either published or in progress. We have endeavoured to keep the questions addressed overtly relevant to the sociology of law, but whenever general issues of sociology are on trial, the sociology of law is on trial also. We may usefully begin the task by reviewing in some detail the nature and rationale of the present call for a sociology of law, and its relationship to existing literature.

THE CALL FOR A SOCIOLOGY OF LAW

We can assume that the recognition of a lacuna in academic sociology developed along with an awareness not only of the importance of law in social life, but also of law as a social phenomenon, itself a valid object of study. Yet this is hardly a revelation. The founding fathers of sociology wrote extensively about the law in their understanding of the primary characteristics of modern society. For Weber, Durkheim and, though to a lesser extent, Marx, law was a social phenomenon of enormous significance. Each sought to comprehend law as an index of the nature of society, both as part of a body of writing encompassing the totality of forms of social relations, and as something to be accorded attention as a topic *sui generis*. Weber,[7] for instance, understood the development of law as one instance of the general drive towards rationality, his characterization of the stages of legal evolution parallelling the unfolding sequence of the nature of social organization—charismatic legal revelation; the creation of law by precedent; the imposition of law—so as to demonstrate in careful, lucid fashion the relationship of law to other forms of social relations and the distinctions to be made between the various types of law.

Durkheim's[8] analysis of law was similarly comprehensive. Law for Durkheim was a social fact par excellence, a set of social norms independent of individual actors in any given historical epoch. It was in this general framework that Durkheim was able to represent, for example, the change from repressive to restitutive law as part of the more general development from mechanical to organic solidarity as forms of social organization. Durkheim was then able to examine in greater detail the nature of punishment; the varying degrees of punishment; the function of crime and its relation to punishment and so on.

The conception of law held by Marx[9] was if anything even more dependent on his general theory than was the case for either Weber or Durkheim. Marx viewed law as an objectified social form, but one only comprehensible when understood as an ideological form, itself contingent upon the configuration of the forces and relations of production, the resultant class structure and the nature of the state. But law remained open to examination in terms of its effects on society, its relationship to social change, and its potential for use by the classes and warring factions of modern society.

If the Grand Masters of sociology paid such attention to law, and discussed legal phenomena in so many of their various guises, they would seem to have provided a foundation for a sociology of law which could be both erudite and systematic. But the callers for a sociology of law seek an alternative framework for their protégé, and this suggests that some other reason than lack of attention to law lies behind the claims that such a sub-discipline remains significant by its absence. Perhaps we can be helped by looking at the type of sociology of law being called for—in what manner is it different from the works of Weber and Durkheim?

Whilst no spurious uniformity need be portrayed, contemporary calls for a sociology of law do appear to stand on one common ground, that of 'relevance'. The sociology of law being advocated and anticipated is one with a potential for being relevant. We should know how the courts operate, in order to reform, criticize or lubricate the mechanism. We ought to know the effects of laws in order to advise the law-makers. We ought to study the operation of the law so that we can articulate demands for higher levels of law.[10]

Perhaps the most chilling statement of the 'relevance orientation' is put forward by Podgorecki.[11] For Podgorecki the 'main objective of sociological investigations into the functioning of law is to provide expert advice for social engineering, allowing for rational and effective remoulding of the human condition. The sociology of law makes an effort to shape its studies so as to make them useful for practical application.'[12] Such explicit acceptance of a handmaiden role for sociology is peculiar to Podgorecki. Other authors are more circumspect, or make claims to relevance more directed to assumed universal ideals rather than the pragmatism of the policy makers. Nevertheless the thrust of their programmes for the sociology of law carries identical implications. For instance, the programmatic statement given by Schur has a sociological framework; this is evidenced both in his assertion that 'relatively few areas of social life can be fully understood in all their complexity without some apprehension of their legal aspects'[13] and in his obviously sincerely held view that 'the analysis and understanding of a legal system as *such*, rather than the mere recognition of legal spects in selected areas of life, . . . is the primary concern of the sociology of law'.[14] When Schur suggests central research concerns, however, the relevance orientation to the sociology of law becomes apparent either in terms of the *effectiveness* of law for promoting social control or social change or, more concretely, in terms of the implications of empirical work for legal policy. Schur urges that sociology has 'at least a legitimate secondary interest in seeing that relevant data are put to socially beneficial use'.[15]

It is clear that there are at least two issues here. One is the issue of whether sociology can decide what is socially beneficial; the other is whether sociology should accept topics for investigation set by lay or professional conceptions of social problems. Schur is not arguing for the first but does seem happy that the sociology of law capitulate to questions allied to a social engineering view of law. The two issues are more clearly brought out if we look to the writings of Philip Selznick,[16] who sets up the sociology of law in such a fashion that, in time, it will be able to suggest 'ends meet for men' from which could be adduced, for instance, criteria of legality. At the same time, Selznick also suggests that for the moment, when choosing topics of research, the sociology of law should use its own methods and insights to answer questions relevant to the more effective operation of the legal order.

Morris's[17] statements about the purpose of the sociology of law indicate the pervasiveness of this relevance orientation. She begins by denying that her intention is to produce work relevant to those whose task is policy formulation and the efficacious distribution of available resources. She sees sociology as having its own perspective, a perspective which engages wider issues and which indeed questions the assumptions which underlie any particular instance of policy formulation or implementation. This questioning inquires into the social nature of law and the relationship of law to social change. We must agree that such lines of inquiry are consciously directed away from the narrow avenue of relevant research. However if we turn attention to the concrete, focused research which they are said to have inspired, we find that the main area reflects a concern with the provision of legal services and the sociological questioning of the lawyer's definition of 'unmet legal need'. Morris stressed the *social* parameters of that concept and one might therefore expect a sociological treatment of the issues. But rather than pursuing a sociological treatment Morris began a programme of research including the investigation of people's attitudes to legal services; the impact of discretion on the implementation of policy; the investigation of pressure groups as forces of reform; and the study of conflicting perceptions of clients and professionals so as to help explain the varying uses to which lawyers are put.

It should be clear that if such questions are provided by a

sociological perspective it is a sociological perspective in a strange guise. It certainly looks very different from Weber's interest in drives towards rationality or Durkheim's concern with forms of social solidarity, and yet both these writers pre-date Morris's concern with the social nature of law and the relation of law to social change. While Morris may avoid the use of sociologists as aids of government, the research provided by her perspective turns out to be totally 'relevance' inclined. The promoted lines of inquiry fail to express the claimed sociological commitment.

Our objection to the relevance orientation amongst the variety of authors calling for a sociology of law does not flow from a disparagement of the concerns which prompt a determination to contribute to useful knowledge. Rather, we feel that over-commitment to the study of legal problems only serves to obfuscate both sociology and also the pursuit of relevant knowledge. Mainly our concern is for sociology. First, the discipline can never serve as a science if it becomes an adjunct to social policy; and this is the case whatever our view of the ability of science to discover and demonstrate the values which a society should pursue. Secondly, sociological methods, to the extent that they constitute a distinctive compartment of scientific research, are designed for a particular purpose. This purpose is necessarily related to the topics of inquiry which this particular social science sets for itself. They are neither designed for, nor particularly necessary, if our task is to solve the problems of people who man the various institutions which as laymen we are willing to accept as important. The sociology of law must be inherently suspect if it is being asked to *acquire* relevant knowledge. We need not relinquish our view as members of society that knowledge be open to use, but as social scientists the criteria for asking questions and finding valid answers must stem from our science and from no other place. We would argue against the acquisition of socially beneficial knowledge, not from any unseemly purpose, but simply because it defeats the grounds on which sociology pursues and validates scientific knowledge.

Before leaving the call for sociology of law we need to note that a concern for 'relevance' is not their only common ground. There is also agreement on the barriers to development faced by the sub-discipline, those most frequently cited revolving around, first, the problems of inter-disciplinary study and second, the absence of any one sociology available for meting out to the sociological study of law.[18] Insofar as the second constitutes a part-recognition that sociology is not an unproblematic tool, we are inclined to view it sympathetically. But it cannot be a problem in respect of the underdevelopment of the sociology of law, for if it were, we would also be faced with under-developed sociologies of education, organizations, family and so on. It might indeed be the case that these sub-disciplines are under-developed, but in that case the 'problem' ceases to distinguish and will not assist in explanations of why a sociology of law in particular should lack maturity.

The first problem, of inter-disciplinary study, appears more sub-stantial, especially when it is borne in mind that lawyers possess their own theoretical discipline of jurisprudence from which to contest issues of interest to sociology. Indeed, jurists such as Pound have taken a lead in offering strong conceptions of the nature and course of the sociological contribution. Such considerations make readily com-prehensible the views of Zwingmann,[19] for instance, when he says that 'the future of the sociology of law in Germany very much depends on the extent to which it will be possible to persuade jurists and sociologists to work together in genuine collaboration'.[20] Zwingmann's position must also be understood in relation to the peculiar position in post-war Germany. Academic concerns in German universities reflected the problems of de-nazification and they were facing the politically central yet sensitive issue of the role of the jurists both under Nazism and under the new regime. The pleas for inter-disciplinary study, however, are not limited to countries with such overriding and immediate concerns. Reisman,[21] echoed by Schur,[22] expressed the same position in America and Vilhelm Aubert[23] has done the same for Europe.

Coming to terms with legal science is seen as taking several forms, be it clarifying the language utilized by sociologists and lawyers, examining the benefits that each discipline will bring to the union, or in general terms, how accommodation can best take place. The crucial distinction drawn between the sociology of law and other sub-disciplines is the idea that a sociology of law somehow faces peculiar problems in this respect. On reflection, however, it becomes apparent that other provinces of sociology have had to face up to the problem of accommodation to competing disciplines. The sociology of the family has accommodated to the psychology of small groups, the sociology of crime has accommodated to the psychology of criminal motivation, and political sociology, after a particularly protracted and bitter debate, has accommodated to political theory. The accom-modation, however, has not been achieved by capitulation. These sociologies have been able to develop autonomously, in opposition to competing theories, without taking their relevance structures from or being coopted by established sets of explanations within their chosen domain of study. The sociology of law can do likewise when it is appreciated that such an enterprise requires neither a union of sociologists and lawyers nor a commitment to intellectual imperialism. The crucial issue in the development of a sub-discipline does not relate either to the social relevance of the work produced or the relation to superficially similar concerns. The crucial issue will always be the types of questions asked and their derivation from a sociological rather than from any other perspective.

'Relevance' is a misdirection, and merely to accommodate or come to terms with a competing discipline can only provide the conditions for co-existence, not a framework for understanding the social world and the place of legal phenomena within it. We are arguing that development of the sociology of law revolves around questions as to the nature of the sociological enterprise rather than questions of social utility or how, as practising sociologists, we can best compete in the academic market place.

THE NATURE OF THE SOCIOLOGICAL ENTERPRISE

We want to make a strong claim that hitherto statements for a sociology of law have failed because they do not succeed in making contact with the subject-matter of inquiry and because they misconstrue the relationship between sociology and its sub-disciplines. We must now specify in more detail the nature and implications of these defects as they will be repeatedly stressed when reviewing contemporary work.

Subject-Matter: The subject-matter is the base in which to ground all inquiry. Most sociologists agree on the nature of the subject-matter, conceiving it as social action. Disagreement arises as to how one should study this subject-matter, both in terms of the correct use of theory and the legitimacy of available techniques of inquiry. To the extent, however, that academics address questions concerning social action they can be construed as sociologists.

Now what do we presume if we say that the subject-matter of sociology is social action? At this stage the important implication is not something to do with social action itself but that the subject matter of sociology is a *unified* subject-matter. If sociology is always construed as sociology of something, then what follows is no more than an everyday breakdown of the world into convenient packages. It is not the case that a sociology of law is an entirely different enterprise from the sociology of organizations. Such should be obvious if only because methods textbooks are not divided on this basis. The criteria for establishing good methods are predicated on the nature of the subject matter and that subject matter is not divisible into the common sense packages of law, family, deviance, organization and so on.

If the subject-matter of sociology, social action, is common to all sub-disciplines, then the sociology of law will fail to mature if it takes 'law' as the subject-matter and thereby fails to pay attention to the epistemological and methodological problems of producing any and all forms of sociological knowledge. Certain problems are central, although they await later sections of this chapter to be fully developed:

(a) the subject matter carries imperatives as to the appropriateness of the methodology used to study it;

(b) conversely, methods can become the master and decide for the sociologist what his subject matter is to be;

(c) presupposing or taking law to be the subject matter leads to an uncritical use of methods.

We can see, then, that if sociologists disagree as to how social action can be satisfactorily studied, the inherent unity of that subject-matter, however conceived, prevents sociologists of law from abdicating responsibility for the legitimacy of their chosen methods and topics of study. If the unity of the sociological subject matter is not to be prostituted to particular theories, particular techniques or particular problem-relevances then the whole procedure of generating statements (that is, the creation of theory, use of theory, creation of techniques and use of techniques, etc.) within the sociology of law must be treated as a methodological problem—one must be able to demonstrate that the statement was generated in a manner that reaches the subject-matter of sociology and therefore allows the sub-discipline to be entertained as a member of the sociological family.

Sociology and its Sub-Disciplines

The unity of the subject matter allows for a recognition, long awaited, of the *relation between sociology and particular sub-disciplines*. This relationship is frequently conceptualized either as analogous to that holding between a tree and its branches, or as hierarchical. In the first case the branch is dependent on the main discipline, though integral to it. In the second, the sub-discipline is subordinate to the main theoretical body of knowledge, from which theory is meted out according to the availability of pure sociological knowledge and method.

In our view the true nature of the relationship is neither of the above; rather the relationship is dialectical. Briefly, we mean that any investigation in a particular sub-discipline should enable one to gain greater understanding of the sociological subject-matter. In turn, this can enlighten the sociological endeavour to the extent that greater understanding of the subject matter will help to refine and reform the methods of study.

So, this far we have argued that the sociological subject-matter is unitary (though people may conceive it in different terms) and that there must always be a dialectical relationship between the studies of any one sub-discipline of sociology and sociology itself (though that discipline may mean different things to different people). We are, however, claiming that these two points are closely related; that the dialectic must reach down to the level of social action. There is no reason why the dialectic will prosper automatically and there is a distinction to be drawn between the dialectic operating with an ability to shed light on the nature of social action and operating but failing to so illuminate. The distinction arises in the varying relationships between the subject-matter of sociology and the statements which we as sociologists make in respect of that subject-matter. A typology of possible statements might include behaviourist, functionalist, Marxist, positivist, interpretive and other types, each type of statement having a particular methodological and theoretical relationship with the sociological subject-matter. The relationships differ, not because *communality* of subject-matter is in doubt, but because the basic agreement that sociology addresses social action is not reproduced at the level of theory or method.

If sociological attention is focused on law through functionalist spectacles, for instance, the dialectic will continue to operate after a fashion, for such study can certainly illuminate the tenets of the theory used. But unless the theory is properly linked to social action in the first instance, it cannot feed back knowledge of any greater applicability. It cannot escape from the assumptions built into the theory—in the case of functionalism, assumptions that social action is captive in a series of functional pre-requisites for social order and that the subjective point of view of social actors is not essential. Bredemeier's investigation of law as an integrative mechanism,[24] research pursued within the functionalist framework, provided a feedback for functionalist theory itself, but was unable to transcend this level. The dialectic operates but is short-circuited because we learn nothing about the nature of social action, only about the content of the functionalist framework.

Harvesting the full fruits of the dialectic depends upon the manner of making contact with the subject-matter. Establishing this linkage is a matter of establishing a valid methodological stance towards the chosen area of concern. Given the nature of sociology contact has to be made with a substantive field, but this should be without the imposition of assumptions which restrict the sociological vision. Such assumptions may take the form of an adoption of a pre-existing theoretical edifice (the functionalist framework), common sense (law is a social constraint) or an assumed applicability of questions taken from a problem-hierarchy (issue of relevance). Within each there are, of course, many levels at which one could attempt to make the necessary contact with the subject matter of study. The five following levels are all to be seen in the literature:

(a) The choice of a particular theory which suggests topics of study. At this level one may take functionalist theory or an aspect of such theory and locate the subject-matter within its terms. This is the method of Bredemeier when adopting a view of law as a societal integration mechanism. It would also be possible to approach the subject-matter with a view to testing a theoretical proposition. This would necessitate locating the subject-matter within the concepts out of which the proposition was constructed. Similar problems would here arise as with the Bredemeier example. The internal logic of a theory is no demonstration that the theory manages to gear into the empirical world.   [Kelsen's Pure Theory of Law]

(b) Perhaps after having chosen a theory or maybe in place of a theory, initial statements concerning the subject-matter may be made to characterize those particular features of the subject-matter with which the research is concerned. 'Law is a form of social control' acts as such a statement for both Parsons and Black.[25] For one it underpins the place of law within an overarching scheme; for the other it serves to generate issues concerning the interaction of this particular form of social control and other aspects of social life. In both cases, however, one construct, 'law', has been replaced by another, 'social control'. The latter stems from sociology and serves to underline that sociology may take a jaundiced eye to constructs such as 'law' that have a place in everyday terminology. It at least gives a sociological gloss. It does not, however, reach social action if it contains, as in this particular example, assumptions as to the nature of the human behaviour representing the construct.

(c) Once having prepared initial statements with or without theory, the researcher will have certain questions that he wishes to be answered. Indeed this may in certain cases be the first step towards the subject-matter. The subject-matter will become lodged in the questions. If the research is to test a theory, the question may be phrased as a hypothesis, perhaps of a more general character (the relationship between law and social change) or of a more narrow character (the impact of a new law on a particular social phenomenon such as family structure or a particular social organization).

(d) Once the question has been posed, and this of course has already limited what the researcher will see as relevant, he will have to formulate a research design. He may decide on the survey, its structure depending on what his theory or his common sense sees as relevant. He may favour the questionnaire or may choose one or other variant of observation (participant or non-participant; open or covert). The choice may reflect a particular conception of sociology, but we need only note that the choice further determines what the researcher will be allowed to see. In the survey and questionnaire he will only have symbolic data and the subject-matter will have to be rendered unproblematic if to be set in a series of questions; with observation the research may be more open but it will still be up to the researcher to provide a scheme of interpreting field notes. The subject-matter will still be lodged within the chosen design.

(e) The design will have to be implemented, and here we can find a reliance on certain specified techniques provided by methodological textbooks (how to ask questions; how to observe) and particular techniques for the research at hand (what questions to ask; what situations to observe). At this level the subject-matter is represented in interviewee responses or conversation notes.

At each and all of these levels the processes used to provide questions and generate answers must be viewed as a methodological *problem*. And the problem must not be looked at as one of resolving bias or avoiding some other gremlin but of ensuring that the subject-matter remains the same at each level and at each level remains social action. It is very common for research to proceed from say 'functional prerequisites' at one level down to 'opinions' at the next without consideration being given to the relation of either to what sociology is supposed to be studying. Without such questioning the research can never allow the empirical world to break through the theoretical, conceptual or commonsensical façade. The dialectic can never prosper. By stressing the methodological problem and recognising that methods are only attuned to particular conceptions of social action, we are more able to allow any exercise in sociology, be it concerned with law or some other sub-discipline, to approach a unified subject-matter with an ability to both enlighten its nature and to question the view of the subject-matter on which the chosen methods are based.

To conclude this section we can recapitulate that neither a relevance orientation nor mere affirmation of a sociological intent can create a viable sociology of law. The reason is that neither necessarily are capable of enlightening the nature of the sociological subject-matter nor the relationship between discipline and sub-discipline which rests on such enlightenment. Making contact with the subject-matter, creating a methodology competent to generate valid statements, is a problematic and tortuous process, but influences everything else that follows. It is a problem too often ignored and one which has bedevilled the development of the sociology of law. In a general sense, the project of this book is to resolve this problem. It has created a fragmentation within the sub-discipline, both between and within levels of analysis, and the theories and techniques employed. To this we now turn.

FRAGMENTATION

Those who glibly take law to be the subject-matter of inquiry and who thereby disdain to enter controversy over the basis of sociological knowledge portray forcefully the misconstruction of the relationship between sociology and its sub-disciplines and bear a responsibility for the sociology of law's lack of methodic character. Lack of methodic character speaks of fragmentation, but in turn fragmentation itself breaks down into several component parts each of which will have to be traced through. The elements of fragmentation are:

(a) starting points for discussion;
(b) depictions of the field;
(c) the application of concepts, theories and methods.

The issues raised by the kaleidoscopic character of the sociology of law are germane to the purpose of sociology, the nature of its subject-matter and the criteria of validity to be utilized in assessing work claiming to be part of that sub-discipline.

The Starting Points

Conventionally, sociologists have taken four types of starting points for their study of law. The first is that which apprehends law as a phenomenon of everyday life. Law, according to this view, is everywhere. If we live an orderly life, then we are, in the main, obeying, consciously or unconsciously, the dictates of prescriptive legislation and case law, and in any event much of our activity is constructed within a framework erected, provided and sustained by law. Even a lack of contact with legal personnel does not obviate our inevitable contact with the law itself. Law constitutes a framework for ongoing, mundane existence. If our lives are characterized by unthinking contravention of legal codes, then our contact with the law is likely to be both more immediate and less satisfying. Either way, the law is held to be clearly of significance for us all. Such a starting point tends to elevate issues of 'relevance' for sociological scrutiny.

An alternative beginning is to be found in those authors taking law as important in itself. The very nature of law is significant to the extent that it finds expression in notions of obligation, of right, and of the legitimate authority of the state—all of which are held to impinge on social life. Topics generated by such a view revolve around issues such as the nature of legality, the attributes of natural law and the necessity for higher levels of law.

The third starting point for sociological study of law has been more sociological, the recognition that law is of importance as an element of one or other social theory. Just as the political system, the educational system, religion and the family are seen as key building blocks of social structure, so the legal system is appended to this anthology as a means of completing the picture, so to speak. Such a beginning produces characteristic terms of reference for inquiries into the relationship of law and social structure, law and social change and so on.

Finally certain authors have promised analysis of the social nature of law, the emphasis being a sociological study of law differentiated from sociological research on law, so as to become a fully-fledged sociology of law. Black for instance, promises 'a scientific analysis of legal life as a system of behaviour. The ultimate contribution of this enterprise would be a general theory of law.'[26] A similar thrust obtains in Schur's statement that 'it is the analysis and understanding of this legal system as such, rather than the mere recognition of legal aspects in selected areas of our social life, that is the primary concern of the sociology of law'.[27]

We have no wish to imply that any one starting point of the above four is *necessarily* linked with a relevance orientation, a natural scientific programme or any other specific approach, though within them we can identify a predilection for asking certain types of questions rather than others. The point to be made is that despite this variety of starting points, sociologists of law of whichever type, have displayed an uncritical acceptance of (or demurred to) the available and developed theories and methodologies. However they start out, author upon author arrives at a collection of topic areas (law and social change, law and social control, the profession, etc.) which are remarkably similar. Such collections of topics have accepted law and presumed sociology in a fashion which treats the sociological subject-matter as divisible and which denies the full possibilities of the dialectic.

Even when such topic collections are eschewed, a similar demur in the face of law and sociology obtains. A few illustrative examples will have to suffice. Skolnick attempts to hang at least part of the sociology of law on a peg taken from the literature concerning organizations. Skolnick says that '(It) is well known that organisations routinely experience a certain amount of deviance from rules. Indeed, empirical evidence from sociological studies of organisations suggests that as a matter of everyday fact organisations cannot function in terms of the rational model of bureaucracy posited by Weber—there is always a certain amount of variance, or so-called deviant behaviour, and much of it is accepted. The interesting question for a theory of law in society is to specify the point at which, or the conditions under which, distinctively legal controls come into operation.'[28] It only takes a little inquiry, however, to see not only that the sociology of organizations points to no such peg of sociological truth as the formal–informal rule distinction (it is, therefore, problematic to tie the sociology of law to such a framework) but also that such a position is even more invidious if it is accepted as an invitation for other sociologists to take alternative established 'sociological problems' and ask 'How does law relate to this?' A more fundamental basis for inquiry is required.

An example from a different source relates to Schur's acceptance of 'functional pre-requisites' for the maintenance of society. Schur in one place claims to question the very tenets of functional analysis and yet he is willing to serve the student not only the 'truth' of functional pre-requisites but also claim that the question of most importance for the sociology of law is '(to) what extent must these functions be served through "legal" mechanisms?'[29]

Finally it might be mentioned that Gibbs, in a fairly influential paper, asserts that the sociology of law has 'lost sight of the original paramount question: what is the relation between law and social order?'[30] Now this may well be a plea against fragmentation, but again if the student is not asked to face questions concerning how he is to conceptualize and treat 'law' and 'social order', then it serves at best only to unify the sociology of law around problematic concepts.

Depictions of the Field

We will continue to discuss the fragmentation within the sociology of law by looking at the manner in which the field is depicted by practitioners themselves. First, there are those authors who avoid any attempt to devine the sociology of law and only provide a picture of the sub-discipline organized around a congeries of substantive topics.

As an initial exercise, pass the eye over the contents pages of many of the available works in the sociology of law, works concerning law and society, the sociology of law, law and sociology, etc. The topics are remarkably similar, being broken down into such elements as 'sociology and jurisprudence'; 'law and social control'; 'law and stratification'; 'legal organization'; and so on. The fragmentation we have pointed to suggests that we should only unwillingly disparage such apparent uniformity of topics. When consensus is so rare, agreement, perhaps should be treasured. Yet, further examination of these works indicates that whilst the level of agreement may be high, the basis for agreement is tenuous. Presumably, criteria for inclusion of works in sociology of law texts or readers are utilized at some stage, and the similarity of topics suggests that the criteria operating are roughly similar. Perhaps then these authors and editors have a fairly clear idea as to what their field of study is. We would expect them to be able to state their principles of inclusion, possibly via the use of a definition of the field which informs their choices. What we in fact find is not only the absence of a statement of guiding principles, but the overt disavowal of the need for such a statement. In other words, there is marked agreement not only in practitioners' views of the content of the field but also in their uncertainty as to the nature of the project which engages them.

'. . . we have deliberately eschewed a formal definition of the field: given the amorphous state of this research such an effort would be premature'.

'Because this area of research is nearly still in its formative stages, at present it comprises a variety of somewhat diverse strands of research and theory . . .'[31]

The apparent paradox between (presumably) similar criteria for inclusion of work and similar topic breakdown on the one hand, and the reticence to state the nature of the project which links these works on the other, can on further reflection be resolved. Sociologists of law may eschew formal definitions, but this does not indicate an absence of guiding principles, merely a refusal to transcend commonsensical and uncritical notions of both law and sociology. It is the hegemony and universality of commonsense notions of the sociological study of law which produce the characteristic terms of reference for substantive topic breakdown. This failure to ponder, critically and reflectively, the nature of sociology provides the basis for an open-handed welcome to all and any of the fragments of contemporary sociology.

The substantive topic breakdown approach is more than a mere depiction of the field: it is fragmentation with two characteristics. First, it is an attempt to divide the subject-matter of the sub-discipline. It may be appreciated that sociology is concerned with human behaviour, but the sociology of law is seen as having *law* as its subject matter. This subject-matter can then be broken down internally (the profession, juries, etc.), and externally (law and . . .). The latter division involves the use of sociological concepts, for instance of class, stratification and power. The two levels may then interact, as in the relation of the profession to class and elitism. Secondly, it has the characteristic of being seen as in need of justification, perhaps in terms of convenience (the hegemony of common sense) or in terms of the stage of development so far reached by the sub-discipline—a stage at which it possesses an armoury of 'sociological methods'. Such methods are then seen as needing the guidance of concepts or a sociological model of society if the data generated is to be contributed to the comprehensive edifice whose existence, fortunately for us all, always lies somewhere in the future, a sort of sociological mañana.

Alternatively there are writers who depict the field by way of explicit definition. What, however, is meant by a definition of the field? In some senses it may be thought that the collection together of the various topic areas, if they are seen as subject-matter areas, should give the boundary of the sub-discipline and hence a definition of its contents. It is clear, however, that the similarity of breakdowns offered cannot stand as a definition. A definition, if it is to serve any purpose at all, must give criteria for inclusion or exclusion of particular work within the sub-discipline. Topic breakdown, however, is either a simple matter of convenience or has the heuristic function of establishing a hierarchy of importance of various topics as against others. In other words a substantive breakdown could never be concerned with the nature of particular studies, nor could it be co-terminous with the boundaries of the sociology of law.

Significantly, the depiction of the field following on from definition diverges from the common form outlined above. We have in mind such writers as Weber, Timasheff and Black.

Weber is perhaps best known for providing a definition of the sociology of law. He has a clear definition of law and a definition of sociology. The two, together, should provide adequate criteria for including work within the field of the sociology of law.

Weber's sociology is the scientific study of social action at the level of meaning. Since social action is meaningful, the study of social action must of necessity be interpretive. Hence the subject-matter provides an imperative in the form of the method of Verstehen (interpretive understanding). At the same time, Weber saw meaning as capable of causal explanation, and thus the relations of meaning can enter causal generalization. By emphasizing methodology, Weber allows us to see what sociology looks like, what it is. What then is Law?

Weber provides simply that law is a particular form of legitimate order which carries with it the likelihood (or possibility) that a group of people, having the special responsibility to do so, will exercise coercion to ensure conformity, or sanction failure to conform. Since the subject-matter of sociology is meaningful behaviour, the sociology of law is the understanding of meaningful behaviour as it relates to this particular social phenomenon; in Weber's words, it is the study of 'persons participating in a communal activity . . . (who) subjectively consider certain norms as valid and practically act according to them. In other words orient their own conduct towards them.'[32] Such then allows that the sociology of law is first and foremost a sociology. Sociology can be defined by its subject-matter and the methodological imperative of Verstehen, and can be directed at a particular phenomenon, identified by its external features.

For Timasheff,[33] who seeks to answer the question, 'what is the sociology of law?', law must be identified before it is possible to appreciate its sociological study. Law, for Timasheff, has a function, that of imposing norms of conduct or patterns of social behaviour on the individual will. These norms are real, but they are not the only reality. One other reality is human behaviour in society, the study of which is the province of sociology, a study whose method is causal investigation. The sociology of law, then, is the causal investigation of the relation of human behaviour to legal norms. Again we are given an explicit scheme for identifying work as being part of a defined and delimited field.

Finally we can note that Black[34] gives an equally explicit scheme in specifying that law consists of governmental social control and that sociology should be regarded as a predictive science, based on a natural scientific model, which studies human behaviour. Thus, 'a purely sociological approach to law should involve not an assessment of legal policy, but rather a scientific analysis of legal life as a system of behaviour'.[35] The purpose of the sociology of law then becomes the prediction of empirical patterns of governmental social control in a manner capable of generating a general theory of the relation of law to other forms of social control.

Several writers, then, have been able to offer definitions of the sociology of law. Within the literature, therefore, we are faced with a conundrum. On the one hand are those who offer a definition of the field and criteria for inclusion. On the other hand we have a series of writers who 'eschew a formal definition of the field' and index only 'a variety of diverse strands of research and theory'. The former encapsulate the field prior to study, the latter do so after studies have been undertaken; the former is based on conceptions of *what sociologists do*, the latter on a reading *of what sociologists have done*. The critical point to raise is that common sense would suggest that criteria of inclusion of work within a sub-discipline of sociology should reflect criteria of validity. Thus, for instance, a determination that the sociology of law engages in causal investigation should mirror an appreciation of the validity of causal explanation in sociology. As we shall see below, the lack of attention received by this and similar issues cannot be understood in terms of a consensus concerning the nature of explanation in social science. That the issue of validity is not given prominence in textbooks on the sociology of law reflects in part a misapprehension that the nature of the sociological subject-matter can be presumed and treated in cavalier fashion, and in part a view of sociology that sees problems of validity to be issues merely of the logical consistency of theory and the correct interpretation of the canons of methodology textbooks. In both cases sociologists of law are seen to have capitulated their responsibility for questions regarding the nature of the sociological subject matter.

The Application of Concepts, Theories and Methods

Our earlier ascription of uniformity to the sociological subject-matter, a view endorsed by a wide range of practising sociologists, might lead us to expect that writings both within and between the various sub-disciplines would reflect this uniformity, if only at the levels of 'theory' and 'method'. That the first of these expectations is likely to be disappointed should be clear by reflecting on the state of, say, the sociology of organizations. Silverman[36] has already documented the disparate approaches characteristic of that sub-discipline, and it is by now common ground that these disparities reflect fundamental conflicts with regard to conceptions of the nature of social action and of the sociological endeavour.

At present there is a dichotomy between theory and method which provides for a form of division of labour. A theorist studies theories, a methodologist studies methodologies. An aspiring researcher chooses a little from both. Put simply the division rests on the varying relationship between theories, methods and the object of study. A theory is about data, a method is a means of gathering data. Such a separation of tasks, however, misconstrues the criteria on which generalizations will stand as valid or invalid. The construction of theory is *always* a methodological problem. It cannot be otherwise if we consider that 'theories' are not God-given and have to be generated, and equally that, once generated, their substantive content (the meat on the theoretical skeleton) has to be acquired through empirical work.

Even adopting a theory/method dichotomy, then, does not allow theory to be isolated from methodological considerations. Although we will spend more time on fragmentation within the two sides of the dichotomy, the dichotomy itself is perhaps the most invidious fragmentation of all. We can best see this by considering conventional depictions of the relation of 'methods' to 'theory'. Theories are the context of discovery; the theory provides relationships between disparate phenomena. Methods are the context of validation; empirical work seeks out those phenomena to see whether they do relate in a manner suggested by the theory. Theories have to be internally logically consistent; methods have to respect the canons of good research practice, usually the canons of statistical analysis. In the division of labour established no one, in the end, has responsibility for maintaining contact with the subject-matter. We can provide a theory of deviance, discover relationships between say class, locality and deviance and we can either support or refine the theory depending on whether our operationalization supports or disconfirms the theory. But in this we gain very little understanding of deviance as a social phenomena. We have forgotten that *people* are deviant, or participate in activity ascribed as deviant; we have not begun to understand how people construct lines of action, deviant or so-called conformist.

We need not however stress the point here. The sociology of law, as with many sub-disciplines, contains very few, if any, studies which follow the logic of the theory/method dichotomy. To this extent it is more pertinent to discuss the fragmentation exhibited within the two camps.

If our neophyte sociologist be a methodologist he will soon learn his subordinate role. The tools of his trade will be a selection from a vast array of techniques and principles for the construction of both research design and implementation. His place will be the context of validation, using his 'neutral' techniques to disconfirm or support ideas. We need not be in the business of establishing notions of truth or falsifiability to recognize that what is at issue here is the view that statements concerning social action can be verified by the use of techniques which both are predicated on underlying assumptions regarding the nature of social action and involve criteria of validation which may not be relevant to the subject-matter of social action. While it may appear appropriate to use an opinion survey if one wants to find out opinions, and further that the principles of statistical sampling are appropriate to reduce error and bias, this does not decide for us the appropriateness of the notion of 'opinions' as a building block for sociology. In other words, whilst we may follow good research practice in discovering people's opinions (e.g. not utilize questions which invite a particular answer), or we may be able to replicate any 'opinion' study (e.g. from two random samples of the same population the same proportion of people thought that 'the law was fair'), what we must know first is the relationship between an 'opinion' and social action. Many sociologists may see the problem as revolving around the meaningful nature of social action and the necessity both to relate symbolic components (e.g. expressions of opinions about a phenomenon) to an interactional setting (e.g. an everyday situation where people apprehend the phenomenon) and to avoid subjecting the phenomenon to research techniques whose criteria of validity leave meaning out of account. It is more central at this stage, however, to understand that using opinions as building blocks would be just as bad sociology even if social action were *not* meaningful. The reason is that such study could never inform sociology as to the nature of social action at all. The dialectic as we expressed it earlier could not operate because, treated in this way, we cannot entertain the possibility that opinions are anything other than discrete and isolatable, and that they are a more or less accurate rendering of the social reality they purport to represent.

There exist any number of means of acquiring data, the number depending partly on where the line is drawn in an invidious distinction between methods and research techniques. Podgorecki, for instance, identifies seven methods to be applied in the sociology of law, including the historical-descriptive, the ethnographic-comparative, the questionnaire, the interview and so on. For Podgorecki participant observation is not a method but a technique, although observation itself is a method 'including such distinct techniques as studying the court files, overt or secret participation etc.'.[37] These arbitrary distinctions we mention simply to indicate the extent of the fragmentation pertaining within the methods camp, and to point to the most serious fragmentation within methods, that achieved between social action on the one hand, and research findings on the other. Using research methods, sociologists study men's activities and discover 'findings'. The problem is that with so many different methods to choose from, we can never be sure just what the relationship is between our findings and the activities out of which they were discovered.

Should our sociologist be a theorist, then difficulties of choice will still haunt him. Will his scheme reflect consensus or conflict? Is his society a system or an atomism of competing, conflicting parts? Whichever, the 'problem of social control' will have to be resolved, on the one hand possibly in terms of normative regulation, value consensus and cognitive consensus (a functionalist view). On the other hand, the society under siege will weather the storm by a manipulation of the concepts of power and authority (usually a Marxist orientation). No doubt the sociologist will claim that by subjecting his theories to the context of validation he will ensure that his construction will be empirically grounded and not mere fancy. To this end he may avoid grand theory in favour of theories of the middle-range, and thus prevent amorphous abstraction. This, however, is no mean task.

Is his theory of whatever range going to be pursued in functionalist, behaviourist or intentionalist terms? To answer this requires an understanding of the nature of social action, but is not this to be achieved by theory? Whether our sociologist chooses to understand in terms of generalizations, explanations or predictions he is obviously in difficulties. Choosing between the available systems or action approaches is unlikely to be of assistance unless he learns to appreciate that the nature of the subject-matter legislates against certain modes of theorizing and dictates that the construction of theory be regarded as a methodological problem—whether the theory is consistent with and can inform sociology of the nature of social action or whether it has taken on a life of its own. Social action must order theory, not vice versa.

The final element of fragmentation refers to the application of concepts. As with 'theories' and 'methods' we do not wish to resolve the problems but merely to sensitize the reader to an undeniable characteristic of work within the sub-discipline. The characteristic is an uncritical introduction of concepts into accounts of legal processes. 'Concepts' may be taken to mean those more or less technical terms which refer to phenomena which cannot be seen but which are said to display themselves across a range of situations. In other words a concept should capture a piece of reality in a concrete expression; it stands as a word which refers to something rather than being an explanation of it. The questions immediately arise; first, how are the concepts used within the sociology of law generated and secondly, to what use are they put? In some instances concepts may be chosen with care, either being taken from a particular theory or being induced from research findings for the purpose of developing or refining a particular theory. In these cases it is quite easy to see the generation and use of concepts and thereby quite easy to be critical should such generation and use be problematic. Unfortunately, the sociology of law displays little of such clarity. Concepts are chosen either for academic pedigree or imagery rather than for ability to communicate. For instance the concepts of class, power, norm, expectation, deviance, stratification, etc., enter at many points into the sociology of law.

For our part the problem is not that there are too many concepts. Sociology needs concepts as a means of apprehending the empirical world. But it is a situation where the concepts fail both in their generation and the uses to which they are put. Concepts only have a place in sociology if they can capture, perhaps highlight, some seg-

ment of reality and if we are clear about the reasons for the conceptualization. But since here communicative value is assumed rather
than addressed we are neither allowed to know what aspects of reality
are being referred to nor whether the conceptualization is for descriptive or explanatory purposes. It is the eclecticism in the choice or use
of concepts which serves to hide these sorts of problems behind a mask
of academic respectability. Black provides a useful, albeit unwitting,
example of what we mean. He is concerned to develop a theory of law
which explains features of social control (law, remember, has already
been stylized as 'governmental social control'). From empirical observation Black constructs a theoretical proposition: 'Law tends to
become implicated in social life to the degree that other forms of
social control are weak or unavailable.'[38] Part of the empirical data is
drawn from research on the police. Black continues, not ten lines
away from the empirical data on police behaviour, 'we can *explain*
(his italics) the behaviour of the police, since it can be *predicted and
deduced* (our italics) from a more general proposition about law'. Now
we ask, what possible status can that general proposition have? The
answer must be, can only be, a descriptive status, a short-hand account of what has been empirically determined.

Even at this level of description the proposition may be problematic unless all the procedures leading to its formulation are
documented. This is going to be very important when concepts such
as 'social control' are contained within the proposition. How do you
recognize social control? Did the policeman use the term? If they did
so is not Black just reproducing the policeman's working knowledge
or *lay theory* about when law should be introduced into human affairs?
If so, is that form of reproduction the purpose of sociology?

Black himself, of course, is intent on portraying the proposition as
an explanation. But a status of explanation is only achieved if we are
willing to take two steps. First, we have to say that the proposition is
not addressed as explaining social action (of policemen) but as explaining 'law' (a change of the subject-matter) and secondly, close
our eyes to the obvious tautology. The obvious nature of the tautology
is nicely supplied by Black in that he provides all the steps on a single
page. First he abstracts features out of an empirical setting (description): secondly he puts those features into a general proposition (conceptualization or construction of a theoretical proposition): finally, he
reintroduces that concept or proposition into an explanation of
the empirically given (tautology).

If issues of concept creation, content and use are ignored then

communication comes to depend on whether or not the reader is willing and able to 'fill in' the concept either in terms of understanding
'what the writer means is . . .', in terms of the meaning of the concept
in other settings; or, more frequently, in terms of his own common
sense. The researcher shirks his responsibilities and the reader has to
make sense as best he can. The conceptual armoury of conventional
sociology perhaps makes it unsurprising that a communicative and
explanatory potential be given to concepts by the youngest of its sub-
disciplines but this is little justification for conceptual anarchy.

If the multiple fragmentation we have described leaves us with
little idea of what a sociological understanding of legal phenomena
would look like, we can be sure that the optic nerve was cut when the
sub-discipline ceased to engage in sociology and assumed the mantle
of a jack of all trades. 'What's your problem? I've the very thing for
you.' You can see the attitude whether the interest in 'problems'
reflects a 'relevance' orientation and a concern with 'legal effectiveness' or a conventional attitude to the fragmented nature of
sociology and a concern with, say, the effectiveness of law as a system
of social control. Whichever it is, practitioners offer conceptual
systems and tools of research which can be adopted for use, the nature
of social action being given no more than a passing reference. This
catch-all role for a sociology of law finds an easy justification in the
reticence to define the project. Lack of sophistication is hidden behind
a mask of modesty.

The problems of fragmentation are the problems of a sub-discipline
which has lost, or has not found, its sociological direction; a sub-
discipline which uncritically accepts and presumes the very topic of
inquiry. The many faceted character of fragmentation is an open
invitation to the student to take an eclectic approach to sociology not
only in his own treatment of law but in his appraisal of work already
undertaken. There is a temptation to organize some form of unity into
the mosaic by ignoring or not fully addressing the fundamental differences between the fragments.

Within the sociology of law, study remains both pedestrian and
intellectually unsatisfying. This position will hold so long as the sub-
disciplines retains 'law' as the subject-matter of study, rather than
social action. The sociology of law is neither more nor less than a
study of how people achieve, in concerted social action, those
activities which we understand as pertaining to law. Law in the
context of social action is the proper object of attention, not law as a
generic notion identifiable independently of social activity. To attend

to this object we need a means of overcoming the problems of fragmentation. To begin to resolve the problem we need to examine the current debates within sociology regarding the form and purpose of methods and theories.

THE DEBATES

So far we have suggested that what sociologists look at is social action. This implies several things. It implies that social action is all that sociologists have to work with in the form of 'data'; that is all that is empirically given, not the constructs or concepts devised by sociology; secondly, it implies that meaning cannot be left out of account for if that is done the dialectic cannot operate and we could never resolve the significance of meaning in social action. We could only assert its significance or deny. Most sociologists would in fact agree that sociology is concerned with patterned features of behaviour that *are* meaningful to the social actor. Further, most would agree that the purpose of sociology is to explain these regularities. It is from this common ground that disagreements arise; sociologists disagree on the methodological imperatives inhering within that subject-matter. It is at this level, therefore, that of *constructing* explanations which are valid for a particular science in the face of a particular subject-matter, that the issues taken up in this section are lodged.

To orient ourselves to these debates let us take an example from the literature on the sociology of deviance. For Merton,[39] the features of a pattern of action are explicable in terms of, on the one hand, culturally acquired dispositions to act in certain specifiable ways and, on the other, sanctioned expectations. These expectations are seen as capable of being taken on board by social actors—of being internalized through socialization—thereby establishing a shared culture of expectations both internalized and sanctioned by other actors.

Common to both these notions of expectation and disposition is the idea of 'a stable link between the situation of an actor and his action in that situation'.[40] Since actions and situations occur and re-occur, the way in which an actor identifies situations and actions is crucial. If social action is to be stable (have features of patterned regularity) different actors must discriminate situations in the same way, or virtually the same way. If actors in situations cannot agree, more or less, on the meaning of that interaction, and recognize whether the action in the situations meets expectations, then the delicate balance between dispositions, expectations and sanctions, cannot operate. Regularity for Merton, then, is explained in terms of a shared cognitive and normative culture; actors acquire purposes and motives in the form of dispositions to act in certain ways in certain situations, and they act in response to legitimate and internalized expectations. Social variability for Merton depends upon the acquisition of characteristic dispositions which vary with differential location within society (social class, gender, etc.) and the differential impact of organizational structures (of different types of schooling, of membership of voluntary organizations and so on).

The above is the basis for Merton's *anomie* theory of deviant behaviour, a theory in which common socialization to an overriding value consensus brings certain structurally located groups to despair of ever achieving these values. If legitimate routes are closed to him, then the socialized actor is faced with a problem, a problem which can be overcome, *inter alia*, by a rejection of legitimate in favour of illegitimate means. The substance of *anomie* theory is well documented and needs no exposition here. The basis of the theory is, however, very important. As refined by Cloward and Ohlin,[41] amongst others, the basis is 'a model of normatively constrained differential opportunity structures influencing rates of crime through variability of socialisation and varying access to legitimate and illegitimate social roles'.[42] The scheme provided would *explain* a specific patterned regularity by showing that it could be deduced from the more general axioms of the theory. Knowledge of the socialization of, say, female white-collar workers, and an appreciation of their access to criminal sub-cultures, could be used to deduce hypotheses about their rate of criminal activity, which could then be operationalized and tested against empirical evidence.

The perspective we have described is known as the normative paradigm—normative not in the sense that the sociologist stipulates canons of behaviour or what people 'ought' to do, but in the sense that social actors are normatively constrained by society stipulating correct behaviour and sanctioning transgressions.

Such an approach to social regularity is not without critics but it is sufficient to remark at this stage that another well-established line of thought in the field of deviancy construes the problem of explaining social regularities in very different terms. Under the 'interpretive' paradigm, stability is viewed as achieved by social actors in their routine everyday activities, rather than created by societal forces external to actors' social being. The meanings of situations are not seen as culturally given, but as constructed in the interaction setting. Whether or not meanings appear at one level to be objectified (we all know murder is a crime), they are none the less established and maintained through the interpretive process of interaction, rather than by reference to a body of culturally given definitions. Looked at in this way, we cannot explain behaviour by showing that it is what we expected (deducible from general theoretical axioms) but rather we can 'only know why people do what they do when we understand what the situation means to them—for such meaning includes the reason for the eventual action'.[43] Explanation, then, is rooted at the level of people doing things, of going about the world continually understanding and reaffirming the meaning of situations. This holds both for 'ordinary' and 'deviant' behaviour.

Clearly, these two orientations reflect different levels of analysis within sociology rather than being of the order of the difference between a sociological explanation and an economic or political explanation, and the disjuncture highlights a number of important issues—issues of theory and method; levels of analysis; ways of handling meaning; and so on. It is notable, for instance, that in moving from the former to the latter orientation, explanation in terms of causal generalization and prediction gives way to explanation in terms of reasons and understanding. In the first, regularities in rates of deviant acts are explained by pointing to an external cause. In the second, deviant action is explained by understanding the reasons why such action took place. Though the issues are complex, an encapsulation of the approaches suggests that the Mertonian stance reflects a view of sociology split between theory (general axioms) and method (operationalization of hypothesis, tested through empirical research). The alternative is closer to a view which sees methodology as the total process undertaken in generating a statement about social phenomena, with the stricture that the statement must in some sense be adequate at the level of meaning.

The problem presented by an appreciation of these alternative approaches is none other than the relationship between what we say about an aspect of social reality, and that social reality itself. Resolving that problem depends upon knowing what we mean by this reality in the first place, before we address it scientifically. Various solutions may be available but we need not adopt any one in particular at this stage to recognise that social reality can not be treated as of similar status to physical reality. We have no objective measuring device for social reality, beyond what is given by the theories and understandings which we develop. If social action is to do with meaning, it can never be treated as an objective phenomenon even if certain actions and certain meanings are so stable and regular that parties to an interaction treat them as non-problematic—to the sociologist, 'objectified'.

Such a recognition clearly places constraints upon the sorts of statements which sociologists can make. In arguing that such constraints do exist, that sociology must have regard to the relationship between what is said of a phenomenon scientifically and that phenomenon as it exists pre-scientifically, we are arguing (not originally) that a division exists within scientific disciplines. We are saying that the natural scientific method (theory construction and principles of verifiability and falsifiability) apply to a subject-matter of a particular nature (intrinsically meaningless: 'The world of nature, as explained by the natural scientist, does not "mean" anything to molecules, atoms and electrons.')[44] and for a particular purpose (explanation and prediction). The social sciences engage a different order of subject-matter ('social reality has a specific meaning and relevance structure for the human beings living, acting and thinking within it')[45] and for a particular purpose (understanding). In other words, explanation in the social sciences is achieved through an understanding of what situations and actions mean to those social actors located within the sociologist's observational field. It can not be argued that we 'understand' patterned action by showing it to be what can be expected from the axiom of a particular theory because what is at issue is the relation between those axioms and the thinking, acting and theorizing which constitute the observed behaviour. When we see the problem at this level, the level of constructing statements which are valid according to our subject-matter, we can see that it makes sense to argue, as Schutz has done, that the role of theory is the same in the natural and social sciences; theory is 'the explicit formulation of determinate relations between a set of variables in terms of which a fairly extensive class of empirically ascertainable regularities can be explained'.[46] The primary goal of theory is organized knowledge; within sociology, organized knowledge of social reality. We have then to look at the nature of that social reality.

THE NATURE OF SOCIAL REALITY

The only common ground so far achieved is that within social reality there are 'empirically ascertainable regularities' or 'patterned features of behaviour' and that these regularities or features are somehow meaningful to the actors themselves. What remains to be established is whether these features carry methodological imperatives. Let us then look at these regularities, and juxtapose the arguments of two authors who have been influential in answering the question of whether in grasping regularities in social science we are on a par with the natural scientists' methods of establishing causal generalizations. The two authors are Winch[47] and McIntyre.[48] Both have been concerned with the 'idea of social science' and the methods used to explain social regularities.

Winch argues that the idea of a regularity implies the notion of a rule by involving judgements of identity or sameness: to 'investigate the type of regularity studied in a given field of enquiry is to examine the nature of the rule according to which judgements of identity are made in that enquiry'.[49] Within natural science the observer is able to supply his own criteria of sameness, and the concepts and criteria basing the 'discovery of uniformities' must be understood in relation to the rules governing natural scientific investigation. Such an ability is predicated on natural scientific subject-matter. Winch, however, makes a claim that for the sociologist the situation is rather different. What the sociologist studies is human action carried on in accordance with rules. In other words, it is these rules of social action that determine whether we can count two empirical appearances as being the 'same kind of activity'.

For instance one could look at a trial situation and a mock trial and think how one would begin to differentiate between the two. If human action is carried on according to rules and if these rules supply the definite characteristic of any species of action, then understanding action means understanding the rules by which it is guided. This is how Winch sees social science grasping the meaning of action. Compared with natural science, social science engages a subjective world whose members provide constructs for signifying the rules in operation. Constructs such as 'law' or 'war' are of this type. Natural science is seen as free to provide its own constructs to explain regularities, constructs such as 'heat' and 'gravity'. Both types enter into the explanation or understanding of regularities but in a radically different manner.

Winch uses the constructs of 'war' and 'gravity' as examples of what he means. 'The idea of war was not invented by people who wanted to explain what happens when societies come into armed conflict. It is an idea which provides the criteria of what is appropriate in the behaviour of members of the conflicting societies.'[50] To point the difference between concepts in the social as opposed to the natural, sciences Winch states that if my country is at war then the 'concept of war belongs essentially to my behaviour. But the concept of gravity does not belong essentially to the behaviour of a falling apple in the same way: it belongs rather to the physicist's explanation of the apple's behaviour.'[51]

Winch, then, is able to erect an impenetrable barrier between the natural and the social sciences at the level of methodology and explanation. We can understand and grasp regularities in terms of rules or meaning but this cannot allow us to predict behaviour as if meaning stood to behaviour as cause to effect, because the relation is internal and conceptual not external and causal. This is the division between acting for a reason and behaving from a cause and provides for the debate within sociology between those who seek to explain patterned action causally and those who seek to understand patterned action interpretively.

MacIntyre's attempt to rebut this argument is important because whilst accepting the necessity of understanding an actor's reasoning, he argues that acting from a reason is not incompatible with behaving from a cause. The idea is best expressed in those situations where an actor is being duped. A wants B to do something. If B knew A's real intent he would not do it. A therefore tells B that his intent is different, or he acts in a way such that a different intent will be ascribed to him. B then does what A wanted. McIntyre argues that A's actions have been causally effective: B may act for whatever reason, but the cause of his behaviour can be located in A's action. Now this looks like a peculiar use of the word cause, for two reasons.

First, cause usually implies some fixity between two phenomena. It is a notion which allows us to order, in a particular way, empirically observed relations such that one phenomenon is both a necessary and sufficient condition for the second to occur. But what we find in McIntyre is the ascription of 'cause' after an initial account of the relations between A and B in terms of motive, intention and so on. In other words, what is gained by conceptualizing the relationship in this way? Perhaps more importantly, what may be hidden and lost? Secondly, the natural scientist is free to place his observations into an enclosed system which contains within it the determinate relationship. The system can specify the rules for judging each observation and in turn the system can be judged in terms of its predictive value and logical consistency, and prediction can then be used as a basis for judging the validity of the system at an explanatory framework. Natural phenomena are objective, 'out there', and can therefore be treated in this fashion. Here we can quote Winch: 'Consider for instance the explanation of a chemical reaction in terms of a theory of molecular structure and valency: here the theory establishes a connection between what happened at one moment when the two chemicals were brought together and what happened at a subsequent moment. It is only in *terms of the theory* that one can speak of the events being thus "connected" (as opposed to simple spatio-temporal connection); the only way to grasp the connection is to learn the theory.'[52]

For Winch it is theoretical knowledge which enables one to explain. It is the particular role of theory in natural science, establishing the connection between events, that allows for location of cause. If we picture a scientist mixing two chemicals A and B, we can ask what caused the resultant chemical X. Was it the scientist or the chemical mixture A and B? The question for natural science is spurious. The theory establishes the connection and the events which are relevant to the theory exist as an 'independent sequence of events'. The theory holds and establishes a connection whether the scientist deliberately mixed A and B, accidentally mixed A and B or whether A and B mixed because of a defect, say, in their containing jars. Independent sequences of events are an important factor in the location of cause in natural sciences.

For social science, theory relates to phenomena of a different order; phenomena which are meaningful. The relationship between such phenomena is intrinsic to them and not to be established by the external canons of theory. Further, correct prediction in the social sciences is irrelevant to the validity of a constructed theory. The validity of a social theory is not to be judged in terms of the internal fit between its parts, but in terms of the 'fit' between those parts and the phenomena they concern. If we accept McIntyre we hide this problem and never attend fully to the social action comprising the phenomena. His use of cause in social science is bound up with an understanding of theory and before concluding on 'cause' it is therefore necessary to look more generally at what is claimed for social theory by sociologists.

We mentioned that Schutz described both natural and social theory as explaining 'empirically ascertainable regularities', and by looking at this notion of 'regularities' we discovered some dissimilarities between natural and social science. Now we look specifically at social scientific theories. We make no attempt to do more than scratch the surface. Social scientists are frequently confused and more often unintelligible when discussing theory—many 'theory' textbooks do not even give an unambiguous statement as to what theory is claimed to be. In any event the word is over-used or its importance under-played. It is over-used when claims to the status of theory are made on behalf of statements barely transcending an account of a single observation; it is under-played by the assumption that this convenient dignity can be indiscriminately invoked without harming the coherence of sociology and its ability to produce 'ordered knowledge of social reality'.

For Cohen, a scientific theory is 'ideally, a universal empirical statement which asserts a causal connection between two or more types of events'.[53] A theory must be universal (which can include statistical probabilities) and open to empirical test. To be open to empirical test necessitates that statements about the empirical world are deducible and can be verified or falsified. Such then are the properties of a scientific theory. A fully acceptable social scientific theory would have the form: 'The degree of social mobility in industrial society varies directly with the degree of industrialisation achieved.'[54] A theory can then be a single proposition stating a determinate relationship between two concepts. The concepts have then to be operationalized in order to test the truth of the proposition. Mere concepts, therefore do not constitute a theory. Homans states this forcefully: a theory consists of a set of concepts or a conceptual scheme *and* a set of propositions which state a relationship in a deductive scheme.[55] If an aspect of a phenomenon can be deduced then it is explained and theory 'is nothing if not an explanation'.[56] As an example of a deductive theory (explanation) we can use one supplied by Durkheim and referred to by Homans, Durkheim's theory of the low suicide rate in Spain.

(1) In any social grouping, the suicide rate varies directly with the degree of individualism (egoism).

(2) The degree of individualism varies with the incidence of Protestantism.

(3) Therefore the suicide rate varies with the incidence of Protestantism.

(4) The incidence of Protestantism in Spain is low.

(5) Therefore the suicide rate in Spain is low.

The logic of the theory is clear. It is composed of a set of concepts or a conceptual scheme. Some of the terms Homans called 'descriptive concepts' (e.g. individualism, suicide) showing what the theory is about, and others Homans called 'operative concepts' (rate, incidence) identifying relationships. The conceptual scheme is insufficient for a theory. The second element is the set of propositions stating relationships, such as 'varies with', between the variables. In the example from Durkheim, proposition 3 is derived from (deduced from) propositions 1 and 2 and proposition 5 from propositions 3 and 4. For Homans when 'propositions are so derived they are said to be explained'.[57] Finally for the theory to be acceptable to empirical science, some of the propositions must be 'contingent' in the sense that experience is relevant to their truth or falsity, e.g. we are able in the example above to check actual suicide rates.

The nature of theory, for Homans, follows this pattern and it has a nature common to both the natural and social sciences. Homans has followed Schutz in a claim for uniformity of purpose between the natural and social sciences but has extended the similarity to include a uniformity of method: a method of explanation by deduction and operationalized research to validate or falsify.

Homans's claim is strong and not without support within general sociology. There is a wide agreement among theorists that a theory is an explanation, one which is couched in terms of a set of propositions containing concepts, stating determinate relationships that can be deduced from more general propositions. These systems are seen as capable of producing 'theoretical' laws and further, that we can locate within that system a notion of cause. So Popper says, 'to give a causal explanation of an event means to deduce a statement which describes it'.[58] In other words, 'explanation' in deductive systems is given to be a 'causal explanation', somehow separate from an explanation at the level of meaning.

The support, however, is not unanimous. Many empirical studies promote explanations contained in simple correlations or statistical laws. Some collate such laws into inductive theory which then suggests further correlations for empirical validation. Other writers, however, have questioned the very basis on which all these methods rest, seeing a prior question of 'how sociologists can recognize and identify the characteristics that social phenomena have'.[59] The methods outlined all require imputations of sameness or uniformity but it is argued that the explanations treat as unproblematic the meaningfulness of social phenomena which alone provides for their identification.

This agreement within sociology as presently practised necessitates that we look into the relationship between theorizing and explaining, a relationship which if properly understood can help resolve the difficulties encountered.

EXPLANATION AND DEDUCTION

The purpose of this section is to untie explanation from the logical qualities of deduction, and to support the contention that theories which 'ignore meaning or ride roughshod over the issues it raises will necessarily remedy the realities to which they purport to relate'.[60] Alan Ryan[61] provides an argument based on a distinction between two types of theories. The first is 'empirical law inside a deductive scheme' (e.g. Boyle's Law concerning gasses); the second is theory properly so called which provides a narrative underpinning to the empirical law (e.g. the Kinetic 'theory' of gasses establishing the natural processes involved in the expansion of gasses). It is the basis of Ryan's argument that from Boyle's law we can deduce that a gas of given volume will expand a certain amount given a specified rise in temperature. Any empirical observation can be explained by the general proposition of the deductive scheme and can support the empirical law by evidencing the latter's capacity to predict correctly the relationship between temperature and expansion in individual instances. Ryan does not wish to fault the deductive power of empirical laws, but wishes to suggest that the deductive scheme can be theoretically underpinned. For Boyle's law the relevant theory is the Kinetic theory of gasses, a theory of how molecules move and are stimulated by heat. Ryan argues that the kinetic theory does not improve the *deductive* qualities of empirical laws such as Boyle's law but allows a more *intelligible* account of causal sequences (natural processes). As Ryan says, 'the role of theory seems to be more in the improvement of causal narratives than in the ensuing deductive vigour'.[62]

Let us now transmogrify the argument to see how this relates to the role given to social theory as the accumulation of ordered knowledge regarding social reality. Given an empirical law concerning the relationship between two factors (say, crime and socio-economic status) the role of theory would then be to fill in the narrative of social processes.

If Ryan's argument is built on acceptable premises it would seem to support a view which both accepts Schutz's statement that the purpose of theory is the same in both natural and social science and rejects Homans's view that the only form of theory is deductive explanation. Are Ryan's premises acceptable or could Homans argue that Kinetic theory has its value based in the fact that, from it Boyle's law can be deduced? If Boyle's law can be deduced from kinetic theory, then the force of Ryan's argument as per the natural sciences is undermined. Unfortunately, the question of whether a deducible relationship exists between empirical laws and theories is a question still being debated with the philosophy of natural science and little help is forthcoming from that direction. The question seems to depend on whether the elements of the theory are simply 'theoretical' or whether they can be witnessed empirically. If we presume that 'molecule' is a theoretical construct then it may be that the only means to chose between the Kinetic theory of gasses and some other theory of gasses would be in the terms of their capacity to allow for the deduction of Boyle's law and the other empirical laws to which the Kinetic theory of gasses relates. We have, however, no wish to presume the future development of the philosophy of science and are satisfied to accept that Ryan's argument, though attractive, assumes the question of the relationship between empirical laws and theories to have been answered. Within natural science the existence of theories beyond empirical laws does not damage the deductive model of explanation and as we saw from Schutz and Winch the natural scientist is free to create theories containing theoretical elements such as gravity, molecules, force, etc., which order his subject of study.

At this stage, then, it seems uncertain whether Ryan has broken the back of deductive explanation but we have begun to untie explanation from deductive rigour. In order to decide whether the social sciences are reliant on deductive systems without assuming developments in the philosophy of science we have to decide whether the logic of deduction is an acceptable form of theory and the only basis on which to adjudicate between competing theories. Since these questions are discussed in Chapter V we need only stress three points here.

(1) *Deductive Theory and Explanation*

Several problems limit the applicability of deductive theorizing to the social sciences. They stem from the pre-interpreted character of the social·world, a world which is made sense of by actors through the concepts they use for its interpretation. It is not for the scientist to provide his own scheme of interpretation unconnected to that of the actors, for how actors understand the situations that face them is implicated in producing their action in those situations. Further, the phenomena of social life rarely have the discrete properties necessary for them to be contained within a deductive scheme.

The social sciences, however, do have an alternative to deductive theorizing, an alternative mode of explanation. It is open to explain phenomena by reference to the actual operating logic (interpretive

schemes) of those whose behaviour we study. Empirical generalizations of the type provided by Black ('police only use law when other
forms of social control are not available'), instead of being subsumed
within a deductive framework, can be explained by showing how
police activity and the decisions taken during that activity are constructed, say, by reference to operating ideas, notions and background
assumptions of those involved. Moreover this procedure is necessary
because the initial statement by Black contains the theoretical concept of 'social control' which stands on a par with concepts of natural
science, such as 'heat'. We have no other index of the concept,
however, except the activity of police and others within those
situations which the scientist has construed as instances of social
control.

Such a means of constructing explanations may be far removed
from systems of deductive logic. But that need not be surprising nor
be treated as unscientific. Social phenomena do not exist in the same
manner as natural phenomena and we should not be surprised to find
that different types of explanation exist as the best promoters of
understanding in the two respective sciences.

(2) *Validating Theory*

Sociologists have often assumed that the purpose of study is to solve
theoretical problems. This gives a particular flavour to problems of
validation. Validation becomes narrowed to issues of theoretical consistency and the empirical verification of theoretical propositions.
Sociologists put the social world into operationalized concepts and
legislate meaning out of existence by an act of fiat. Again we can use
Black's general theoretical proposition as an example. The proposition allows a prediction that police do not use the law to settle family
disputes, the family being seen as available for social control. This
proposition could then be empirically validated to support the more
general initial statement. But we can see, however, that more than
deduction is being used. The problem of indexing social control
within family organization, though not made explicit, is a necessary
process for the initial proposition to be verified. If the police are
operating by reference not to any notion of social control but to, say,
conceptions of 'proper police work', organizational directives or constraints, or promotional considerations, Black's explanation would be
inadequate. As it is the issue is hidden. The method of Black does not
address social processes and its status as sociological explanation is
thereby put in doubt.

(3) *Adjudication Between Competing Theories*

If deductive logic were the end to explanation in social sciences then we would have difficulty in deciding between explanations offered by competing sociological perspectives. By relinquishing deduction, however, the alternative mode of explanation provides a relatively unproblematic criterion of choice. The social phenomena studied by sociology can speak back to the science; social actors construct the meaning of events and situations and this understanding of social phenomena provides an underpinning to our theories and constructs. If we can establish an empirical law in terms of actual patterns of behaviour and particular types of situations, competing theories can be addressed in terms of their ability to subsume social actors' understandings of the situations they themselves meet.

Given the foregoing we are now in a position to reopen the debate between Winch and McIntyre. If we go back to Winch, we see that the important difference between a causal connection and a meaningful connection is that a causal connection asserts a contingent relationship between two phenomena that can be independently identified. The meaningful connection, on the other hand is internal and conceptual. We can, then, only establish laws if we can identify and describe phenomena which are not conceptually linked to any other phenomena. Winch argues that connections which hold between social actions are conceptual connections and that language is indispensable to our ability to identify and talk in terms of *social action* as opposed to mere movement or behaviour. To the extent that we have identified social action as the subject-matter, connections between events and observed regularities require analysis at the level of meaning for their very discovery. We are not permitted to establish causal connections between them without destroying the very subject-matter of sociology.

CONCLUSION

To place these debates more firmly within sociology we can now return to the normative-interpretive debate within the discipline. The major critique of the normative approach (of, for example, Merton) concerns issues already raised. They include the division between theory and method, and the acceptance of the natural scientific mode of theory, operationalization and deductive explanation. Because of this, the normative paradigm is seen as failing to underpin empirical generalizations at the level of social processes and as engaging in a form of explanation which renders social processes non-problematic. The explanation is incapable of informing the sociologist as to the nature of anything but his accepted theory. Further criticism involves the notion of rule. The normative paradigm, as seen with Merton, uses the notion of rule to explain observed regularities. The social world is seen as rule-governed. But this in a different fashion to Winch. Whereas Winch says you cannot identify a regularity except in terms of a rule operating within social life, the normative paradigm begins with the assumption that social action is normatively regulated; the social world is *rule-governed*. Rules *explain* regularities rather than being involved in their recognition.

Against this position, the interpretive paradigm asserts that such a reliance on rules settles *a priori* the nature of social action and prevents sociology from addressing the question of how social order is achieved by the everyday reasoning and interpretive practices of people actually living and going about day-to-day tasks. Secondly, it asserts that meaning does not oust concepts of rules but raises as an issue the question of how we can as sociologists conceptualize and use the notion of a rule within explanation. Further, the rule-governed character of action is a topic of investigation not a resource for explanation. How people negotiate rules and decide for practical purposes what it would take to see a rule operating and act in accordance with it becomes a central sociological problem.

If, then, the debate involves questions concerning the rule relatedness of social phenomena, then we can use a discussion of law to enlighten us.

Indeed, an appreciation of the historical development of sociology reveals a seminal role for law in the creation of social theory. Take the work of Durkheim.[63] There, an ability to discover a truly social level of explanation depends upon the identification of phenomena which can be treated via a natural scientific methodology. The phenomena chosen by Durkheim were social facts, a category consisting of 'ways of acting, thinking, and feeling, external to the individual, and endowed with a power of coercion by reason of which they control him'.[64] Legal rules were of enormous significance in this scheme, illustrated by their place in Durkheim's investigation of the division of labour in society. Did law require Durkheim to create the category of social facts, or did the category, once established, point to law as having this particular social status? The question is unnecessary at this point. We need only see that law was an integral feature of the Durkheimian vision of sociological understanding and note that his position is either echoed, or reproduced, among the work of contemporary sociologists. Consider also the discussions of 'social norms' which are to be found in most contemporary introductory textbooks. Norms here are instances of socially sanctioned behaviour, involving mutual expectations and, generally, supported by values. For most sociologists norms (and values) may involve conflict, either between or within individual actor or groups, but the basic picture is the same. Norms are 'out there', external to the actor, providing through his own and others' expectations the constraints which make social order possible. From such initial propositions flow a myriad of distinctions between prescriptive and proscriptive norms, 'sent' and 'received' norms and so on. Law is seen as the acme of this normative regulation, the cherry on the cake layered in terms of the hierarchy, law, rule, custom, habit, etc. The apparent facticity of one end of this continuum, and its easy identification through a written legal code, is held to endorse a view of the rest of the cake as treatable as being 'out there' also. Just as Durkheim used law to index types of social organization, and a view of the sociological project, so law is used here to index the nature of social order.

The use does not go without philosophical justification. Goldthorpe[65] for instance, is explicit in finding support in a Popperian approach to knowledge and places social phenomena such as law in the world 'of objective content of thought', constituting an 'autonomous domain' within this area. Such thought interacts with the subjective world but is independent of it. It is knowledge in an objective sense and is 'totally independent of anybody's belief, or disposition to assent; or to assert, or to act'. So objectified, knowledge can be manipulated, immersed in causal relations and becomes subject to the tortures devised by natural scientific methodology and statistical analysis. Social actors may apprehend such knowledge, but cannot deny it. Their social activity might collectively constitute such knowledge, but it is independent of them. It is made by men, but outside of them.

The philosophical underpinning of a view of social order as normatively regulated and the part law is held to play in such regulation should be enough to confirm our interest in epistemological issues if we seek to address law as a social phenomenon. A commitment to investigate such issues is all that is necessary at this stage, and we take them up in more detail in later chapters. For now, merely note that embracing a view of social life as normatively regulated, as controlled by social norms, legal rules and so on, cannot be justified by successful prediction of behaviour on the basis of knowledge of the rules. Assume that we can identify the rules—an important assumption which underlines the significance of law—and that we accurately predict behaviour. The successful equation does not justify the imputation of cause. Moreover, it tells us nothing about how meaning intervenes—unless we further assume that it intervenes neutrally. At which point meaning (and social action) become unproblematic and we deny the potency of the dialectic to talk back to our appreciation of the subject-matter itself.

In any event, academic suicide is unnecessary. Twenty years ago Blumer supplied a suggestive dichotomy when he said that '(it) is the social process in group life that creates and upholds the rules, not the rules that create and uphold group life'.[66]

The issue, then, becomes simplified into this dichotomy between normative and interpretive research; between research which has to accept the normative character of social action for the purpose of explanation and those that would elucidate those features of social action that themselves explain the regular and ordered appearance of social life.

The sociology of law has a role of potential significance to play in advancing sociology beyond its present state. Whether this potential is realized will depend on the sociological component of empirical work. The sub-discipline can either accept the responsibility of investigating the nature of social action or it can approach law in a way that can lead only to knowledge with no established connection to the social world.

CHAPTER II

Déjà Vu

In this chapter we review the work in the sociology of law of Émile Durkheim and Max Weber, two authors who are rightly regarded amongst the founding fathers of sociology. In the review we hope to establish two propositions. The first is that the sociology of law has a history and a history somewhat neglected in the present profusion of work in the sub-discipline. The work of Durkheim and Weber shows, if any demonstration be needed, the legitimacy of the study of law within sociology. The second is the intimate connections between:

(a) the methodological concerns of sociology;
(b) the construction of sociological theory and substantive sociological analysis; and
(c) the sociological study of law.

ÉMILE DURKHEIM

If the fragmentation of sociology is both widespread and destructive of the enterprise itself, there is much comfort to be obtained from studying the work of Émile Durkheim. Durkheim demonstrates that sociology is not fated to fragmentation, and we do not have to agree with his particular conclusions to value the fundamental unity with which he viewed sociological investigation. Not only do we find in him a true appreciation of the epistemological debt of social science, but we also discover a refusal to exile any part of the sociological endeavour. In his study of suicide he forced home the implications of statistical technique only after first considering deeply the validity of such a treatment. Similarly, his analysis of the division of labour in society entailed a grant to law of a particular status within sociological knowledge as a visible index of intricate social processes, but that grant was considered and measured and was not given in a capricious or an unreflectively pragmatic spirit. His diversity of sociological interests was matched by his determination to explicate the linkages between them.

The symbiotic character of Durkheim's sociology in all its various

45

guises is nowhere more apparent than in his study of law. Law oc-
cupies an important place in the study of the rules of sociological
method and in the establishment of the nature and type of phenomena which it is the task of sociology to investigate. Laws are social
facts, treatable by positive science, a doctrine finding implementation
in *The Division of Labour in Society*, an attempt to 'treat the facts of
moral life according to the method of the positive sciences'.[1] But
moral phenomena were hardly the stuff of science, so that Durkheim
substituted for the moral phenomena of social solidarity 'the external
index which symbolises it . . . This visible symbol is law.'[2] It was in
this fashion that Durkheim carefully created his edifice, matching and
relating his methods, data and problems to form a complete
sociology.

An explanation of this organic embrace of the discipline can be
found in Durkheim's intention to base the new discipline of sociology
on a peculiarly social level of investigation, separate from an ethical
or psychological science, and to explore the limits of this new type of
explanation. It is therefore appropriate that in examining his
sociology of law we should look first to his vision of sociology and in
particular to his statements on methodology and on the subject-
matter.

SUBJECT-MATTER AND METHODOLOGY

For Durkheim the problem of a social scientific methodology and
its solution was rooted in the apparent refusal of social phenomena to
be treated adequately by the methods of positive science. Positive
science had successfully handled natural phenomena, and the rationality which Durkheim saw as underlying such a method he wished to
transfer to social phenomena. The transference, however, could
hardly be automatic. Natural scientists had experienced severe difficulties in contradicting the theological and political dictates of earlier
eras. But if the theologians had invoked the scriptures against natural
science, at least the scientific subject-matter did not answer back.
Durkheim's new science on the other hand faced a double intransigence, that of the university politicians and that of its subjects.

Intransigence was to be defeated by drawing lessons from the history of natural science, particularly of biology, and by according a
greater weight to scientific than to lay knowledge—'the aim of all
science is to make discoveries, and every discovery more or less dis-
turbs accepted ideas. Unless then sociology attributes to common
sense an authority which it has not enjoyed for a long time in other

sciences—and it is impossible to see how such authority could be justified—the scholar must resolutely resist being intimidated by the results to which his researches lead, demanding only that they be conducted scientifically.'[3]

The natural scientific method was seen as both a means of acquiring data and confirming it. Before Durkheim could explicate the stages of the method he proposed, however, he had to show how that method could be made immune to the distortion created by sociologists' own presuppositions and existing commonsense theories. Durkheim recognized that men had theories and notions about the world and that in this respect sociologists hardly differed from other human beings. Moreover, the thoughts men held about social phenomena had greater force than mere neutral ideas, and differed markedly from ideas about natural phenomena. He argued that 'our political and religious beliefs and our moral standards carry with them an emotional tone that is not characteristic of our attitude towards physical objects; consequently this emotional character injects our manner of conceiving and explaining them'.[4] Durkheim found a solution to the eradication of insidious presuppositions in three ways. First, he vehemently exhorted sociologists to discard 'renascent mysticism'. But this in itself was little more than mere assertion and could hardly support a solution reliant upon the sociologist's commitment to ethical ideals of truth and honesty—compare Weber, for instance, for whom the pursuit of knowledge was in the final analysis, 'a persisting moral effort'. Rather, Durkheim's entreaties simply gave eloquent weight to what was in effect a two-pronged, and for him a more definitive, solution; establish a sociological subject-matter capable of scientific treatment; treat it by the scientific method.

Durkheim concluded that sociologists should study 'social facts' which by virtue of their externality were independent of lay or sociological theories and were hence amenable to a positive methodology.

This category of social facts was justified in part by an appeal to common sense. In fulfilling my obligations as brother, husband or citizen, Durkheim argues, I perform duties which are defined, externally to myself and my actions, through law and custom. Even if they conform to my own sentiments and I feel their reality subjectively, this reality is still objective, for I did not create them. Moreover, these types of conduct are endowed with coercive power. If I fully consent and conform to them the constraint is barely noticed, but the constraint is there none the less, the proof being that it asserts itself as soon as I attempt to resist it.

These social facts were seen as lying along a continuum, from the structural (the number and nature of the parts of society, distribution of population, etc.) through more, or less, formal social rules (law, custom, religion, financial systems), to those which 'without presenting these crystallized forms have both the same objectivity and the same ascendency over the individual'.[5] These latter are the social currents which 'impel' people to rates of marriage, for instance, or which turn a peaceful gathering into a lynching mob. The definition of social facts was given as 'every way of acting, fixed or not, capable of exercising on the individual an external constraint', or again 'every way of acting which is general throughout a given society; while at the same time existing in its own right independent of its individual manifestation'.[6] The definition thus embraced a wide range of phenomena. But if the definition was this encompassing, Durkheim clearly saw some social facts as more relevant to sociology than others, since sociology was duty bound to address the facts which were the best indicators of the underlying social reality. In his early work particularly he chose to address law. Law was taken as the paradigmatic instance of a social fact on account of its visibility, codification and extremely overt resistance to contravention. In *The Division of Labour in Society* he even excludes customs and folkways which whilst of similar character to law were seen as subservient social phenomena. Even where custom and law conflict, this 'arises only in rare and pathological cases which cannot endure without danger . . . If then there are types of social solidarity which custom alone manifests they are assuredly secondary; law produces those which are essential and they are the only ones we need to know.'[7]

At times Durkheim even appears to be arguing that law is more than an index of social reality, that it is the true reality in itself. Whereas the 'visible symbol (of moral phenomena) is law' and we find 'reflected in law all the essential varieties of social solidarity'; it is also the case that 'social life, especially where it exists durably, tends inevitably to assume a definite form and to organise itself, and law is nothing else than this very organisation in so far as it has greater stability and precision'.[8]

It is easy to see why law should occupy such an important place, for it provided a solid phalanx of data on which to base the inevitably tentative first steps in the still uncertain exercise of sociology. Social facts had to be studied from an aspect independent of subjective assessments, and since a 'legal regulation is what it is and there are no two ways of looking at it',[9] law clearly seemed to fit the bill.

The principle throughout, then, is to lock the sociologist into a level of data of sufficient permanence and tangibility to survive the vagaries of ethical and philosophical contamination. It finds expression in both the notion of social fact and the exhortation to treat 'social facts as things'.

At this point, a point at which Durkheim had fully established a subject-matter for sociology, it will be useful to pause and comment on the achievement. As we have already mentioned, all the stages of this method took a lead from the positive methodology of natural science. Such guidance was a means of injecting rationality into social science, and he rejected criticism of his methodology as 'positivist' by arguing that 'what our critics have called our positivism is only one certain aspect of this rationalism'—though this in itself could not resolve the issue since it left open the nature of the relationship between the two. In any event, what Durkheim never achieved was a coherent account of the general suitability of social phenomena for this positivist, rationalist method. He argued, quite rightly, that if social life was to be amenable to a positive methodology, then the data of social life would have to be construed in a particular way, but he failed to demonstrate adequately that the purpose of that construction was legitimate. Such demonstration as he gave exhibited a series of excesses. One excess was to assume that having recognized philosophy to be incapable of addressing sociological questions, sociology should insulate itself from philosophically informed reflection as to the nature of social life. He proposed 'not to anticipate the conclusions of sociological science by a philosophical view but simply to indicate by what external signs it is possible to recognize the facts of which it must treat'[10]—as if the nature of the knowledge which sociology sought to organize could be separated from epistemological and philosophical concerns. Anyway, he as much admitted that philosophy was of importance in his investigation by opting quite firmly for an inductive mode of reasoning and constantly sniping at those favouring deduction—'. . . in the absence of . . . empirical proof, only deductive reasonings are possible, whose conclusions can have no other than presumptive value'[11]—a debate clearly within the compass of a philosophy of knowledge. The assumption that positive methods were suitable for the study of social life was itself a part philosophical assumption, and one which Durkheim perhaps failed to justify.

A second excess was perpetrated in his delineation of the social from the psychological. The two for Durkheim were quite separate and every time a social fact is explained psychologically he considered it as certain that the explanation was false. Psychology he considered as individualistic and introspective. He identified social life as a collective phenomenon, and furthermore as a collective phenomenon which was by and large a prisoner of history. As he said, 'we must remember that the greater part of our social institutions were bequeathed to us by former generations. We ourselves took no part in their formation and consequently we cannot by introspection discover the causes which brought them about.'[12] In this Durkheim was quite right. Social actors cannot create a social world. But this did not entail that social activity should be stripped of the subjective. He erected a false and excessive dichotomy between introspection and the objectified data which was the stuff of his sociology, a dichotomy reinforced by a matching division between the individual and the collective.

Each of these excesses led Durkheim to a philosophically illiterate view of the nature of social phenomena. Whilst recognising that a distinction of importance obtained between, say, the level of molecules and that of living cells, such that they required separate sciences, and whilst using this distinction by way of analogy to justify the need for a peculiarly social level of explanation for 'social facts', he failed to give sufficient weight to the more fundamental division between natural and social phenomena in general. He was so intent to part the social from the psychological that he all but ignored their communality as social vis-à-vis natural sciences. In any event he neglected to pursue his own logic, for if each of the sciences was so different, addressing fundamentally diverse subject matters, it might also have been the case that the methods to be employed should be different: if there was to be a peculiarly social level of explanation, what of a peculiarly sociological method, rather than massive borrowing from positive science? Instead the natural scientific method was given primacy and the social world construed to make that primacy appropriate. Hence the need for a sociological equivalent to the discrete data of natural science, and the genesis of the category 'social facts', whose objective reality was 'our fundamental principle'.[13] This was the scene of Durkheim's greatest intemperance. The category cleaved the Gordian knot between fact and value in a fashion which ill compares with Weber's determination analytically to untie the two only as far as was necessary to achieve a sociological science. Durkheim's sword was a far too vicious instrument. Durkheim equated values with subjectivity. Limiting the former was therefore considered to necessitate the exclusion of the latter, but this conflated the need for objective social treatment of social phenomena (i.e. the elimination of bias) with the need to treat such phenomena as objectified (i.e. 'out there', with a reality of their own).

This conflation was reinforced by the early reliance upon legal codes as the paradigmatic social facts. Law fitted the criteria of 'social fact', appearing incontrovertibly to possess a supreme facticity, an ultimate externality and an obvious element of constraint. But on reflection that facticity, at least for a sociologist divested of common-sense assumptions about the reality of law, was both tenuous and contingent. As Rex has argued, from a neo-Weberian standpoint, we should be wary of assuming that laws are simple empirical facts. 'We are too readily impressed by the image of rolls of parchment or stone tablets and hence tend to think of law as a quasi material object. But the essence of the law is not in the material through which it is published but in its meaning.'[14] Unlike Durkheim, Rex appraises the social world as meaningful and construes law as an object of sociological study in a fashion corresponding to that appraisal. Durkheim appraises law in the context of his positive method, and finds an endorsement of the suitability of that method from the apparent objectivity of the data itself. Now, it must be noted that Rex is not merely pointing to the fact that people can interpret the law differently. Though that does happen (indeed, it is one of the assumptions built in to an adversary system of justice) the implication need be no more than that to be attached to the fact that we differentially identify an object, as, say, a sea-shell, an ornament, or, more fancifully, a sailboat for a mermaid—a case in which we would still all be happy to agree that 'the object' had a real existence in time and space. What Rex is saying is that the fashion in which social actors understand law as a 'real' fact in social life, is itself dependent on a certain subjective attitude towards it. What Durkheim did was to consider that, since law was acted towards in society as if it were a fact, then sociology had leave to treat it as such in general analyses involving law and other social variables. In other words he took a contingent feature of social life and adopted it as a methodological (and philosophical) maxim. In the words of Rex, he was taking over lay or participant theories about law and perpetrating a type of sociology (based on the commonsense world) that he himself had so disparaged.

SOCIAL FACTS—THE NORMAL AND THE PATHOLOGICAL

Social facts were considered to be of at least two types; 'those which conform to given standards and those which "ought" to be different'[15]—the normal and the pathological. The distinction arose in the following way. First, Durkheim's sociology was comparative, both within and between societies and over time. One problem then was to find a valid basis for comparison. Secondly, it was necessary to show how sociology, whilst remaining true to itself, could none the less be of use to society. For if sociology had to avoid value judgements in its practice, it had to be of value through the applicability of its conclusions in terms of a practical effectiveness.

The solution to both problems lay in an adequate differentiation of the normal and the pathological since 'for societies as for individuals health is good and desirable, disease on the contrary is bad and to be avoided. If then we can find an objective criterion, inherent in the facts themselves, which enables us to distinguish scientifically between health and morbidity in the various orders of social phenomena, science will be in a position to throw light on practical problems and still remain faithful to its own method.'[16] Durkheim's solution had the virtue of apparent simplicity and 'instead of aspiring to determine at the outset the relations of the normal and the morbid to vital forces' he elected to 'simply seek some external and perceptible characteristic'[17] to enable the differentiation of the two orders of facts. That characteristic was the level of generality. Social facts of the widest distribution were to be the normal, or average type, others morbid or pathological. The distinction was methodological, and intended to have no moral connotations. Thus the fact of crime was normal for Durkheim, since crime was found in all societies and is moreover 'bound up with the fundamental conditions of all social life'.[18] And not only crime, but a certain kind of crime was normal and if the crime rate should drop noticeably below the average for that type of society in a given epoch 'there is no occasion for self congratulation . . . for we may be certain that this apparent progress is associated with some social disorder'.[19] At the same time, it was open to sociologists, as to others, to abhor crime from a value standpoint. In this way, knowingly choosing an exposition of his taxonomy calculated morally to affront, Durkheim brutally enforced the separation of science and ethics.

Since both normality and its converse were valid categories only in relation to a given group of phenomena, it was necessary to classify the various social species, such classification based upon 'the nature and number of the component elements and their mode of combination'.[20] This in turn enabled the explanation of social facts to achieve maximum precision.

Explanation was to take a dual form, having to account for both the causes and the effects of social facts. Such explanation was to be *social* explanation, couched in terms of preceding social facts (cause) and social ends (effects or functions). Though his position changed on this, in Durkheim's earlier works it is the facts of social morphology which are given prominence. In *The Division of Labour in Society* Durkheim identified the number of social units and the degree of social density as key aspects of the social milieu to be used in sociological explanation and, though these were not to be taken as exhausting the *possibilities*, they did in his view exhaust the need for further *explanations*.

The ability to give causal explanation in this way was itself dependent upon the fundamental principle of the objective reality of social facts, which displayed the exteriority and the discreteness necessary for the juxtaposition and establishment of determinate relations. Again we find ourselves returning to this remarkably ubiquitous category—truly the touchstone of Durkheim's method. He began with a subject-matter that would exclude the subjective from sociology and concludes his method by erecting explanatory principles which, for him, required that exclusion. As we shall see below in considering Weber this was in some ways a gratuitous requirement, for Weber both subscribed to the notion of cause existing in sociology yet retained a commitment to viewing the social world as inherently meaningful, and adapted an epistemology which relied throughout on data as meaning-related. Successful or not, that method demonstrated that cause and meaning should not be construed as mutually exclusive without extensive prior cogitation.

Durkheim thought that a scientific attitude entailed a positive method. He had sufficient imperialism to demand a peculiarly social level of explanation, but insufficient to demand a unique sociological method. In saving sociology from philosophy he committed it to an excessive scientism. Like all scientists, Durkheim wanted to find a level which would provide ground rules for talking and disagreeing about sociological propositions. But this need not have entailed the endowment of phenomena with a tangibility itself contingent on a certain subjective attitude. Durkheim failed to differentiate properly the value question of objectivity and the epistemological question of objectification—Weber will show that a refusal to construe social facts as objectified does not necessarily deprive us of grounds for debate and assessment. To be sure, the construction of sociological theory containing truth-like propositions demands the independent identification of phenomena. But this should open up the possibility of reflection as to the validity of such theorizing for social phenomena, rather than persuade us to accept their legitimacy *a priori* and to arrange the social world, perhaps perversely, to meet that purpose. As Durkheim said, man cannot create the social world as an idiosyncratic project, for it is prior to him. A sociologist, as observer, has rather more latitude to describe the world in whatever terms he chooses—subject only to the restrictions placed upon him by the academic market place. That, however, is his scientific responsibility not his scientific licence and in the final analysis we must have a weightier endorsement for the methods we employ than that they have found success at the hands of a science investigating a quite different order of phenomena from that which we address.

SUBSTANTIVE WORK

We turn now to consider Durkheim's substantive work on law. Characteristically, that work entailed no sterile pursuit of a defintion of law and neither was it limited to a particular legal regulation. Law was rather treated sui generis. In a wide sweep through the histories of several societies Durkheim adduced evidence from legal codes for the themes of his treatise on social solidarity given in *The Division of Labour in Society*. The problem that book was to address is stated early on in the work and, without tantalization, the solution is stated there also. 'This work had its origins in the question of the relations of the individual to social solidarity. Why does the individual, while becoming more autonomous, depend more upon society? How can he be at once more individual and more solidary?' [21] Durkheim's curiosity was aroused by these contradictory yet parallel movements. If this was the problem, then Durkheim saw its resolution in 'a transformation of social solidarity due to the steadily growing development of the Division of Labour. That is how we have been led to make this the object of our study.' [22]

The method employed was to be that of the positive sciences, with law as a source of data, considered in accordance with his strictures to study social facts and to study them as things. Whether social solidarity produces law or whether the relation was the reverse was not important at this stage. It was enough to recognise that the 'two orders of fact are linked and vary at the same time and in the same sense. The more solidary the members of a society the more they sustain diverse relations ... Moreover, the number of these relations is necessarily proportional to the jurisdictional rules which determine them ... we can thus be certain of finding reflected in law all the essential varieties of social solidarity.'[23]

There is then, a tripartite relation between law, social solidarity and the division of labour. Durkheim gives marriage as one example. In a given society the state of conjugal solidarity is symbolized by the totality of juridicial rules which constitute it. The stronger the marriage ties the more numerous and complex are the legal rules expressing this union. As history progresses, so too does the importance of marriage, and 'it is certain that at the same time sexual labour is more and more divided'.[24] A woman's role, claims Durkheim, has become more specialized as she has withdrawn increasingly from public life and 'consecrated her entire life to the family'.[25] This exposition on marriage was necessarily tentative since all that it and other examples established was that a correlation existed between the three orders of facts. To determine whether the division of labour was an essential as against an epiphenomenal feature of social life, this type of social linking had to be compared with others by classifying and juxtaposing the different types of social solidarity. This was to be achieved through the study of law. Since 'law reproduces the principal forms of social solidarity, we have only to classify the different types of law to find therefrom the types of social solidarity which correspond to it.[26]

The juristic distinction between public and private law he rejected at once, because it involved the notion of the state and 'it is not scientific to make a fundamental classification repose on a notion so obscure and badly analysed'.[27] Instead, he founded a taxonomy on the varying sanctions attached to legal rules. Differences in sanction were based on 'the place they (legal rules) hold in the public conscience, the role they play in society',[28] so that here then was a criterion sufficiently social and objective to be used in assigning legal rules in a classificatory scheme.

Sanctions are of two kinds, those which involve suffering or loss, and those which do not intend (though they may gratuitously entail) suffering, but merely strive to return things to their previous state. The first correspond to repressive, penal law, the second to restitutive law, including civil, commerical, procedural, administrative and constitutional law (after the penal elements have been abstracted). Each type in turn corresponds to a particular type of social solidarity, respectively mechanical and organic.

To break a penal law is to commit a crime, calling forth punishment. This is so in all societies, says Durkheim, but not because members of society must impose such laws for their own or other's benefit. The function of criminal sanction is not to rehabilitate. Such a view would accord too much weight to calculation and reflection in the determination of penal laws and punishments, and further would fail to account for the fact that the amount of harm done to society by criminal acts is not related regularly to the amount of punishment. For Durkheim, the 'only common characteristic of all crimes is that they consist in acts universally disapproved of by members of each society'.[29]   See Deming quote Royal commission on Capital Punishment

Crimes attack the common sentiments of the *conscience commune* (common conscience) held by all socially healthy individuals. It is for this reason that the rule 'ignorance of the law is no defence', as applied under the penal law, entails no fiction—only the pathological do not have the penal law 'engraven in their consciences'. The legal rules are known and accepted by everybody. In this they display certain similarities with moral rules but are differentiated from the latter by virtue of their organized character.

Punishment and crime are but two sides of the same coin. Legal regulation and sanction are inseparable and thus penal law, in codified form, prescribes both the obligations and the sanctions whereas civil law 'and more generally in every type of law with restitutive sanctions, the legislator takes up and solves the two questions separately'.[30] The general nature of criminal acts, as provoking the conscience commune, gives rise to two other specific characteristics of penal law. First, 'the functioning of repressive justice tends to remain more or less diffuse'.[31] The whole society has been shocked and the whole society participates in meting out justice, hence the institution of the jury to represent 'the people'. Secondly, because of the strength of the sentiments at issue, penal law evolves very slowly. 'The collective sentiments to which crime corresponds must . . . singularize themselves from others . . . they must have a certain average intensity.'[32] It is insufficient that sentiments be widespread; they must also be strongly felt and persist over time. Only slowly do they find expression in penal law.

It is this *conscience commune*, then, which is the key to understanding crime and punishment—acts do not shock the *conscience commune* because they are criminal: they are criminal because they shock the *conscience commune*. Likewise, it is the nature of the *conscience commune* which explains the nature of punishment. Essentially, punishment consists of 'a passionate reaction, of graduated intensity, that society exercises through the medium of a body acting upon those of its members who have violated certain rules of conduct'.[33] The collective reaction derives from the communality of held sentiments.

So far as penal law expresses a form of social solidarity, therefore, it expresses one based upon resemblances amongst the individual conscience. Social cohesion is founded upon conformity. It is a 'solidarity sui generis which, born of resemblances, directly links the individual with society'.[34] Punishment has the effect of maintaining this solidarity by enforcing similarities. Penal law protects the force of the *conscience commune* from enfeeblement, 'both in demanding from each of us a minimum of resemblances without which the individual would be a menace to the unity of the social body, and in imposing upon us the respect for the symbol which expresses and summarizes these resemblances at the same time that it guarantees them'.[35]

Here then is the firm basis of comparison of social solidarities, for 'in determining what fraction of the juridical system penal law represents we at the same time measure the relative importance of this solidarity'.[36]

In that restitutive differs from repressive law, the social solidarity it represents is different accordingly. Restitutive sanctions are far from being wholly or mainly expiatory in character, but consist of a simple return in state. The judge speaks of law, not punishment. Such law, moreover, has no direct relation to the *conscience commune*, and for this reason restitutive law is implemented by ever more specialized agencies and can change rapidly and dramatically. None the less, restitutive law in the form of say, contract law, is not on these grounds to be denied a social character as if it were relevant only to the parties it governs. All law is a social thing. This was important, especially in regard to contract, since part of Durkheim's self-ordained remit was to contradict scholars who, without concern for empirical history or science, had elevated the notion of contract to a key place in a theory of society. Durkheim allowed no such 'metaphysic' and gave primacy to society even in the face of the social contract theorists' modal example. Contract depends upon the non-contractual, and if 'the contract has the power to bind, it is society which gives this power to it'.[37] Without societal sanction, contracts simply become promises without moral authority. 'Every contract thus supposes that behind the parties implicated in it there is society.'[38] Society does, however, play a restricted role in restitutive law, intervening only through the intermediary of specialized agencies.

Restitutive law takes two forms and there are two types of corresponding solidarity to be located, the negative and the positive. Negative relations are engendered by that law which unites only people with things, positive relations by law uniting people with people. The categories derive from the juristic distinction between rights real and personal. Real rights, including the law of property, signify a relationship with things and only these give a 'preferential and successorial right'. The person is bound to the thing directly without the mediation of other people, as compared with claims on a debtor's property, for instance. As a result of this character real rights preclude hostility between people, but cannot promote consensus. A complete legal system of this type would 'resemble an immense constellation where each star moves in its own orbit without concern for the movements of neighbouring stars'[39]—and in this case law would contribute nothing to social cohesion.

Taking away from restitutive law the negative and abstemious rules of real rights we are left with a corpus of law expressing a cooperation 'which derives, in essentials, from the division of labour'.[40] Thus, for instance, domestic law symbolizes the 'particular solidarity which unites the members of a family in accordance with the division of labour'.[41] Contract law especially is the essence of cooperative and complementary relations, for the exchange implied, 'presupposes some division of labour more or less developed',[42] but commercial, procedural and other forms of restitutive law also promote cooperation.

To sum up then, cooperative law governs a social solidarity which results from the division of labour. Therefore, there are two systems of the interlocking elements of law and social solidarity, penal law and mechanical solidarity, with cohesion based on social resemblances embodied in a forceful *conscience commune*; cooperative law and organic solidarity, cohesion being based on complementary relations signified by the division of labour. Durkheim found that the two systems varied inversely and according to a more or less unilinear progression. Solidarity based on the division of labour was found to be ever the more predominant form and as it developed mechanical solidarity declined accordingly.

The explanation given for the development of the division of labour was that such specialization and complementary relations as it entailed were a necessary means of restoring the increased competition for scarce resources which arose as societies got larger. However, gross size as such was less significant than the higher levels of contact and interaction that generally characterized a more voluminous society. Greater social density, then, constituted the key variable in the transformation from mechanical to organic solidarity.

This substantive thesis has come in for a great deal of questioning over the years and still gives rise to empirical research and theoretical wrangles. The indictment laid most regularly concerns the empirical adequacy of the thesis. Merton stated the basic problem in an early review of the first English translation of *The Division of Labour in Society*, pointing out that the transition from mechanical to organic solidarity was adduced from defective ethnographic data. 'With Maine and Steinmetz, he affects to note the preponderance, even the exclusive existence, of *penal* law in primitive society. In point of fact, as recent field studies have demonstrated, primitive societies possess also a corpus of restitutive civil law, involving rights and duties between individuals, and kept in force by social mechanisms.'[43] More recently Schwartz and Miller,[44] while not claiming to have disproved the thesis, have also questioned its empirical basis on the evidence provided by a cross cultural survey of legal processes. They scaled societies according to the dimensions of mediation, police and specialized counsel, the three being found to exist hierarchically, i.e. whilst some displayed none and some displayed only mediation, where the police existed as an agency mediation was also present and where specialized counsel existed both of the others were present. To the extent that mediation is taken as an index of restitution the findings appear to run counter to Durkheim's claims.

Against this, Baxi[45] has pointed to the need for reticence in accepting Schwartz and Miller's findings. Part of the problem resides in the very general nature of Durkheim's propositions and the difficulties in achieving an adequate operationalization of them. The categories of repression and restitution are somewhat taken for granted—many authors would, for instance, wish to question whether the presence of an overt sanction exhausts the category of repressive law. There may be more to restitutive law than mere restitution (as in the non-contractual, societal, element in contract): there may also be more to repressive law than penal sanctions, and more law that is repressive than contains such sanctions.

However, the thesis can be seen to be problematic even without levelling criticisms at this general level, for at a number of points

Durkheim provides counter evidence to his own assertions or goes directly against his own method.

Durkheim specifies, for instance, the dual purpose of every written penal law; 'to prescribe certain obligations and to define the sanctions which are attached to them',[46] this being contrary to the practice in civil law of treating the questions separately. Yet he notes, apparently without embarrassment, that the Pentateuch, an ancient Jewish criminal code, fails to mention sanctions in many of its precepts, for which he gives the witless explanation that it was not 'a code properly speaking' and if it prescribed 'duties which assuredly were sanctioned by punishments, they were not ignored or unknown to the Jews nor was it necessary to make them manifest. On the contrary, since the book is only a tissue of national legends, we can rest assured that everything that it contains was engraven in every conscience.'[47]

This complacent attitude to recalcitrant data appears again in his discussion of the functioning of repressive justice. Supposedly the whole society participates in this exercise, yet the recognition that in certain cases this function is exercised by a privileged class or a specialized agent is bypassed. Such 'facts do not lessen (the force of the argument). This delegation may be due either to the very great multiplicity of affairs which necessitate the institution of special functionaries, or to the very great importance assumed by certain persons or classes and which makes them the authorized interpreters of collective sentiments'[48]—which merely raises more issues than it solves.

Finally, consider this treatment of crime under mechanical solidarity. Crime offends the collective and it is the collective which seeks retribution. Yet what of the institution he points to of delicta primata, those Roman delicts where punishment depended on the decision of the offended individuals, and this for a wide range of criminal offences? This was by no means an idiosyncratic case for, as Durkheim himself indicated, similar practices were to be found in Greek and Hebrew law. Durkheim's answer was to locate these legal rules between his two major categories of repressive and restitutive law as intermediate forms. But this ran totally contrary to his own method. His taxonomy of law was supposedly based upon the accumulation of empirical data into true 'natural' categories according to the nature of the sanction, but in this case he turned his method on its head and used the taxonomy itself to adjudicate the data.

Overall it is difficult to avoid the conclusion that Durkheim's substantive work on law must be faulted along similar lines to those suggested for his methodology and view of the subject-matter.

Respect for the boldness with which he helped to carve out a new discipline must be tempered by recognising that such a coup was only achieved at the cost of a number of excesses. Those of his methodology and view of the subject-matter were mentioned earlier: severing instead of simply distinguishing sociology from philosophy and psychology; and the de facto exclusion of subjectivity. In *The Division of Labour in Society* these excesses manifest themselves in an over-ordering of the empirical data into Durkheim's own conceptual schema. An initial determination to deal only with 'facts' as empirical data led to a divorce of the theory from empirical nourishment.

MAX WEBER

In treating Max Weber's sociology of law we will need to trace through his own understanding of sociology, its subject-matter and his method, as we did for Émile Durkheim. This will allow a conclusion which can bring together the work of these two writers around the themes documented in Chapter I. It is not our intention to present the full flavour of Weber's originality nor the reflection in his work of the then prevailing views of the nature of scientific knowledge. We will simply address the character of Weber's work and juxtapose the types of statements he makes with regard to law with his own account of the nature of sociology. His writings on law have to be seen in terms of methodology because only in the latter do we gain a clear impression of the operating concept of his sociology. As with Durkheim, Weber's work on the substantive area of law is built upon a coherent sociological edifice utilizing modes of explanation justified by an appreciation of how social science can study social phenomena. The diversity of study even in relation to law is great; from an interest in the relation of law to structures of social action to a view of law as indexing a historical movement towards increasing rationality. With each interest, however, modes of explanation are used which have been fought for in the face of a particular understanding of social action. The unity of sociology is never undermined. We must not imagine that discrepancies will not arise nor that substantive investigation and general statement will flow directly from methodological considerations. Given the extent of Weber's work such harmony would have been a remarkable achievement.

For the purposes of exposition we will break down the discussion as follows: general framework; Weber on sociology; Weber on methodology; Weber on law; Conclusion.

GENERAL FRAMEWORK

Weber's sociology of law is contained within his work published in 1922 entitled *Economy and Society*. The work carried the 'ambitious plan to investigate ... the inter-relationships between economic institutions and relationships, and all other phenomena and relationships of society, of the present and past'.[1] Legal institutions and relationships were basic to the scheme, but the scheme is not only of substantive but of methodological relevance as well. The questions of interest here are:

(a) how are social phenomena and relationships between them to be identified in a manner fitting the logic of scientific discovery?

(b) what is the logic of scientific discovery?

(c) how are relationships between social phenomena to be explained?

(d) what is the purpose of such an explanation?

The first three questions will be addressed in the sections on sociology and methodology but a few words on (d) will be given here.

It must be the case that, in one sense, the purpose of putting forward explanations derives from the methodological imperatives residing in particular forms of scientific activity. By methodological imperatives we mean those considerations which provide for the *validity* of statements generated by a particular form of explanation. In this sense, explanation serves nothing but the truth, and demonstrable truth at that. But it is equally clear that Weber did not believe in a single truth, a truth which could embody reality in one statement or many statements generated by a single form of explanation. Weber required all types of explanation to meet the canons of scientific inquiry, but by denying to himself and to others the ability to lay bare social reality by a single root of inquiry, he was enabled to develop and justify his own particular orientation to this infinite and varied social world.

By paying attention to the totality of phenomena constituting the fabric of society, Weber sought to highlight and understand the peculiar features of Western capitalism then prevailing and in particular the relationship of legal development to economic development. In the words of Rheinstein, 'what was needed even for the limited goal of understanding the rise of Western capitalism was an analysis of society as a whole'.[2] This limited goal represents part of the 'value-orientation' of Weber and since Weber was adamant that no one method of explanation was necessarily superior to any other, it was open to him to formulate a method satisfying his inquiry into the rise of Western capitalism. For Weber any one explanation serves a *particular* value orientation and can be judged through its utility in enlightening the segment of reality such chosen orientation seeks to study.

Value-orientation: Most students of sociology in the West associate the name of Weber with value-neutrality in science. Value-neutrality ranges from strictures concerning the conduct proper to the teaching profession (a warning against cooption by the authorities) to issues more closely related to the conduct of scientific research. Science is concerned with establishing the truth of propositions and such an endeavour must eschew value-judgements. A scientist can be pleased or displeased by the facts as found but such evaluation enters not into their discovery. The distinction between fact and value is one of logic and a logical necessity for science. Ethical neutrality is linked to the notion of objective validity, such validity not being open to question by subjectively held moral beliefs, but it is equally closely linked to the notion of value-orientation which acts as a limiting factor on the applicability of ethical neutrality.

Even if we accept that values are irrelevant to the veracity of scientific propositions there remains the issue of why certain questions are asked by science. For Weber, value-orientation suggests the question the scientist addresses to reality and goes further in guiding the conduct of inquiry. Value-orientation is not a simple question of what appears to be of interest, but guides the scientist by requiring him to seek the reasons why a particular phenomenon or question seems important and important in relation to what. For instance, Weber considered legal rationality to be important in relation to the mutual influence obtaining between the legal and the economic phenomena of society. This in turn was important with regard to the development of one form of economic organization (capitalism). This value-orientation guides the study of legal rationality to make it relevant to the general consideration and means that one cannot trace Weber's substantive sociology from 'pure' methodological considerations. Value-orientation chooses the topic, provides criteria for the choice of relevant materials and only after such selection has taken place is the scientist encapsulated in a value-free vacuum concerned solely with the objective validity of the statements he makes about the world.

Weber limits value-orientation to the human sciences and this gives a particular thrust to the argument. The argument assumes that values do not inhere in nature but do inhere in society and that by referring, or being oriented to different aspects of societal values, each human scientist can give us a new perspective on a problem because importance is attached to elements neglected by an orientation towards other values.

In some places Weber seems to say that value-orientation is endemic in, and specific to the human sciences because the latter operate at an individualistic level of explanation, that is, relate phenomena together specifically in terms of their individual characteristics as opposed to subsuming that relationship under a general rule. Weber accepts the distinction between the logic of statements of generalization and the explanation of the unique but does in fact, at different points in his substantive interests, utilize both forms of analysis. For instance he was interested in understanding the development of *particularly* Western modes of legal thought at the same time as the *general* drive towards rationality. In his work, Weber does not limit general (as opposed to individualistic) explanations to the natural sciences nor individualistic explanations to the social sciences. Both forms of explanation may be used in the social sciences so long as they further the analysis of the phenomena to be studied in a causally adequate manner. Weber is able to counter arguments that the subjectivity of social phenomena precludes the scientific goal of objective knowledge while stressing that only partial knowledge is available to any science. Partial knowledge alone is attainable because science must use concepts, and concepts are by their nature abstract and reality can never be equated with the totality of the concepts in which it finds expression. Weber was quite convinced of the 'futility of the idea . . . that it could be the goal of cultural sciences . . . to construct a closed system of concepts which can encompass and classify reality in some definite manner and form and from which it can be deduced again'.[3] The main goal of the social sciences is to understand why particular historical phenomena came to be as they are. But this presumes an abstraction from the complexity of social reality. Both social and natural scientific forms of analysis involve and are dependent upon a guided selection from the 'infinitude of reality'.

By demarcating the area of ethical neutrality via an understanding of value-orientation, Weber is not, therefore, advocating a single methodology meet for the human sciences, only a characteristic of all scientific methodologies in the quest for truth. Truth in science is not a synonym for reality. Science cannot grasp the infinite and extensive reality but can gain partial knowledge by being oriented to particular types of question. If Weber warns against anything, he warns against academic imperialism. The types of questions to be addressed by the social scientist do not spring automatically from the 'nature of things' but are consequential on a value-orientation.

This will be of considerable importance if one is to make a claim that the nature of sociological study springs from the nature of phenomena to be studied. For Weber this does not follow. There is not only the distinction between looking at a form of social action sociologically; psychologically; from the point of view of physiology; etc., but within sociology itself distinctions between various methodologies (say qualitative and quantitative; generalizing or individualistic) are not open to evaluation in terms of the nature of social action per se but in terms of their efficacy in forwarding study from a particular value-orientation. This must continually be borne in mind when looking at the particular methodology which Weber used in the study of social phenomena and the methodological imperatives which seem to flow from his own characterization of the nature of social action and social relationships.

For Weber, then, methodological imperialism is tantamount to raising the God of cognition above its proper place: methodology is a heuristic device or combinations of such devices to be assessed on grounds of utility rather than scientific protocol or over-confidence in the ability of concepts to grasp the elusive reality of things. Explanation does not serve only truth, it serves the partial knowledge opened up by a particular value-orientation.

WEBER ON SOCIOLOGY

Reflecting the European tradition within which he worked, sociology for Weber was concerned with discovering, first, the basic units of society—those phenomena and relationships which constitute the flesh on the demographic skeleton—and, secondly the empirically observable regularities within such phenomena and relationships. Weber realized, however, that social phenomena cannot be grasped by simple observation and enumeration of external behaviour. The subjective meaning attached to behaviour is necessary to the identification of that behaviour. Weber called such an understanding of social phenomena 'interpretive understanding' and sociology is a science 'which attempts the interpretive understanding of social action in order to therefore arrive at a causal explanation of its course and effect'.[4] That interpretation is required merely reflects our inability to make social phenomena comprehensible by the naturalistic method of observation and enumeration. Weber's use of *rational interpretation*, as we shall see, allowed the *individualistic* relation between phenomena (a meaningful relationship) to be subsumed under *general* rules.

Weber establishes action as the basic reality addressed by sociology. As Weber says: 'In "action" is included all human behaviour when and in so far as the acting individual attaches a subjective meaning to it.'[5] The term social action is reserved for activities whose intent is related by the individuals involved to the conduct of others and is oriented accordingly.[6] At this stage we can see that a normative orientation is given to social action which will be important when we turn to discuss the means Weber used to generate rational interpretation. Normative orientation means that social actors act with regard to the expectations of how other social actors will act, or more properly with regard to the probability that others will act in certain ways. The notion of normative expectation will mean that all rational interpretation remains at the *probabilistic* level. For Weber social structures have to be analysed as the *probability* that men under given conditions will 'orient their conduct to a meaningful precept' which in itself 'furnishes them with a reason for so orienting their conduct'. Action will then be *causally adequate* when there is a probability that a certain course of behaviour will result from other courses of behaviour whose subjective meaning we can subjectively grasp. With this idea of probability (or meaning-causality) and its relation to social structures, Weber shows how action develops; gives rise to other actions; and finally, bases the political, economic and legal organization of society. Meaning-causality refers to Weber's belief that an awareness that social phenomena depend for their identification on an understandable meaning, does not preclude sociology from engaging in causal analysis. But he does utilize a peculiar dualism with regard to meaning. The first type refers to the 'actually existing meaning in the given concrete case of a particular actor'. The second is a 'theoretically pure type of subjective meaning attributed to the hypothetical actor'.[7] It was this pure type of meaning which Weber used to construct models of action. In the construction of such models Weber further distinguishes between four types of action depending on the orientation attributed to the hypothetical actor. The types were 'affectual' (action driven by emotion); 'traditional' (action driven by routinized practice); '*wertrational*' (action expressing or realizing values); and '*zweckrational*' (action driven to serving rationally calculable ends, where the ends and the means to the ends were both calculated and taken into account by the actor). Rational interpretation of action is only possible, says Weber, if the scientist builds a model of the ends and goals of the actor and the situations in which he is placed. From this the scientist can derive how the actor would act if he pursued his ends using a 'purely rational cause of action'. If in reality, the actor did not so act then the scientist could locate the causal significance of 'irrational factors' on the construction of action.

Sociology, then, refers to the interpretive understanding of social action. Social action is meaningful, but to enable sociology to reach objective knowledge it is necessary to conceive pure types of meaning and rationally interpret actual conduct by reference to a rational ideal type of conduct. In his substantive work, Weber is concerned both with explaining the existence of certain phenomena and with detailing uniformities in social and economic organization. In each case he is guided by a value-orientation which limited his ability to see reality. Within the area of ethical neutrality, he is concerned to formulate objectively verifiable general principles and generic types of concepts but such had to be built up from an understanding that sociology must grasp the meaning of action and render it intelligible. More specific detail on how this is done will be taken up in the next section but we can now see how this framework is related to substantive issues.

Concern with the interrelatedness of social phenomena as producing the fabric of society leads sociology to encompass the study of the whole of society, and societies past and present. Weber's value-orientation led him to consider the problem from the point of view of understanding the particular structure of one particular society at a particular time. The primary task of analyzing the relation between social phenomena is subordinated to the understanding of the particular structure of one form of capitalism. We may expect a certain tension, therefore, between analyzing the relation between social phenomena by the method of interpretation (which should enable us to grasp the status of any particular phenomenon within a society) and analyzing social phenomena in such a way so as to explain the variance that can be empirically seen between differing societies or the same society at different times. It was Weber's belief that he had resolved this tension and in a manner which retained the interconnectedness between social structures and the multifarious activities of men, that is, had neither reified social phenomena nor engaged in structural explanation.

WEBER ON METHODOLOGY

For Weber the purpose of science is explanation by locating cause. We now have to see what was given as the logic of such discovery of cause in the human sciences. The distinction of importance lies between the generalizing and the individualistic methods of science. The generalizing approach seeks a rational relation between two separately identifiable phenomena that can be intellectually grasped. We intimated above that the human sciences proceed along individualistic lines, seeking the *relation between phenomena* for the purpose of explanation. We further saw that such relationships between phenomena of the social world have to be grasped interpretively. Further, this interpretive understanding had to be causally adequate. We now have to see how this, for Weber, is achieved. Weber stresses that interpretive understanding has to be causally adequate if sociology is to establish generally valid rules. He is not then eschewing generalized explanation. For Weber both approaches can be useful and neither can claim to be the only route to scientific truth: 'a method must advance knowledge rather than be faithful to an imaginery ideal of cognition';[8] the choice between the methods given above lies within the domain of the type of knowledge sought which in turn reflects the sociologist's particular value-orientation. As Siddens argues, it is invalid to consider that 'causal "explanation" is only possible through classification of events under general laws . . . the formulation of good explanatory principles is not so much an end in itself as a means which may be used to facilitate the analysis of the particular phenomena which are to be explained'.[9]

Both the generalizing method and the individualistic method in sociology, however, must handle three important requirements. First, they must be causally adequate; secondly, in order to be able to identify types of social action or types of social relationships and to trace the nature of relationships between such social phenomena any method must pay attention to the subjective meaning of behaviour; thirdly, this subjectivity must be contained within the theoretical categories which are essential to the logic of the proof of causal relationships. The logic of such proof is one of description, categorization and comparison. As Parsons says, 'Weber's problem was to define the kinds of generalised categories which met the logical requirements of this scheme'[10] and at the same time embodied the use of subjectively meaningful categories. The type of generalized category which Weber used was the 'ideal type'. The 'ideal type' was to enable Weber to generate general propositions concerning the relation between phenomena which themselves were addressed by their specific individual characteristics.

Ideal types were necessary not only to fit the scheme of logical proof, but also to serve the first stage of scientific inquiry: the construction of a taxonomy of the phenomena within the scientist's observational field. Weber recognised the need to provide definitions of social phenomena not only because sure and unambiguous terminology is a pre-requisite for scientific discourse but also because it is a characteristic of social phenomena that they exist only in terms of our definitions of them. In other words if we use collective terms in social science, they are of our own making, and not given in the nature of things. If study is addressed to the inter-relation between social phenomena then we must provide concepts which relate to those phenomena. There may be many ways of providing such concepts; the ideal type was used by Weber (as opposed to the average type of Durkheim[11]) because it met the other requirements of the logic of the proof of causal relations. For Weber, historical and social uniqueness results from the specific combination of general factors. These general factors could be identified by and embodied in ideal types. An 'ideal type' is then an artificial construct but one which can be used to grasp the relationship between different phenomena by means of comparison and causal imputation. In other words the evolution of specific complexes of social phenomena can be causally treated by reference to their departure from the 'ideal type'. As Freund remarked, therefore, ideal types play a dual role. First, they allow for clarity of expression, and secondly, they allow the imputation of causal relationships between social phenomena.[12] Ideal types, however, are not fixed substantive entities which 'capture' reality; they are simply heuristic devices. A change in the content given to the ideal type, a change related to, say, its use by a sociologist with a differing value-orientation, would allow science to view the relationship between phenomena in a different way, or view the relationship between different facets of the same phenomena and generate knowledge which is both fresh and insightful yet meets the logical requirements of the type of demonstration of proof allowed by the use of ideal types—a logic as we said of description, categorization and comparison.

It is only by understanding the ideal type that we can see what is original in Weber's notion of interpretive understanding. Let us refer back to Weber's own words on the relation between adequacy at the level of meaning and causal adequacy. The former is a 'subjective interpretation of a coherent course of conduct' to the extent that 'its component parts' can be recognized as constituting a 'typical mean-ing complex'.[13] If for instance we observe a sequence of events, sub-jective interpretation is achieved when we can intellectually grasp the observed events as representing an intended meaning; we reach an understanding of what is going on.

As we have already noted, sociology is concerned to grasp the meaning of action and the 'interpretive grasp of meaning' means that the particular action to be analysed 'is placed in an understandable sequence of motivation, the understanding of which can be treated as an explanation of the actual course of behaviour'.[14] What does Weber add to this dimension by causal adequacy? In fact he adds something rather simple. Weber says that the 'interpretation of a sequence of events will be causally adequate in so far as, according to established generalities from experience, there is a probability that it will always actually occur in the same way . . . causal explanation depends on being able to determine that there is a probability . . . that a given observable event will be followed by or accompanied by another event'.[15] Putting the two together allows that a '*correct* causal inter-pretation of a concrete course of action is arrived at when the overt action and the motives have both been correctly apprehended and at the same time their relation has become *meaningfully* comprehensible. A correct causal interpretation of typical action means that the process which is claimed to be typical is shown to be both adequately grasped on the level of meaning and at the same time the interpreta-tion is to some degree causally adequate. If adequacy in respect to meaning is lacking, then no matter how high the degree of *uniformity* and how precisely its probability can be numerically determined, it is still an *incomprehensible statistical* probability, whether dealing with overt or subjective processes. On the other hand, even the most per-fect adequacy on the level of meaning has causal significance from the sociological point of view only insofar as there is some kind of proof for the existence of a *probability* that the action *in fact* normally *takes* the course which has been held to be meaning-adequate.'[16] Weber continues by saying that statistical uniformities constitute understand-able types of action and therefore constitute 'sociological generalisa-tions', only when they can be regarded as 'manifestations of the understandable subjective meaning of a course of social action'. Con-versely, 'formulations of a rational course of subjectively understand-able action constitute sociological types of empirical processes only when they can be empirically observed with a significant degree of approximation. It is unfortunately by no means the case that the actual likelihood of the occurrence of a given course of overt action is *always* directly proportional to the clarity of subjective interpretation.'[17]

There may be more than one way of arriving at such *correct* interpretation, but for Weber all such methods involve some use of ideal types. Weber insisted on recognizing the use of ideal-types and confronted the problem of achieving an ideal type of social action fitting his schema of proof. Weber's problem was, in Freund's words, one of how 'to establish, on the basis of interpretive understanding, a rational and accurate ideal type of social behaviour which would be compatible with . . . rational interpretation'.[18] It was for this purpose that Weber drew the four ideal types of social conduct; traditional; affectual; value-orientated; and goal oriented. By the ideal types of social action Weber located a particular state of mind as being represented in action. This state of mind represents in one sense the meaning of the action and, in the ideal type, has the form of 'theoretically conceived pure type' embodied in the hypothetical construction of social action. Goal-oriented (*zweckrational*) action is the ideal type which Weber gives as most susceptible of causal explanation, and this ideal type of rational conduct was, therefore, used to understand the *actual* cause of actions by studying the departure of the actual subjective meaning from the meaning residing in the ideal type. Relating back to value orientation, however, we can see that ideal types served the purpose of interpreting and explaining a particular historical configuration. The ideal types used by Weber were 'specifically delineated for that purpose and . . . do not reflect universally "essential" properties of reality'.[19]

There are problems with the formulation in Weber's use of the terms 'causal explanation' and 'causal interpretation'. For instance we could say that these represent two very different methods. Causal interpretation would stand as the simple probability of events following meaningful patterns understandable to the observer. Causal explanation, on the other hand, is made possible by the processes of categorization, description and comparison. It is clear, however, that whether this differentation serves to clarify Weber's position or not, both forms of scientific investigation are used by Weber to tackle the problem of meaning in a manner that allows sociological knowledge to be objective and demonstrable, not as truth, but as part of the truth.

CONCLUSION ON METHODOLOGY

The approach Weber adopts to the unique constellations of social material and the method of ideal-types both relate to the method of comparison contained within his logic of discovery, a logic designed to explain the particular characteristics exhibited by Western capitalism. The research determined the method applicable. To understand a sequence of empirical events causally, Weber needed to be able to examine comparable conditions. This required extensive and intensive historical documentation from societies past and present, plus the use of ideal types whereby similarities and differences between social phenomena or complexes of social phenomena could be located and explained. By a comparative analysis of causal sequences Weber tried to find the necessary and sufficient conditions for the rise of capitalism. But to highlight the 'real' causal relation between two phenomena or a sequence of phenomena Weber said we must construct 'unreal ones'. These unreal causes he termed objective possibilities representing ideal typical constructs. For instance, by using ideal types one can locate the causal effect of irrational or unforseen factors. Similarly if we know that A and B_1 happened and C followed, we can reconstruct an objectively possible idea of history in which B_1 is replaced by B_2. If we can intellectually grasp from our knowledge of history that result C would now no longer obtain then B_1 stands in relation to C as cause to effect. The nature of cause remains probabilistic because the particular relation between phenomena is a meaningful relation, and meaning is only graspable, for Weber, in the probability that men in like circumstances will orient themselves in a particular way. We are not therefore entitled to make judgements of *necessary* sequences, but simply to gather an appreciation of the significance of various phenomena or aspects of a single phenomena (for instance the ascetism of protestantism) in an unfolding sequence of events. The notion of 'objective possibility' allows the sociologist rationally to interpret social action and rational interpretation itself is open to causal explanation by the comparative method of ideal types.

In his methodology, Weber is always trying to relate the interpretation of particular social relationships to an understanding of the general relationships between social phenomena. Causal explanation is achieved by 'rational interpretation' which itself is facilitated by the construction of ideal types of social phenomena and objectively possible courses of events.

WEBER ON LAW

Weber, himself a lawyer, used historical documentation of legal developments to index both particular movements towards the rationality of modern societies and affinities between developing legal and economic orders. His approach to sociology would also lead one to expect a discussion of the various ways men can be oriented towards laws; a discussion of the causal importance of men orienting themselves to legal precepts, a discussion of legal rationality; and a discussion of law creation and its relationship to the economic structure of society. We should also expect such discussions to highlight the peculiarities of the nature of law creation and legal rationality in the West and their relation to the rise of capitalism. Weber is not found wanting, although the first two questions receive scant treatment when compared to Weber's interest in legal rationality.

WEBER'S IDEA OF LAW

Sociological inquiry seeks 'what actually happens in a community owing to the probability that persons participating in communal activity . . . subjectively consider certain norms as valid and practically act according to them, in other words, orient their own conduct towards those norms'.[20] Certain of these norms are legal norms, and Weber provides a means of distinguishing legal norms from the norms of ethics, custom, tradition, etc. To do this Weber provides a working definition of law generated from the concept of social action. One form of social action is action oriented to the idea that there exists some legitimate order. The probability that action will be so oriented Weber calls the 'validity' of the order in question.

Weber analyses different forms of legitimate order and their bases of validity in relation to the motives of those actors subject to the order, but he confines the term 'law' to that form of legitimate order which is guaranteed by the likelihood that coercion will be exercised by a group of people especially holding themselves ready to enforce conformity. Law, for Weber, 'is simply an "order system" endowed with certain guarantees of the probability of its empirical validity'.[21]

For sociology the task is to understand the action of members of society in relation to the legal order—to determine the nature of the belief in the validity of legal norms. In other words, part of Weber's sociology of law is to determine the bearing of a legal norm on the social activity of individuals. The central idea is that law is a 'set of "ought" ideas'[22] which are held in the minds of certain people, though not necessarily regarded as obligatory by them. A rational interpretation of the belief in validity enables Weber to discuss law without departing from his conception of history as a causal succession of unique events. The causal analysis looks not to what people do but to what they think about their actions. For the sociology of law the question becomes one of locating the reasons why the order comprised in the 'ought ideas' is regarded as legitimate. Since 'legitimacy' refers to subjective orientations, and 'law' merely to the availability of a coercive apparatus, 'legitimacy' and 'law' need not always go hand in hand. The existence of law is satisfied if the coercive apparatus is available to guarantee an order of norms to which people orient their action, but the particular orientation need not be one of legitimacy. It can include tradition, habit, efficacy, etc., but of course if people act from, say, tradition, then the legal order ceases to exist as a subjectively meaningful phenomenon.

It is clear that Weber is building up a taxonomy of *ideal* types of legitimate orders. Our inability to work out the *empirical* relation between the existence of a legitimate order, orientations to that order and its means of guarantee, is not therefore surprising. The ideal types do not appear empirically but provide a means for comparing actually existing orders. Within the area of law, it is then open to Weber to study the increasing rationality of legal concepts and practices as they developed in Western civilization.

Weber presents a theoretical construction of the general development of law and procedure. This development passes through the following stages: 'first, charismatic legal revelation through "law prophets", second, empirical creation and finding of law by legal notables . . .; third, imposition of law by secular or theocratic powers; fourth and finally, systematic elaboration of law and professionalised administration of justice by persons who have received their legal training in a learned and *formally logical* manner'.[23] These 'stages', acting as ideal types, can be used to locate the forces operating to effect or resist rationality in law and the development of legal domination. *Legal domination*, as opposed to charismatic or traditional domination, exists where the rules of legal order are implemented in the belief that they are legitimate because they conform with the statutes of a government that monopolizes their enactment and the legitimate use of physical force. By the method of ideal typical analysis, Weber attempts to show the conditions that led to the development of the particular type of law creation existing in the Western model of legal domination and the relation of this development to the economic structure of capitalism. In other words legal domination as it exists in the West represents only one method of law creation and the existing form of formal rationality of Western law only one avenue for the development of legal thought. Weber was particularly interested in the relation of such developments to the emergence of economic orders and this is perhaps why he gives so little attention to the question of the interpretive understanding of the creation of particular laws and the motives by which men oriented themselves to such laws. He was interested in the relationship of the development of law to the development of capitalism. The relationship between the two spheres is not a determinate one but relates people's belief in and expectation of a legitimate order to their economic activities. Weber gives especial attention to two issues. These were first, legal rationality, and secondly, 'subjective rights' such as freedom of contract.

LEGAL RATIONALITY

Weber is here concerned with the general process of legal thought and sought to explain the particular development of Western legal thought along lines of *logical formalism*. To understand this process Weber constructed four ideal types of legal thought according to whether it is rational or irrational with regard to formal or substantive criteria. Such ideal types are reflected in the model of the development of law and procedure given above, but it must be remembered that this is a device to facilitate understanding and not a chronological table of history nor a table of necessary evolution.

Formal irrationality in the law reflects the use both in the process of law-creation (in modern form the legislative process) and law-finding (in modern form the judicial process) of set criteria (the formal aspect), but criteria not open to the control of reason. Examples given include such means as prophetic revelation and trial by ordeal, for instance trial by battle. Irrationality is substantive if no set criteria are applied and legal thought proceeds along an inquiry of emotional evaluation or pure caprice.

To the extent that rational considerations base the activities of legal personnel they can in turn be formal or substantive. Freund suggests that substantive law rationalizes itself on the basis of utility whereas formal law rationalizes itself along lines of pure logic, but Weber is more specific and makes finer distinctions in order to understand the peculiar character of Western thought. Substantive rationality exists when the law does not acknowledge the limitations of formal procedure or logical consistency, but proceeds by way of the application of clearly conceived and articulated principles. To be rational formally the law proceeds by applying general criteria to operative facts in a generic manner.

Law is formal to the extent that 'only unambiguous general characteristics of the facts of the case are taken into account'[24] but by emphasizing the 'operative facts' basing legal determinations Weber was able to sub-divide formal rationality and to highlight the particular development of *logically formal* rationality. Rational formalism, then, can be of two kinds, the distinction depending on whether the legally relevant characteristics are of a tangible nature (i.e. perceptible to the senses) or not. The adherence 'to external characteristics of the facts . . . represents the most vigorous type of legal formalism'.[25] Law making and law finding are *formally rational in a logical sense* where the 'legally relevant characteristics of the facts are disclosed through the *logical analysis of meaning* and where, accordingly, definitely fixed legal concepts in the form of highly abstract rules are formulated and applied'.[26]

According to Rheinstein the problem of the relation of legal formalism to the growth of capitalism is the main problem addressed by Weber in his sociology of law. If we remember the ideal types of social action it is clear that logically formal rationality in legal thought corresponds to the purposive rationality which Weber regards as the quintessential feature of modern capitalism. The relationship between these two spheres, however, never delved into an economic or legal determinism. Weber understands the relation between economic and legal phenomena as representing similarities in mental states without identifying a *necessary* causal nexus between the two styles of thought. 'Cause' is always addressed as the rational interpretation of activities using ideal types of legal and economic organization to see the operative factors in their relative courses of development.

Weber gives body to his theoretical over-view of legal development by a remarkable documentation of legal processes both ancient and modern, and the influence of the secularization and bureaucratization of law on the drive towards rationality. Indeed these 'influences' take on the flavour of pre-conditions for rationalization, these pre-conditions themselves reflecting the historical development of the modern state with a form of legal domination in which legitimacy is given to a legal precept on the basis of its enactment by a constituted political authority. We must, however, be watchful of any attempt to assimilate historical analysis and ideal-typical analysis. It is probably the case that no society has ever existed representing a pure ideal typical character and, although Weber gives great weight to the growing logical formal rationality in legal thought and its relation to the development of capitalism, the latter phenomenon developed first in England where the logical rationality in legal thought never reached the level of development that was attained by continental jurists. Further, when Weber discusses in more detail the basis of beliefs in the legitimacy of legal orders he sees the conflict between formal and substantive criteria as ubiquitous and ongoing rather than just marking a stage in an evolutionary process. For Weber, it remains one of the functions of the sociology of law to understand this conflict and the various ways legal thought has developed in attempts at its resolution. The formal and substantive aspects of law give rise to competing views of justice, the antagonism between the two not being open to either judicial or sociological resolution. Sociology can merely see the extent to which the legitimacy of a legal order favours formal or substantive criteria and explain the departure of a particular order from the rational ideal type by reference to factors which causal analysis can show to have hindered or facilitated its development.

Weber concludes that the modern legal order is sustained by incompatible sets of belief in its validity. This ambiguity continually dilutes even its most formal aspects as reflected for instance in the judicial acts of interpretation and the emergence of social legislation. The conflict between formal and utilitarian values was seen as existing in all forms of domination and for Weber remained irreconcilable. In characterizing this basic conflict Weber formulated 'a frame of reference for analysing the struggle for power that occurs under each and any system of domination'. He became concerned with the relation of bureaucracy to the *utility* of the law's formal aspects and moved the sociology of law into the political arena.

SUBJECTIVE LAW

It is in his discussion of subjective law that Weber comes closest to positing a determinate relation between law and economy. Subjective law implies the possibility for an individual to appeal to the apparatus of coercion for the protection of those of his interests which exist independently of the rights which the law gives to all members of society. As Rheinstein says, 'in consequence of his general position in society a person can find himself as factually occupying a position in which he is likely to be able to exercise a power of disposition over other persons or over economic goods. This factual position can be fortified by the likelihood that the members of a special staff of the community will go into action to guarantee him his position. The situation in which he thus finds himself is that of having *a right.*'[27] Subjective law confers subjective rights, such a right being defined by Weber as the probability that a man occupying a certain position in society can call to his aid the coercive apparatus in order to guarantee him his position. 'The circumstances under which the community's staff will go into action on his behalf are indicated by the rules of *law.*'[28] Through the guarantee of legal protection, he who is in the possession of the 'power of disposition over a thing or person obtains a specific security for the permanency of his position; for instance one to whom a promise has been made obtains through the legal guarantee a super-added security for the performance of the promise. Such is, indeed, the most elementary relationship between law and economy.'[29] But it is not, as Weber points out, the only one. Law, as a set of prevailing norms controlling the operation of the coercive machinery, can have such a structure so as 'to induce the emergence of certain economic relations'.[30]

The subjective right to which Weber gives special attention is freedom of contract. It should be clear, however, that his sociology of law conceives of such a right not in terms of 'freedom' but as being a particular type of guarantee of contracts made between individuals. By remembering that Weber bases his discussion of subjective law on a particular type of guarantee, we see that contractual freedom stems not from law per se but from political authority. The development of this guarantee is traced in detail and related to the needs of a developing capitalism through the institutions surrounding contract such as agency, assignment and negotiable instruments. Weber noted that 'even after the creation of actionable contractual claims capable of assuming any content we are still far from that legal state of affairs which is required by advanced and completely commercial social intercourse',[31] but the treatment is not intended as a mere legal analysis of the status of the law regulating contractual freedom but as a rational interpretation of their development and their relation to the economic activity of individuals engaged in commercial enterprise.[32] The relation between expectations in the legal and the economic field are analysed in terms of the conditions facilitating the development of capitalism. It was Weber's intention to trace in a causally adequate manner this particular relation. By analysing the relationship between expectations in the legal and economic field Weber facilitated the identification of the conditions of capitalist development while avoiding reification of the inter-linked aspects of politics, economy and sociality.

CONCLUSION TO DURKHEIM AND WEBER

As a preliminary comment on Durkheim and Weber it can be seen that there is to be found in their work a significant contribution to the sociological analysis of legal phenomena and an undeniable corrective to those whose advocation of a sociology of law implies the lack of attention to law or particular difficulties confronting the sociological apprehension of law. A lot of attention has been paid to the law and this attention, in the works of Durkheim and Weber, displays certain significant features.

First, it is quite clear that the organizing frameworks used to direct attention to specific areas and questions were not generated by any reliance on what we have termed a 'relevance' perspective—the order of questions and levels of analysis are quite distinct from those that would have a direct and intended benefit to social policy. Secondly, Durkheim and Weber brought to bear on legal phenomena a logic of scientific discovery established on an understanding of social action. They themselves determined the questions of sociological importance which a study of law could be used to provide answers. By engaging in analysis which retained the wholeness of their sociologies, both authors allowed their substantive analysis to be assessed according to their idea of social science.

To an extent these are the most significant aspects of the work of Durkheim and Weber when viewed against the contemporary sociology of law and the sub-discipline's struggle to achieve its own renaissance. It is necessary, however, if we are to claim any special competence for sociological midwifery, to trace the relation between the works of Durkheim and Weber and the normative-interpretive debate introduced in Chapter I.

We may have given the impression in Chapter I that a conception of social action as normatively regulated entailed analysis unmindful of the significance of meaning and that an awareness of meaning led necessarily to an interpretive mode of analysis. As a gloss this is superficially correct but we can now be more specific. To do this we will make certain points concerning the work of Durkheim and Weber; indicate the specific features of normative and interpretive modes of analysis; and relate each of the authors to primary developments within sociology.

Durkheim and Weber are quite distinct in the importance attached to meaning. Durkheim believed that sociology had to ignore meaning in order to be scientific; Weber believed that if sociology did ignore meaning it would have nothing to be scientific about. Both authors, however, worked with the twin concepts of 'norm' and 'cause'. Durkheim believed that norms existed as social facts; they were external to men and constrained their action. This was underpinned by a particular view of human nature. Mankind was a species whose individuals were essentially social beings. As non-social beings, individuals exist only as a set of inordered impulses incapable of sustaining any social order. The social aspect is the norms governing conduct and the norms establish the order of social life. Types of social life can be distinguished by reference to the types of norms by which they are sustained. But Durkheim's use of norms also reflected a particular conception of sociology. The conception of normative regulation has already been portrayed and needs no more attention but it can be seen as basing a distinction commonly made between sociological and psychological analysis. Psychological analysis asks 'why did this person do this action?', where the action is say a crime, for instance a suicide. Sociological analysis asks the question 'why does this society at this time display this rate of activity?' Analysis at this level, if we accept the distinction, is obviously less interested in motives and is concerned with the 'social facts' determining societal rates of specified activities. This was Durkheim's approach and led, as we have seen, to an emphasis on normative regulation and on acquiescence in the terminology of motive-less functionalism.

Weber's treatment of 'norms' was in part distinct. He utilized a conception of social action in which each actor was oriented to the expectation of other actors vis-à-vis himself and his expectations of those others. The mental expectations build up into a normative framework and the conception of social action is to that extent a normative one. We will leave further comment on this until after discussing the normative and interpretive modes of analysis.

Normative and interpretive analysis can be viewed as two competing methods for analysing and explaining patterned features of social life represented by sociology as social order. We gave the dichotomy in the words of Blumer as between those sociologists who see norms as sustaining social life as against those who see social life as sustaining the norms. If we take the first view, then social order can be explained by reference to norms; with the latter view, this is not possible. Interpretive analysis proceeds by assuming that norms are problematic; that whatever order adheres in social life is essentially tenuous however much a 'fact of life' it might seem to social actors. Social actors create and re-create the order by interpreting the meaning of significant aspects and significant others in a way sufficient to establish those features of regularity which other sociologists have attributed to an external normative framework. This portrayal of the analysis is of course too simple and is taken up in detail in Chapter V. It does, however, indicate the particular features with which we are presently concerned. The features are an emphasis on norms as against on emphasis on meaning; an analysis utilizing the logic of an external structure of norms as opposed to an analysis utilizing the logic internal to the social action of those under study.

WEBER AND DURKHEIM AND DEVELOPMENTS IN SOCIOLOGY

Durkheim can be placed squarely in the forefront of normative analysis. He was not particularly interested in the nature of social action. He was only concerned that if sociology were ever to be scientific it had to treat social phenomena, including species of action, as 'things'. Weber, we would argue, was in life a normative sociologist but his ghost sits on the sidelines applauding interpretive analysis. In turn interpretive sociologists take from Weber not only inspiration, but the mantle of sociological propriety.[33] The paradox which exists if we draw such tight boundaries is based in a tension exhibited within Weber's own work. We can begin to display this tension by reiterating two aspects of Weber's concept of social action. Social action is meaningful and patterns of social action are built up within a structure of normative expectations. We can not then simply dismiss normative features from analysis cognizant of meaning. It may be said that in Weber's twin features of social action lies the possibility that analysis should proceed by way of seeking the meaning given by actors to the normative structure which they superficially construct.

In part this is what Weber did. Normative structure was regarded as a scheme which social actors used to project and build their own action rather than being an external sociological tool of analysis. But Weber was not concerned with specific actors' meanings and understandings; he did in fact impute into typical social action a typical orientation to the normative structure via the use of ideal types. The use of ideal types brought to bear on the very large-scale questions he was attempting to answer allowed Weber to contain both normative and meaningful aspects of social action without ever resolving the tension between the two.

This characteristic of his work is developed again in his particular mode of explanation. Weber was adamant that explanation had to be causally adequate and that it must contain meaningful relationships. Neither was itself sufficient. For his own purposes this was resolved by saying that a sociological interpretation has to grasp the meaning of the action and also to show a probability that it will always recur in the same way. Probability talks of the actor's own predictability in the face of a normative framework and meaning talks to the typical meaning actors give to the expectations inhering within the normative framework. Again the tension is displayed but of central importance is the fact that Weber never reduced social action to causal terms and never reduced it to action as deducible from an external normative framework. Meaning and interpretation are not subsumed within any form of systems analysis.

If Weber's own work conceives social action to be normative, and tentatively embraced within causal connections, his ghost remembers that the social action he was speaking of was meaningful and that this was its central feature, and the definitive feature, for the purposes of social science. His ghost would not be incredulous at the idea that sociology should come to view the problem of order as resolvable independently of any assumed belief in a normative structure beyond that held in the minds of social actors themselves.

Before concluding finally we want to state in brief the tensions in Weber's work identified by another sociologist, Dick Atkinson, as a corrective to our own particular emphasis, and to indicate the level of criticism of Weber which we are seeking. Atkinson[34] emphasized Weber's rational interpretation mode of analysis and was concerned that this mode, which correctly understood was a heuristic device, might be misinterpreted as a model of society containing model men. The blueprint attained by interlinking the various ideal types of social phenomena indicates the possibility of analysing the whole of society in terms of an abstract model. Ideal typical man had only one choice in a particular typical situation and this may lead to a picture of real man as equally determined, his action being simply a response to or an output from a particular configuration of societal forces. Perhaps Weber may have invited such an interpretation by his open pessimism in the face of an historically destined move to rationality in all walks of life.

Atkinson, however, is convinced that Weber would, and did, reject any such an interpretation but this view is given as based on 'methodological grounds'. Atkinson says that 'Weber was certain on

methodological grounds that his model of different types of actors and
different aspects of social structure could not adequately explain the
great wealth of empirical diversity solely in terms of the irrational
deviation from these models ... There was no logical way in which
those types necessarily had to relate to one another and there was no
way of deducing empirical reality from them.'[35] Sociology is, then,
immune to systems analysis but at this level the immunity is achieved
independently of any reference to a concept of social action as interpretively constructed. The methodological pitfall here is not taken as
inherent in the nature of the object under study and it is only when
sociology asserted that its subject matter carries methodological imperatives that the interpretive school finally divested itself of normative connotations.

Our argument, then, is distinct from, though not in opposition to,
that offered by Atkinson. We would say that Weber did have an
interpretive conception of social action that was never resolved with,
nor subsumed under, the normative conception. The former conception is emphasized in the very definition Weber gave to sociology and
in his discussions of adequate explanation. This adequacy, however,
did entail a model of action built up from the premiss that norms and
expectations mediate between individuals and action and allowed
Parsons[36] to argue, later, that Weber was almost perverse in not
evolving to a full systems analysis of normative explanation. But it
was no perversity. Weber may have had a view of action hard to
distinguish from that of Parsons, and the Mertonian theory of
deviance given in Chapter I may appear to have a similar picture of
action built up in the face of particular orientations to normative
expectations. But in Weber, meaning kept on reappearing; it
remained the centre of attention too long in his analysis for it ever to
be forgotten.

In Parsons and Merton meaning was acknowledged but in the final
analysis of particular action situations a theory of deviance rates saw
meaning as a troublesome and none too essential travelling compan-
ion. It was then discarded. Weber was never so imperial. Though
he, like Durkheim, may never have allowed his substantive work
to talk back to his science sufficiently for research to aim at
fathoming out whether social action *was* interpretively or
normatively constructed, his use of interpretation, his idea of
normative structure as the social actor's rather than as the
sociologist's framework, and his modesty in the face of meaning,
retained the power to show how a more refined appreciation of the

construction of social order could approach subjective meaning as a topic of investigation for sociology.

From Durkheim developed the normative explanation of social order. Explanation was based on deduction and the imposition on social life of a sociologist's own structure of normative regulation independent of subjective motives. From Weber, interpretive sociology took on the interpretive understanding of social action and derived methodological imperatives, including the rejection of normative systems analysis, independent of any particular value orientation inhering within a substantive topic selection.

As a potential, Weber shows that the sociology of law *can be* a sociology and, further, one that takes seriously a commitment to a subject-matter of social action. Weber developed the implications of a voluntaristic concept of social action to his own satisfaction and although one may disagree with his treatment of meaning in terms of ideal-typical analysis, his commitment ensured that he treated in a sophisticated manner the notions of cause and explanation. It was because Weber took such issues as central that he was able to develop a sociology of law which was both illuminating as to the nature of social action, especially in terms of an understanding of the development of social institutions and their relation to the economic order of society, and one which rose above the mere collation of 'social facts' or the problematic language of systems theory, functionalism or some other overarching framework.

PART II
INTRODUCTION

If the contemporary sociology of law boasts an abundance of literature, then we must ask whether the substance of such literature reflects hard and resolute sociological knowledge or whether it exists, as in the manner of the fabled Emperor's flowing raiment, by mere proclamation. It is perhaps wise not to be prematurely assertive on this point and the following two chapters seek only to review available published work and to interpret them in the light of the discussion in Chapter I. Two preliminary points, however, are required.

First, some indication is needed of the criteria used to include or omit work from review and for directing work either into Chapter III or into Chapter IV. In general the concern of Chapter III is with work setting broad terms for debating the relation between law and society. As such, it is concerned with sociologies of law which take a particular concept of society in terms of which to generate knowledge of law. The work bears a certain resemblance to the writings of Weber and Durkheim in having the flavour of a wide ranging interest in the relationship of legal phenomena to other aspects of society. Chapter IV carries work of a different order and covers those trends in empirical work which seek to generate more or less theoretical knowledge of the relation of law to society from statements regarding fairly narrow and specific empirical concerns.

Secondly, the purpose of the following two chapters is to review work available and not to attempt any assimilation. The field of the sociology of law is both large and amorphous. The work reviewed is representative and illustrates certain problems we find with the field as a whole. The only themes of unity we seek to establish are those which bear on the nature of the sociological component of the subdiscipline.

CHAPTER III

Law and Society

The concern of this chapter is to give an impression of the work of recent years which has retained in general an aim to trace the relations between law and society. Although mainly undertaken in theoretical terms we do not identify such an ambitious aim with theory, counting empirical work as capable of generating only particularistic knowledge. Such a neat division would be both unfair to empirical research and unwarrantably laudatory of theory—it is the case, however, that a basic division exists in the present literature and it is simply to this that we point. To the extent that the work is theoretical it at least has the merit that the concepts used operate within that theory by which their meaning is established. The relation of this meaning to anything we can recognize in the empirical world is another issue.

The writers discussed are Parsons and Bredemeier, representing the functionalist school, Renner and Chambliss, as two rather different versions of the conflict perspective, and Selznick who by disavowing sociological entrenchment contributes a unique brand of theorizing about the nature of legal systems and legality. Having given an exposition of the main lines of analysis, we will draw out certain implications according to the central issues identified in Chapter I.

TALCOTT PARSONS

Parsons is particularly significant for the sociology of law because he saw his general sociology as representing a convergence of the main themes in the works of Durkheim and Weber. This convergence is partly reflected by the two names used to denote Parsons's work— 'functionalism' and the 'action frame of reference'. This is not the place to delve unduly into their complexities but we can highlight their central features.

For Parsons, man is a socialized animal. Society is built on certain common values and these are internalized by its members during socialization. A person learns through socialization how to act in particular situations and the norms governing social life become part of his psychological make-up. So given, the person is set with a particular relation to social order. Social order is not accomplished by external constraint, but internally through obligation. The concept of a norm is central to Parsons's sociology and he states that a norm represents a 'verbal description of the concrete course of action which is regarded as desirable' by the actor together with a 'social injunction to make certain that future actions conform to this course'.[1] An actor, through socialization, takes on the norms and his commitment to them not only solves the problem of order but leads to a particular way of analysing society called the 'action frame of reference'. Parsons criticized positivism within sociology for omitting 'all reference to an understandable normative system of rules and expectations as understood from the subjective point of view of the social actor'.[2] His remedy was to include such reference in the base unit of analysis. This unit Parsons called the 'unit act' and comprises an actor in a situation, the actor being in possession of values and a normative structure in common with other actors. Many such unit acts make up the orderly operation of society—a 'web of interwoven strands'. Voluntarism meant that the actor was able to appreciate what behaviour was expected from him. This, Parsons believed, acknowledged Weber's view that the actor was important.

The importance, for our purposes, is that the action frame of reference was given as a synthesis of converging themes in the work of Weber and Durkheim. Durkheim's organic approach to society saw the primary modes of differentiation in the structure of a system as being related to its functional needs. Weber had rejected such an approach, but Parsons claims that was because Weber failed to realize that starting from the 'frame of reference of subjectively interpreted individual action' it was open to use functional analysis to develop a 'generalized outline of social systems of action'.[3] Parsons's sociology becomes an attempt to analyse society as a system of functionally interrelated variables. Society is seen as a set of recurrent unit acts which are interdependent. A change in one must be reflected in a change in another. Social action, then becomes ensnared in the 'web of interwoven strands'.[4] Once this is accepted Parsons was able to say that the 'subjective point of view is irrelevant' because functional analysis looks for the necessary conditions for the continuation of society—the maintenance of the system—these being located in a set of 'functional pre-requisites'. The primary modes of differentiation within society stand in a functional relationship and the human being whose behaviour is embedded in one or other functional prerequisites is analysed by the concept 'role'. Individuals occupy roles in society and to each role is given a set of obligations, norms and expectations which must be fulfilled if the system is to be maintained. The system, seen in functional terms, allows objective motives to be attributed to the actor in the situation while retaining its status as a set of 'unit acts'. The action frame of reference has been replaced by functionalism.

We may say at this stage that Parsons's functionalism, far from representing a convergence of Weber and Durkheim, is itself divided. The division is represented by the separation of functionalist method and functionalist doctrine. As method, functionalism sees society as a system consisting of sub-systems. These systems and sub-systems have needs and 'when these needs are satisfied the system trundles along; when they are not satisfied the system experiences strains and eventually breaks down completely. In order to satisfy needs, social systems develop social structures (or institutions) ... (which) ... permit system needs to be satisfied in patterned, regular and expected ways.'[5] From this, whether we wish to explain the existence or the persistence of some social phenomena (institution or pattern of behaviour) 'the functionalist method would direct ... attention to the consequences of the phenomena for the system within which it occurs'. That then is the *method* and should not be confused with functionalist *theory*, which consists of explicit statements of the processes and institutions meeting specified societal needs.

With these provisos in mind it is now possible to look at the fate of law within such forms of analysis. Parsons constructed a functional social system in terms of a set of 'functional processes'. These processes he called 'pattern variables'. They represent the primary modes of differentiation within society and are the processes with which to relate society's institutions to the part they play in the operating social system. The relationship of law to such processes should provide a functional account of law. The four processes are 'integration', 'adaptation', 'goal pursuance' and 'pattern-maintenance'. Each process can be looked at internally or as it relates to the other three. While law represents 'integration', Parsons never gave a comprehensive account of the place of legal phenomena in the wider social system. He did, however, provide one particularly important essay which stands as an internal look at the structure and needs of the integrative process itself. In *The Law and Social Control*[6] Parsons analyses how law functions to maintain an ordered set of social relationships.

First, law is in one important sense neutral. It can have any content. Parsons states that particular legal rules apply to individuals who occupy specific roles in society, for instance father, employer, judge, and that since law is 'non-specific with respect to the fundamental content',[7] any social relationship (where the roles intersect) can be regulated by law. For Parsons law is not important for its content but for the way it structures relationships. Law is not 'a category descriptive of actual concrete behaviour but concerns patterns, norms and rules that are applied to the acts and to the roles of persons and to the collectivities of which they are members'.[8] Normative rules, therefore, stand in a definite relationship to the roles occupied by members of collectivities and an analysis of these relationships should show 'the conditions on which the effectiveness of a system of rules rest'.[9] These conditions Parsons wishes to analyse, as they are necessary for the integrative process to be maintained. He is interested not in the content of law but with the mechanism as it exists as an institutionalized part of the social system. The mechanism is a normative phenomenon dealing with 'normative patterns to which various kinds of sanctions are applied'.[10] It is also a neutral phenomenon; it does not necessarily represent any particular content but functions to integrate social actors into those stable social relationships which constitute *any* given society.

Secondly, at one level we have been given no information about law that our common sense might not have equally well provided. Law is composed of prescriptive and proscriptive rules; the content of the rules is in some manner independent from the essence of the law; and the normative structure of law is institutionalized, if we mean by this that certain collectivities are intentionally created with the express purpose of applying sanctions and deliberating case law. We feel no difficulty as lay men in appreciating that a judge represents the law in court but not on the golf course at weekends; that is, the 'judge' is analytically separable from the physical person occupying that position in society. Once this commonsense picture is analysed in functional terms, however, Parsons feels that a step of sociological importance has been taken. We are enabled to address the *function* of normative regulation of social relationships and are then directed to the functional needs which must be met if the process is to continue. Law we are told should be treated as a 'generalized mechanism of social control' and having established the 'place of law in society as an integrative mechanism' we can move on to demonstrate how the law achieves this objective.

Thirdly, Parsons analyses the basis of law's effectiveness and the problems a legal system has to solve if it is to regulate social interaction. Parsons gives some general considerations on the basis of law's effectiveness. Starting with the assumption that 'it is only by adherence to a system of rules that systems of social interaction can function without breaking down into overt or covert conflict',[11] Parsons uses law as the objective visible tip of the societal pyramid of normative regulation (i.e. a pyramid of habits, customs, norms, rules, law). This gives a particular thrust to the process of integration. Integration is achieved by normative regulation and if law is to be effective in pursuing this goal then a pre-requisite will be consistency in the normative (legal) apparatus and a level of acceptability of the apparatus within the collectively to which it applies.

Since Parsons sees society as displaying a genuine consensus on fundamental values, the acceptability of the apparatus can be presumed. The second base of effectiveness—normative consistency— is more problematic and leads Parsons to investigate the problems facing a legal system before it can establish a normative body of rules with which to regulate social interaction. The problems to be solved are those of legitimacy; interpretation; sanctions; and jurisdiction.

Legitimacy

Parsons states that a legal system which is not legitimate in the eyes of the population will not be able to achieve the function of integration. He saw normative patterns being legitimated in particular ways but assumed that law and the sanctions behind the law are legitimately applied. If they are legitimately applied then law can pursue its task successfully even if certain people must feel that the law has been used in some particular case against their own interests. Legitimacy, as a problem for law's effectiveness, must remain a psychic accreditation given to the law by the members of society, rather than merely the courts and Parliament following previously accepted procedures, but the distinction is not pursued by Parsons.

Sanctions

Parsons asserts that inducement and coercion operate in all social relationships. For instance if you withhold certain expectations that I count on from the relationship, I can do the same to you—the image of exchange is not accidental and bases the impression of market control of interaction. Where the law departs from the role of social expectations (norms) in interaction, is in the use of force. Whereas social norms are binding by being an integral part of the personality of role players, certain norms or certain norms at certain points must

Law and Society 91

have their bindingness asserted by a display of physical force. Now physical force, as Parsons notes, is in its nature disruptive and so it is not only the ultimate sanction but one which must lie as a monopoly of the state. Such a monopoly is the primary characteristic of political organization but it would be wrong, Parsons argues, to conceive of the law as a political phenomenon. Nevertheless it is linked to the political apparatus in that force is marshalled to the requirements of the law. The legal system must have an adequate connection with the state in order to use its agencies as the administrators of physical sanctions in the enforcement of legal norms. Such allows the consistency in *legal* norms to over-ride any competing *social* norms.

Jurisdiction

Parsons seeks to base the problem of jurisdiction in the use of sanctions. Tied to the state as enforcement machinery, this sets limits on the geographic application of legal norms. It is necessary to set limits on territorial jurisdiction which are coterminous with the extent of effective enforcement. Without such a correspondence, law, as a system of normative regulation, will undermine its own legitimacy.

Interpretation

In the discussion of interpretation, Parsons points to certain aspects of Anglo-American legal systems which reflect how the particular organization of legal systems functions to provide the means to secure the goal of integration. He is mainly concerned with the legal profession. The judicial function is centred in a 'special type of social organisation' (the court) that 'directly institutionalises the process of arriving at decisions by the authoritative interpretation of rules'.[12] The manner by which the profession performs the interpretive function is facilitated by certain structural devices such as judicial independence. In their interpretive function the profession is subject to the 'strains' of 'maintaining a difficult balance in a tradition which is exceedingly complex'.[13] The response to such strain may be an overidentification with the client and an emphasis on subject law, or an exaggerated formalism, but over and above such responses there are structural devices which serve both to overcome this strain and to maintain the interpretive function as an aspect of integration. Such devices are the principles of due process; the dilatoriness of proceedings; the mystique of the law. These serve to separate the profession from the client; retain the profession as an intermediary between legal norms and the community; and encourage the acceptability of legal decisions to those to whom they apply.

So far we have been given an internal view of the law as an integrative mechanism, a view pointing to certain needs that must be satisfied for effectiveness; certain problems to be solved; and the possible sources of strain experienced by the system. Parsons has pointed to certain facets of the legal system which allow it to perform its integrative function but we now turn to Bredemeier who within the theoretical edifice of Parsonian sociology, sought to display the relationship of this integrative function to the other 'pattern variables' of the social system.

BREDEMEIER [14]

'Integration co-exists with the other pattern variables of adaptation (economy); goal pursuance (polity); and pattern maintenance (sociality). Identifying law with the integrative process, Bredemeier analyses the way that the other processes act as 'inputs' to the law in return for which they receive the 'outputs' of organic solidarity, interpretation and justice, respectively.

Law and the Adaptive Process

Adaptation is society's need to be able to overcome obstacles which may block the achievement of system goals. Bredemeier extends Parsons's identification of the adaptive system with the economy to include also science and technology.

Law takes from such a system knowledge concerning the function of various species of behaviour as well as devices to ascertain the relationship between certain actions and certain outcomes. As examples of specific inputs from the adaptive system Bredemeier mentions forensic science; mortality tables used in calculating civil damages; public opinion; and all devices for ascertaining truth. These inputs of knowledge are used in making a decision. The decision of the court is an output to the system. It is an output of organization or structure, the 'imposition of rights and obligations in the interests of efficient organisation'.[15]

Cryptically put, Bredemeier is saying that the integrative process of law denotes efficient organization and that the adaptive process tells the law what efficient organization is.

Law and the goal-pursuance process

The polity provides the legal system with policy goals, or standards for 'evaluating the "efficiency" of a given or anticipated role structure'. The legal system, in return, applies 'general policy statements to the specific conflict at hand'.[16] In applying the policy (legislative

enactment) the legal system must perform the creative act of interpretation. In return for this output of interpretation, the legal system
receives from the polity enforcement procedures.

Law and the pattern maintenance process

For the courts to operate at all conflicts must be brought to their
attention: 'people must be motivated to turn to the law for the protection of their interests'.[17] The relationship between pattern maintenance and law is therefore a fairly simple exchange; in return for
motivation and conflicts the legal system gives an output of justice
meeting the demands of individuals' 'internalised expectations'.

It would be unfair to Bredemeier to leave his analysis at this point.
Two other factors are significant. First the relation of law to pattern
variables is not given in a static fashion. The set of functional pre-
requisites exist in a dynamic relationship such that they can accommodate to changes in society and show how changes in one section of
a social system can be functional or dysfunctional for another section
of the system. Secondly, Bredemeier is concerned to show that the
internal balance between the functional processes is not an automatic
feature of the system as a whole. Indeed he goes into some detail
concerning the various ways in which the balance can break down,
mentioning in particular 'the development inside the law of goal-
conceptions inconsistent with the polity's'; 'the development in the
pattern maintenance system of values resistant to "justice"'; and a
'lack of communication of accurate knowledge to the courts'.

These caveats notwithstanding, he is in general less concerned to
question the whole or any part of the functionalist edifice and
throughout he sees his task as applying functionalism to the job of
understanding the various aspects of the legal system mentioned.

RENNER

Recent years have seen a revival of interest in the attempt by Karl
Renner[18] to give an account of law in terms of a Marxist analysis of
society.

Marx himself, did not write extensively about the law, nor, in what
he did say, is there to be found even a brief systematic exposition of
the nature and function of legal phenomena. In Marx's scheme, law,
like politics, was considered part of the superstructure, that being the
'more or less clear expression of struggles among social classes'[19] corresponding to the sum total of relations of production. At the same
time law could influence economy, the manner depending on close

analysis. But though stressing that 'influence of laws upon the conservation of the relations of distribution and consequently their influence upon production must be specifically determined',[20] Marx never proceeded with that determination. Apart from these and other remarks of similar generality there is little sustenance for scholars poring over the pages of *Capital* in the hope of distilling a genuine Marxist exposition of law.

It is therefore a little surprising to find Renner giving Marx the credit for undertaking in that work 'a comprehensive exposition of the functions fulfilled by the legal institutions at every stage of the economic process'[21] and for providing the methodological hint which was the springboard for his own efforts to document the relations of law and economics. This hint was to point to the problem of 'how the relations of production as relations of the law enter into disparate development'.[22]

At first glance, the idea of Marx providing more than the barest directions appears to possess a highly original and inventive cast. Nevertheless, to accompany Renner on his trip in the *Institutions of Private Law* is to be convinced that the experience is equivalent in all major respects to one that Marx himself might have offered. It is organized around the key methodological and substantive categories which Marx made his own; the economic analysis for the most part is indistinguishable from that found in *Capital* and, throughout, the work is peppered with statements from Marx and Engels—indeed it occasionally takes on the appearance of a legally annotated version of quotes from *Capital*. That, however, is illusion. The work is insightful and original yet enjoys an intimate relation with Marx's own. To understand how Renner's account of law in society is so close to Marx's project, whilst unable with justice to claim more than the vaguest assistance from him, we must get to grips with Renner's view of law and its relation to economy.

Renner will have no truck with extra-legal definitions of law. We must not 'cloud over the difference between legal and economic institutions with psychological and ethical jargon'.[23] The law is the law, its real content is 'given by the constituent norms; and there is no other'.[24] Such norms have an objective content, confronting and demanding obedience from the individual. Law is given by the state. Law is a crystallized form. It is inscribed on parchment with a factual existence—in this way 'the notions of the individual are removed from the control of his floating psychology and are made permanent. The law appears thus to be established, stable and fixed.'[25] Though derived from individuals it none the less transcends and imposes upon them.

As an analyst of legal institutions, Renner takes his stand with scholars of the positive law school whose purpose is to 'analyse the legal norms contained in the sum total of positive legal provisions, arranging them in accordance with their inherent nature and, to reduce them to a system'.[26] These inherent natures are revealed in the jurists' distinction between public and private law and the various categories of property, obligation, family and successional law. Questions as to the social effects of these norms, on the other hand, 'transcend (the) legal structure' and 'lie outside the province of systematic legal analysis'.[27]

In the preliminaries to his own exposition of the law/economy relation, then, Renner sought to create a yawning abyss between the analysis of the two. Methodologies must remain separate and purified for 'there is no greater stumbling block in the path of knowledge than the mingling of various methods'[28]—this in reply to scholars who would depict the essence of law as social. For Renner this was inconceivable. Law was to be understood initially in terms of the legal, not the social system. The truth of this lay in the fact that legal relations could express an infinite number of political ideals, be implicated in situations demanding moral praise or blame and provide sanctuary for both exploiter and exploited. Contract, for instance, 'remains one and the same legal institution though it may serve a variety of purposes . . . marriage as well as prostitution'.[29] From the varieties of social/legal relations there were to be extracted the enduring normative nuggets to be analysed and treasured. In so approaching law, Renner was far from preparing the ground for legal isolationism. The separation of law from economics was merely a pre-requisite for exploring more exquisitely the relations between the two. 'The unity of a legal institution derives from the unitary character of the norms from which it is built up. How such an institution affects social life is quite another matter.'[30] This other matter was in fact the core of Renner's own inquiry, for whilst we must refuse to study the law itself in a way which requires it to transcend the logical limits of legal structure, positive analysis is no more than a starting point for a complete theory of law. We must also be concerned with the social functions of that positive law. In doing so we will begin to see that any 'legal institution is the end of one process, that of the evolution of law, and the beginning of another, that of the social effects of the law'.[31] A positive analysis alone can only provide a truncated theory.

Like the wooden head in Phaedra's fable 'it may be beautiful, a pity only that it has no brains. Both at the beginning and at the end of legal analysis there is a social theory of the law . . . co-ordinating it like a cog to the whole machinery of social events.'[32]

Of the exact relation between law and economy, Renner at this stage is certain only that law is part of the superstructure based on the sub-structure of productive relations. These terms, 'borrowed from architecture' are designed 'only to illustrate'.[33] Exact relations are to be determined by the detailed analysis which Marx never found time to undertake, and which cannot be exhausted by simplistic notions of cause and effect. They are of little interest in the positive analysis of law which for Renner proceeds by way of teleological explanation. Neither can they assist analysis of economy. Marx will provide the explanatory method here. To say that law affects economy is 'mere platitude', whilst the mechanism by which economy generates the effects of law is obscure. We must purge such primitive categories and recognize that social life 'is not so simple that we can grasp it, open it and reveal its kernel like a nut, by placing it between the two arms of a nutcracker called cause and effect'.[34] Rather, Renner recognises the two autonomous systems of law and economy, the first to be revealed by positive and the second by Marx's analysis, their relations to be investigated historically.

Viewed statically in a given epoch, the two appear 'mutually conditioned and subservient'. Marx's contribution was to grasp the historical process of systems' interaction. The historical dimension, through analysis of the transition of one social order to the next, lays bare the tension between the two systems and 'the inherent laws of development' which 'can only be revealed if the events are seen in motion, in the historic sequence of economic and legal systems'.[35] Renner thus establishes a dialectic in the disparate development of legal and economic institutions. Both sides of his dualistic inquiry— law seen positivistically as stable normative regulation, economy seen through *Capital* as the engine-room of societal change—combine to give primacy to that aspect of the dialectic which is economy outstripping its legal counterpart.

Here then, is the explanation for our earlier difficulties. Renner gives primacy to Marxist categories since analysis of economy as it relates to a more or less fixed normative form is the question at issue. Renner does not engage in a positive analysis of law as such—he takes it for granted, using it as the starting point for his own inquiry. *Capital* has revealed for Renner the key features of social orders and their transformations: his task is to document how law plugs in to those features. As we said, the union is not achieved and maintained by simple, causal determination of law by economy. Instead, certain necessary processes in economy and society require a legal correspondence, which is met by changes in the configuration of several legal norms and their functioning.

The idea that legal norms function in certain ways and in so doing fulfil societal functions runs throughout Renner's inquiry.

The most important function to be met for instance concerns the 'preservation of the species, the production and reproduction of the material conditions of life'.[36] Every economic and legal function is held of necessity to fulfil a function in this process and all legal institutions, taken as a whole, 'fulfil the one function' which comprises all others, the preservation of the species. This in turn is composed of subfunctions of social and economic organization. Social organization includes the functions of replacement of one individual for another and the provision of socialized individuals for this substitution. Further, all societies require orders of labour and of power, the function of coordination. Various legal institutions provide for this and have an organizing function in that 'they integrate the individual into the whole' (shades of Bredemeier!!). As to economic functions, these provide for an order of goods and are to be seen as corresponding to the three stages generally identified: production, distribution and consumption. Contemporaneously (i.e. about 1900) the legal institutions of property and contract of employment fulfil the first, sale and purchase fulfil the second and property (though not by itself) fulfils the third.

In any one epoch, argues Renner, there is a natural order relating legal institutions as composites of norms to a variety of social and economic functions. No one to one correspondence is entailed; one institution can serve more or less than one function: nor are relations unchanging; the functions of a norm may increase, diminish or disappear; alternatively the norm may change without the function. But 'no function can remain unfulfilled permanently without involving the destruction of society itself'.[37] Should we find that a legal institution no longer serves a certain function 'another must be substituted in its place; there is no vacuum in the legal system'.[38]

Armed with these basic propositions about functional necessities and the inevitable implication of legal institutions in fulfilling them, Renner directed attention to what had to be seen as the subtle fiction perpetrated by bourgeois society that it could operate without that direct regulation of goods, labour and power that he knew to be necessary. Feudal society had contained a normative order vigorously expressive of the hierarchical relations between peasant and master, its character worn on the sleeve of legal relationships. The bourgeois legal order, however, made a fetish of personal liberty and endowed everyone with an equal capacity to own tangible objects. Without compulsion to work, how could there be an order of labour? Without legal endorsement for concentration of property and industrial capital how was the order of goods regulated in capitalist society? To Renner the absence of overt legal regulation was a mere mask, the recognition of which pointed to the presence of a more compelling imperative, that of the 'law' of value in capitalist production. Neither was law itself to be thought an irrelevance in this overt domination. Law was implicated and of necessity contributed to this domination. If the nature of that contribution was by no means as clear as in feudal times it was at least as intimate.

Here we see again how it was that economy, courtesy of *Capital*, assumed such importance in Renner's work. Not only did static objective law invite a law/economics analysis in terms of changing economy, but since in bourgeois society it deliberately eschewed involvement with critical social functions, an analysis of normative law was even less likely to reveal its true role in society. It became necessary to 'start a journey through economics in order to obtain a clear understanding of the efficacy of the law'.[39] The journey excluded public law since capitalism construed the state as a mere guarantor for private institutions. Why that construction should have been given more weight than that relating to the modest overt role of law in enforcing capitalist domination is unclear—the latter was dismissed as fiction. Certainly public law could not be so easily ignored if Renner's analysis were to be re-done today. None the less, he restricted himself to the institutions of private law and in particular, took as his focus the functional transformation of the law of property.

Through an historical analysis of the institutions of private law, from the hypothetical social order of simple commodity production to the point of high capitalism (circa 1900), Renner propounds the following basic thesis: these institutions, especially property, have undergone drastic development in terms of their social function, without noticeably corresponding changes in their normative content. Now this is virtually a corollary of the propositions on which Renner's inquiry is founded. To that extent it is the flesh on his analytic scheme which is most interesting.

Simple commodity production has the house as the elemental unit of social and economic organization. House connotes family, occupation, production (especially agricultural), distribution, consumption, succession and socialization. All the material conditions of production and reproduction and 'nearly all their material components, are physically combined into a universal self-contained and organic world of objects which derives its individuality from the person of the owner'.[40] Economic purpose gives unity to the cosmos of persons and goods, a cosmos which adequately fulfils all societal functions. Appropriation and alienation are unknown in the universe, for man is directly tied to his relevant material world.

The legal endorsement of this microcosm is given by the norms of property law, allowing absolute rights of disposal and preventing any interference of any house-unit by another. These norms express actual relations perfectly, and 'house and farm provide the type to which (this) legal institution was consciously or unconsciously adapted'.[41] Law and economy organically embrace. One comprehensive legal institution governs the comprehensive microcosms, addressing itself to each household wherein the order of goods, labour and power find regulation.

This somewhat romantic, part imaginary, epoch is undermined by developments in the order of labour. Labour becomes a market commodity, but since this can only happen if individuals are legally free to sell themselves for part of their day, such development is underpinned by the right to personal freedom. Man becomes free to become a wage slave. Traditional regulation of employment, through service on the land or apprenticeship is 'smashed up by revolutionary methods' and the private contract of employment, a previously little used legal institution, takes the part of providing an order of labour in society. This is the beginning of the critical transformation of simple commodity into capitalist production.

The norms of property law remain stable throughout this transformation, but their functions change in several ways and for many reasons. First, property itself accumulates in relatively few hands. Though the law gives to all the right to own tangible objects, the 'laws' of society generate huge concentrations. At the same time, the character of these objects needs increasingly to be taken into account. Whereas 'property de jure is nothing but the power of disposal of a person A over an object N, the mere relation between individual and natural object which, according to the law, affects no other object and no other person', the social connection between objects and people, as regards machinery perhaps, makes this a 'relation among men, disguised as a relation among things'. The capitalist substratum is such that control of things is control of people and hence of society. Law has been left behind by development in the economic base. By granting freedom of action, law does not abolish regulation, but simply paves the way for economic laws to hold sway.

Each of the mutually supportive components of simple commodity production is precipitated out and alienated from itself. Economic development has 'dissolved the microcosm into its component elements'. The house is merely rented. It is a dwelling place only. Work takes place elsewhere. Labour is simply another commodity.

Transformation of the property function follows accordingly. Capitalist production demands a technical expertise which owners as such cannot provide. Technical use and legal ownership must therefore become separable—the institutions of loan and rent expand to meet this need. Similarly ownership must be transferable to ensure that property is fully technically exploited. Sale and purchase rapidly mature as institutions and are the source of legality for this economic imperative.

Property law, which was an inclusive set of normative regulations in simple commodity production, itself divides functionally, uniting with complementary legal institutions, newly matured to regulate each alienated component of social life. Laws of property and contract of employment combine to regulate productive capital; combined with the institution of loan, property law governs interest bearing capital, and so on. 'The property object has become specialised and assumes specific functions . . . in the hands of an owner it becomes in turn a title to power, to profit, to interest, to profit of enterprise and to rent. And this is capital or an equivalent of capital. Accordingly the object of the right of ownership is now industrial capital, merchant capital, money changers capital . . . The thing which from an economic point of view has become converted into capital remains, as an object (in property law) unchanged . . . the change is due to a changed function, to wit, to rule over a whole society of individuals . . . The title to surplus which is directed against others on behalf of the owner is attached to the thing in its capacity as a social object.'[42]

Property is title to surplus value through more or less direct appropriation of the efforts of alienated labour. Surplus unconsumed and reinvested generates accumulation. Accumulation is therefore, says

Renner, a function of property. Appropriation, accumulation and, finally, expropriation—the dispossession of owners and their conversion into proletarian wage slaves—completes the process by which the patrimony of simple commodity production is irrevocably shattered. The property norm has been transformed through participation in economic development from the legal mirror of the household as social and economic unit into one of the tools of the expropriation which destroy even the last remnants of that historical phase. Here we see how a change of functions can reverse the social effects of the norm. Peaceful enjoyment of one's own property has developed into draconian control of alien labour power.

Through its own functional transformation the property norm helped to usher in the new social order of capitalism. As an unresolved issue, Renner suggests that the time may have come to dispense entirely with its services. Since private property has ceased to be private, and functions, albeit in underhand manner, to create public destitution, should we not recognize the social correlates of the property norm and demand that it be made public? He speculates that the contract of employment might be the seed of a new normative order for a meritocratic society, nestling in the womb of the old. True to his method he discounts contract of employment as of necessity functioning only in deletorious fashion. Under capitalism it combines with property to regulate alienated labour, but this is not inherent in the norm. Can we not use this norm, with which to break the old? Or has society lost the power to contribute to its own emancipation? With such questions Renner lays down a gauntlet for his jurist descendents.

CHAMBLISS AND SEIDMAN

In discussing the work of Chambliss and Seidman[43] we need to appreciate that they do not bear the same relationship to Renner as does Bredemeier to Parsons. Between the two functionalists can be discerned an academic division of labour insofar as Parsons stated the general relations of law to society from a functionalist standpoint and Bredemeier subsequently detailed these relations in terms given by the general statement. Renner bears this kind of relationship to Marx but Chambliss and Seidman are concerned with conflict in society sui generis rather than as an expression of historically and materially determined class interests.

Chambliss and Seidman make a conscious stand against the functionalist tradition within sociology and make an issue of the confrontation around three points. First, while functionalism sees society as a system with needs to be met if it is to be maintained, conflict theory sees society as held together by powerful interests monitoring their own position. Secondly, while functionalism sees society as a well integrated set of elements representing a profound consensus on fundamental values, conflict theory sees society as experiencing large amounts of social conflict which are resolved by constraint exercised by some of its members on others.

Thirdly, while functionalism views the elements of society as maintaining the equilibrium of the system and thereby promoting its maintenance, conflict theory sees the elements of society as contributing to its change over time.

Although Chambliss and Seidman demarcate the difference between the conflict and functionalist views they see each model of society as composed of 'individuals occupying positions that are determined by the normative structure' each position as 'defined by obligations to be fulfilled by the occupant'; and 'the complex of obligations that define a social position' being the main unit of analysis, collectively called 'role'.[44]

The legal system in both models of society is implicated in the social structure by functioning to establish an important section of the normative structure, by enforcing and changing norms and by adjudicating disputes between members of society.

From this relative consensus, Chambliss and Seidman argue that three possible views are available.[45]

(a) Society and its legal structure represent a common consensus and the legal structure is itself value-neutral;

(b) Society is racked by value antagonisms but the legal structure is value-neutral;

(c) Society is structured on conflict and the law is a weapon in the hands of the dominant class.

Chambliss and Seidman choose the latter, the conflict perspective, for generating their analysis of law and for interpreting empirical research on legislation, courts, police and criminal law, but they also wish to provide support for that perspective *through* the analysis and interpretation of such work. At one instance the writers urge that the conflict perspective is a heuristic device for analysing legal systems but they give the lie to this themselves. For Chambliss and Seidman conflict is a sociological reality and it is 'inevitably' so. The consensus view is not device but myth. The myths are embodied in the functionalism of Parsons and perpetuated in the current teaching of law. The fallacy that law can be represented as a normative structure providing a value-neutral framework is a fundamental means by which the state legitimizes itself. It is the contention of the writers that far from being a value-neutral framework 'the power of the State is itself the principal prize in the perpetual conflict which is society. The legal order ... is in fact a self-serving system to maintain power and privilege in society. In a society sharply divided into haves and have nots ... not only is the myth false ... it is inevitable that it be so.'[46] So what can both give the lie to the consensus myth *and* explain the character of law? Chambliss and Seidman pursue their analysis into the major functions that they have given to the legal system; law creation, enforcement and interpretation.

(1) *The creation of rules:* Chambliss and Seidman distinguish rule creation in primitive and advanced societies. Primitive societies are based on a consensus achieved by the common experience of its members; in advanced societies, prevailing conditions, because of the diversity of experience enjoyed by members of such societies, cannot provide the source for norms or normative change. As a result specialized institutions are created to implement changes advocated in the normative structure. Such changes must affect the experience and status of members since status is based in the normative structure. The process is not one way and changes in the social structure are reflected in the normative system. As Chambliss and Seidman say, 'a change in the economic conditions of society will necessarily bring about a change in .... the normative system'.[47] When we look to the research on the emergence of legislation Chambliss and Seidman point to the role of interest groups in promoting change; such change naturally 'makes things better for some people and worse for others'. The legislature is not, therefore, a neutral forum where pluralistic interest groups bargain out a compromise solution. Like every bureaucratic organization, 'it responds to the pressure of the powerful and the privileged. It is a weapon in the struggle.'[48]

(2) *Appellate courts:* Norm-enforcement versus norm-creation. When looking at the work of legislatures, Chambliss and Seidman see a change in the character of law from primitive societies to advanced societies from law representing compromise to law as norm-enforcement. The consensus of primitive societies ensured that the legal order reflected current values and took on a give or take or conciliatory nature when individuals came into conflict. A lack of

value consensus occurs when societies became stratified and 'it becomes necessary for dominant groups to enforce through coercion the norms of conduct which guarantee their supremacy'.[49] Hence the character of law in advanced societies as 'norm-enforcement'. When Chambliss and Seidman turn to the judicial function they give three separate arguments for a conflict view of law.

First, they reject a view of the judicial function as law-finding (value-neutral) by showing that both in their interpretation of case law and the evolution of case law to reflect changing conditions in society, the courts are involved in some manner in rule-creation.

Secondly, Chambliss and Seidman provide an argument which is designed to show the logical impossibility of the judicial function being value-neutral. They put the argument in a set of propositions.[50]

(1) Every decision-making structure necessarily limits the range of potential inputs with respect to the problems to be considered, the potential hypothesis for solution, and the data to be examined.

(2) By these limitations, decision-making structures necessarily pre-determine the range of possible outputs.

(3) Every decision-making structure is therefore necessarily biased against a particular set of potential outputs.

(4) Therefore, every decision-making structure is necessarily value-loaded, it cannot be value-neutral.

Thirdly, the inputs of the judicial function (issues, personal attributes of the judges, rule of law) together with the organizational interests of the courts, costs and so on, ensure that the courts are institutions 'more available to the wealthy than to the poor, and tend to produce solutions in the interests of the wealthy'.[51]

(3) *Appellate Courts' Decision-making:* In both their interpretation and evolution of case law appellate court decisions are only a mild reflection of the 'permissible rules of law'. A full understanding of the process, Chambliss and Seidman assert, requires that the court itself be seen as a small group 'making decisions not merely on the basis of the merit of the problem to be solved, but also in terms of the personal relations between the judges themselves'.[52] Small group analysis is necessary to show the emergence of value-preferences and their introduction into the decision-making process.

Small group analysis not only allows the value-laden nature of decision making to be opened to scrutiny but also shows the limitations of judicial freedom. These limitations are not to be seen just as the legal rules but also as the interests on which such rules are based. We are asked to reject too legalistic an analysis and to see that the structural location of judges in the judicial process ensures that they remain a bastion of the status quo.[53] Ensnared within the rules authoritatively produced by the legislature the judges become puppets of a body whose 'outputs' mean 'rags or riches, servility or power, weakness or strength to every interest group of society'.[54] A legal system with these characteristics cannot be an impartial framework for struggle—it is a tool to be used to the advantage of some and the disadvantage of others.

At this stage Chambliss and Seidman have established a description, albeit threadbare, of certain aspects of the character of law—the aspects are the promulgation of law by a legislature serving the interests of society's dominant groups; a judicial role of norm-enforcement characteristic of stratified societies; and a judicial role of norm-creation within narrowly defined limits. Chambliss and Seidman then review empirical work on, *inter alia*, police behaviour and the emergence of criminal laws, both tending to show that the content of criminal law is a political phenomena controlled by dominant interest groups and police enforcement is carried out in a manner that reflects society's prejudice against the poor, the weak and the black. To the extent that this completes a marshalling of evidence across a spectrum of the legal machinery it establishes in their view the veracity of the conflict model with which they began.

SELZNICK [55]

Although Selznick shares with other authors reviewed in this chapter a broad concern with the relations of law to society, he is alone in his overt concern to locate his analysis against the background of a developing sociology of law.

Selznick regards the sociology of law as an 'attempt to marshall what we know about the natural elements of social life and to bring that knowledge to bear on a consciously sustained enterprise governed by special objectives and ideals'.[56] We already have, then, a governing idea of law; that it is a conscious determination to satisfy basic objectives and ideals.

The sociology of law is that discipline which applies knowledge of 'natural elements of social life' to those objective ideals. Selznick states, and he does not seem to find any fault with the situation, that the sociology of law has a 'double intellectual commitment';[57] commitment both to the problems of greatest theoretical concern in sociology, and to problems of the legal order itself.

On the one hand, sociology can tend its own garden, and the knowledge produced will 'automatically have legal relevance'.[58] There are few incontrovertible sociological truths and sociology should be guided by the practical knowledge of the lawyer while at the same time forging some basic knowledge with regard to the nature of man and society. 'From this standpoint the sociology of law can contribute both to the science of society itself and to the self-knowledge of legal practitioners.'[59] At this stage it is right for sociology to avoid low-level research by emphasizing the basic sociological ideas of socialization, value systems, stratification, etc., but it is equally necessary to generate knowledge of relevance to the legal order. Here then we have the 'double intellectual commitment', a commitment which in effect takes both law and sociology for granted. We can visualize the types of work which might fit the commitment—the social background of the profession; disparities in court decisions; access to the legal system across class boundaries; etc.

On the other hand sociology can study the legal order itself from the position of both its own formulated and documented concepts (such as 'bureaucracy') and from the point of view of problems of the legal order (such as the fate of legality in bureaucratic organizations or the problem of justice in mass society).

In this guise the sociology of law is to attain its 'autonomy' from the legal order while taking on the characteristic of a critical discipline. 'At this point we should be ready to explore the meaning of legality itself, to assess its moral authority and to clarify the role of social science in creating a society based on justice.'[60]

Legality for Selznick has to do mainly 'with how policies and rules are made and applied rather than with their content'.[61] Legality as a phenomenon has to do with the reduction of arbitrariness in the procedures of rule generation and application. From this follow two corollaries. First, legality is a variable phenomenon, and secondly legality extends to administration and is not concerned only with adjudication. Selznick finds a third corollary, that being the application of 'legality' to public participation in rule making and rule-applying. On each of these counts a legal order can be more or less reflective of legality; legality is a normative ideal, much like democracy, it is both a phenomena of legal systems and a yardstick against which legal systems can be measured.

Selznick however, also strives to depict the distinctively legal. He argues that the 'legal' is based in *obligation*, an obligation to act in accordance with authoritatively determined norms. The authoritatively determined norms are the positive law, but positive law is itself part of a legal order striving towards certain basic objectives and ideals. These objectives and ideals comprise the idea of legality against which the positive laws can be measured; the ideal of a legal order is 'progressively to reduce the degree of arbitrariness in the positive law'.[62]

From this position Selznick points the sociology of law in three different, but not necessarily incompatible, directions.

(a) First, the normative ideal of legality can be used both to conceptualize as legal systems normative orders which because of their private nature had not before been conceived as being 'legal', and to judge such orders from the standard of legality (e.g. rules within organizations).

(b) Secondly, legality stems from the positive law itself. As positive law holds within itself the ideals of legality it should be allowed to develop this potential.

(c) Finally, legality stems from the nature of man, and sociology should be able to fathom this nature with regard to imperative directions for the development of legal orders.

The first point is relatively uncontentious. Just as the ideal of democracy was used to show that concepts such as 'participation' and 'accountability' were not to be solely applied to central government decision taking, so Selznick uses legality to point to arbitrariness and lack of participation in the promulgation and application of normative regulations by private as well as public legal orders.

The second point refers to Selznick's call for responsive law, a law which can adjust and reformulate in the light of changing social conditions, a purpose which in turn is constructed in terms of a natural law philosophy. A natural law philosophy is required to take the call for responsive law away from rampant relativism.

After all, the development of purposes and ideals is only as good as those purposes and ideals. For a legal order to be reflexive about itself requires a more objective standard. This then requires Selznick to inquire into the position of values in social science, and into the potential of such science to underpin natural law value systems with knowledge of the essential nature of man. Having identified the fact-value distinction as a master ideal of sociology, Selznick finds little difficulty in demolishing its importance. The findings of modern science, we are told, 'do not refute the view that generalisations about human nature are possible . . . Nothing we know today precludes an effort to *discover objective standards* of moral judgement.'[63] Sociology then needs to discover the ends meet for man in order to sustain an objective judgement on legal orders. This clears the ground for further inquiry into the nature of legality, which Selznick conceives in three ways. First it is part of the positive legal order to the extent that (1) its absence denies the existence of law, and (2) the positive law is itself an attempt to realise the ideal of legality. Secondly it reflects a condition of man as essential to his well-being as that of freedom. It is this examination of the nature of men leading to the discovery of the ideals located in such a nature that bridges the gap between the sociology of law and a natural law philosophy. The difference remains that natural law acts as a code of ideals which sociology may support and in so doing sociology looks at the implementation of such ideals in changing social conditions. For Selznick the ability of legal orders to fashion the ideals of legality in changing social conditions requires that law ceases to be treated as an autonomous norm-governed structure and be treated as a purposive enterprise allowing these purposes to keep positive law responsive.

Sociology of law has a commitment to foster this process by establishing incontrovertible truths concerning the nature of man. Rather than taking a sociological look at law in the manner of a Weber or a Parsons, Selznick is concerned to promote a critical appraisal of the historical development of the welfare of man which will 'automatically have relevance for the legal order'. This means of relating law to society by discovering the 'proper ends of man' leads to a view of the relationship which denies the position of both functionalism and conflict theory. Law is not a neutral normative mechanism but neither is it a vehicle for oppression. It is a purposive enterprise but one which involves the evolution of ideals open to scientific scrutiny and advancement. Whether these ideals be located within positive law or within man's history, Selznick is insistent that 'a modern version of natural law philosophy is required both for a proper understanding of the law itself and for the fulfilment of sociology's promise'.

LAW AND SOCIETY: COMMENTARY

We do not wish to criticize in detail the contribution of any one of the foregoing authors. We can, however, spell out certain points at which they encounter the barriers to the development of the sociology of law specified in Chapter I. We will assess their approach to the sociological subject-matter and the extent to which their work displays the dialectical relationship between sociologies of law and general sociological knowledge. Examples from substantive work will be used to illustrate the issues.

Subject-Matter

In Chapter I we stressed the importance of appreciating the unified character of the subject-matter of sociology and the dangers involved of taking 'law' as the subject-matter of the sub-discipline. The work reviewed in the foregoing analyses can be regarded as encountering two distinct forms of subject-matter. First, there is a tendency to approach law itself without any recognisable sociological cast; secondly there is a sociologically conceived subject-matter of law as a species of social norm.

(a) *Law as law:* This orientation is best seen in the work of Selznick. The central issue he raises of 'legality' is one germane to law itself and its boundaries are established in terms comprehensible only to legal theory. Certainly it is Selznick's wish to extrapolate from understandings of legality in the legal system to other areas of social life such as organizations, but the key issue is supplied by law as subject-matter and not by sociology. We might expect that this election for a role for sociology as a form of socially aware jurisprudence would create difficulties and these do display themselves. The social organization of legality does sound like an issue which could be handled by sociology. For instance a due process model of law could be used as an ideal type. Deviations from such a type, empirically demonstrated, could then be causally located in aspects of the structure of an existent legal system. In this way legality as a value-system would be open to analysis in the same manner as any other value-system and would not of itself dictate any mode of conceptualizing society nor any assumptions on the nature of social action. By taking legality as subject-matter, however, Selznick begins with a conception of society as being an holistic-homeostatic system. In order, further, to discover 'ends meet for man', Selznick has to engage in analysis far removed from questions of social action and undertaken at a high level of abstraction.

That the work of Selznick retains an inner coherence is testimony to his total commitment to the construction of a modern natural law philosophy. But in the work of other writers the selection of law as subject-matter causes difficulties of confusion. We can take, for instance, the discussion by Parsons of legitimacy and jurisdiction. In his discussion of legitimacy Parsons trespasses on the territory of jurisprudence. Legitimacy in jurisprudence is a difficult notion but at least we can accept that law is law if it meets certain legislative conventions and procedures. We also know that such procedures can change. At any one time, however, the courts recognise a law-making apparatus and an enactment following these procedures is law and the courts' enforcement and interpretation of such law is legitimate. Now this is acceptable to a jurisprudence which is looking internally to the structure of the legal system. Parsons, however, does not have this view of legitimacy. As we said legitimacy for Parsons seems to be a psychological response from members of society. This poses a problem if we conceive of a situation where such a response is withdrawn. Such situations often occur and the apparatus recognised by the courts as law-making bodies change. If a situation arises whereby force ensures obedience without the apparatus being seen as legitimate by the society's population, then Parsons would be forced to say either that the enactments of the new legislature are still law, thereby denying the place of 'legitimacy' or that they are not law, thereby setting up for sociology a competing definition of law far removed from his own consideration of law as a content-non-specific normative apparatus.

The confusion stems from Parsons posing questions of the effectiveness of mechanisms of social control but approaching the questions from the point of view of 'law' rather than from a sociologically conceived subject-matter. Similar problems arise with the discussion of 'jurisdiction' as a base-line of law's effectiveness. Parsons does not approach the question of how legal actors decide issues of jurisdiction but seeks to settle *a priori* the role of jurisdiction, a role which he says it must have if law is to be an effective integrative mechanism. The result is again that we make no contact with the sociological subject-matter of social action and end with statements that cannot deal with common legal phenomena. An identification of territorial jurisdiction with the extent of effective enforcement may for certain purposes be a close approximation to the operation of most legal systems but to set it up as a necessary condition for a theoretical role for law produces a theory which does not handle the common legal phenomena of diplomatic immunity and also those occasions when one Parliament seeks to legislate for territories which have declared non-Constitutional independence. Is sociology to say such enactments are not now law? Again we find an unwitting trespass on to the theoretical problems of jurisprudence, and a diversion from the base sociological concern of social action.

(b) *Law as a Species of Social Norm:* To the extent that the analyses discussed in this chapter conceive law sociologically, the conception is in terms of a species of social norm. Law is apprehended as a series of imperatives associated with a machinery for enforcement, playing a role of normative regulation. We see this in both the works of Parsons and Bredemeier and of Renner and Chambliss and Seidman. Within both functionalist and conflicts schools of thought analysis is undertaken from within the normative paradigm.

In Parsons the commitment to the normative paradigm is explicit, as is his view of normative regulation as an imperative for the stable functioning of social systems. Although criticizing functionalism, Chambliss and Seidman are also caught by the normative paradigm when they provide the key concepts for analysing society. The concepts chosen for use are those of role, role expectation and role-performance. The social system is given as a system of roles normatively constructed and sanctioned, inter alia, by the law.

The phenomenon of law (norm-creation and sanctioning) is identified in a manner similar to that of functionalism and underpins an analysis of society within the normative paradigm. Both functionalism and conflict theory are using the same root images of social phenomena, which are remarkably consistent in their insistence that meaningful social action is not the stuff out of which societies are made. Here we see the election of a subject-matter (law as a species of social norm) closing off the possibilities of analysing social action itself.

The Dialectic

It is the propensity of authors to engage analysis of law at the conceptual level of 'social norm' that serves to divorce study from empirically observable activity of men and thereby short circuit the dialectic operating between sociology of law and general sociology. The dialectic cannot operate because social action is never encountered as such, only social action coopted by the concept norm and cocooned within the statements provided by functionalist and conflict terminology. We can spell out the processes whereby the dialectic is thwarted by reference to the work of both conflict and functionalist theorists.

(a) *Parsons:* First Parsons closes off the analysis of social action by gradually excluding its relevance to the analysis of social phenomena. Parsons solves the problem of order by identifying social actors with the norms that govern their roles in society. At this level social action may have remained important. But Parsons then resolves the problem of order again by looking at problems of system maintenance and functional processes. At this level he is committed to explaining social phenomena in ways which are unrecognizable at the level at which they occur. Consider his discussion of confidentiality within the legal system. 'Confidentiality' is given as a device allowing for the freedom of expression required for the profession to act as agents of social control. This makes sense within the terms of Parsons's theory, in which law is regarded as social control, with confidentiality and other mechanisms contributing in some way to this functional process. Yet one imagines that the profession itself would offer a rather different account of the role of confidentiality, couched possibly in terms of client confidence in the advocate. We need not simply accept the profession's account but we do have to be able to explicate a linkage between actors' accounts (and the activities to which they refer) and sociological statements themselves. It is not simply that 'client confidence' may be a necessary process for the integrative function but that any such interpretation is provided by the theory and is not given in the empirical activity to which the theory is supposed to relate. A conflict theory may give an alternative role to 'confidentiality', perhaps as contributing to the necessary mystification of law. Here again the interpretation would be offered by the pre-existing theory and, in the absence of empirical linkage, choice rests more on political persuasion than on sociological propriety.

(b) *Bredemeier:* Bredemeier provides a similar example when discussing features of the legal system such as *stare decisis*. Bredemeier looks to the function of *stare decisis* (the doctrine that commits courts to be bound by their own precedents and the precedents of higher courts) within the integrative task in terms of a contribution to the judicial function of interpretation. Such analysis remains problematic, however, unless it can be related to the working conceptions of the judges who operate the decision-making process. Without such a relationship not only may the analysis misconstrue the judicial function but also we will be unable to adjudicate between the analysis as offered and any available competing analysis—such as, for instance, a contention that *stare decisis* helped the courts resist claims that the law should respond more adequately to changing social conditions. Bredemeier's discussion informs us as to the operations of Parsonian sociology as applied to a particular area of social life but it cannot inform us as the nature of that social life itself.

(c) *Chambliss and Seidman:* We have already commented on the normative character of the work of Chambliss and Seidman. But we can also point to two further areas where their work thwarts the dialectic and elects to interpret social activity by reference to pre-existing assumptions about the character of society. First, Chambliss and Seidman say that in advanced stratified societies it is necessary for dominant groups to maintain their supremacy by the enforcement of norms. The character of law must be norm-enforcement. From empirical comparative studies they adduce evidence that law today is characterized by norm-enforcement rather than compromise. From this Chambliss and Seidman assert the conflictual, stratified character of society and thereby support their conflict theory. For this to be legitimate one would have to be able to infer stratification from the norm-enforcement character of law and from stratification infer a conflictual society. It is clear, however, that such steps cannot be taken. Rule-enforcement *could* operate just as easily, perhaps more easily, in societies with a great degree of consensus on the operative norms. Breach of norms, and therefore the operation of enforcement, does not *necessarily* entail a lack of consensus on the norms unless we assume that people act in full knowledge all the time and with complete foresight of and control over the course of their own actions. Many authors have seen the basis of norm-enforcement to lie in the extent to which a consensus in society exists that adjudication be taken to settle once and for all the relationship between parties. Further, with stratification and conflict, the latter *may* be a concommitant of the former but is not necessarily so. Functionalist writers have had no difficulty in accommodating stratification within concepts of society displaying a wide ranging value consensus. In this situation we can see that the interpretation given by Chambliss and Seidman does not have the logical force that their mode of writing assumes. In fact the only way of so interpreting the data analysed is by taking on a commitment to the conflict perspective. It is the assumptions built into the perspective that provide the interpretations and dictate the analysis.

The second example taken from Chambliss and Seidman refers to their accumulation of empirical research on the police into their conflict model. Many of the studies had been undertaken through an understanding of social activity sui generis. The focus had been social activity rather than a pre-ordained sociological concept. To uproot such studies into a theoretical manipulation of the concepts 'role' and 'norm' is to risk an assimilation which neglects to appreciate that the studies represent a view of sociology several stages removed from the maxims of the conflict perspective itself. The attempt to use the theory to order empirical studies, rather than allowing empirical work to order theory undermines any potential such studies possess of increasing our knowledge of the nature of social action and does so in the name of the false God of theoretical power and persuasion.

CONCLUSION

Further discussion of the problems inherent in the mode of theorizing analysed in this chapter will be provided in Part III of this book, where we will also address the potency of the interpretive paradigm to provide a more fruitful avenue for generalizing about social phenomena, generalizations which are empirically grounded and ordered. So far we have tried to show how superficially opposed accounts of law converge at those places we identified in Chapter I as barriers to the development of the sociology of law. As a conclusion we wish to reiterate the point but by choosing work from within both Chapter II and Chapter III. The two authors chosen are Durkheim and Renner. At one level these authors could hardly be more different. Renner stands firmly within the tradition of the Marx of *Capital* and establishes the nature of law as domination, and the development of law as dependent on materialist struggles between the forces and relations of production. Durkheim is the forerunner of the modern consensus school. He sees the nature of law as cooperative and the development of law as concomitant upon a progressing and progressive division of labour.

Yet on closer scrutiny a number of points of similarity emerge. First we can point to a difference in their substantive foci which masks an instance of their convergence. Renner considered that the analysis of the institutions of private law, and especially property, could best reveal the true relation of law to society. Durkheim regarded property law as gratuitous to the foundation of social solidarity. Property law could prevent conflict but not sponsor solidarity. The convergence lies in that both were able to put to one side the modal analysis of the other. Just as Durkheim could reject a consideration of conflict ridden societies as an 'abnormal form' so could Renner dismiss apparent consensus as a result of successful bourgeois fiction—they in fact each choose at an early stage to focus substantive analysis at a level considered by the other to be irrelevant.

Secondly, both regard the status of law in social life as normative regulator. They both approach law as a species of social norm, possessing an awesome and objective facticity. The law is the law, a crystallized form beyond the consciousness of man. Law is imperative and impervious, having a tangibility in its normative structure. Law for both could be, had to be, divorced from man as an active subject.

Equally for both, law serves functions in society, it keeps society going and facilitates the adaption of society to changing underlying conditions of the social order. The substantive functional analyses differ but the conceptual structure is strikingly comparable. This is especially ironic in that both Durkheim and Renner sought to avoid functionalist theorizing. Durkheim stressed the identification of causes and effects as the key explanatory device of natural science against the teleological explanations of functionalism. Renner rejected any idea of society as biological organism and stressed that social systems are communities conscious of their own existence. Neither however succeeded in avoiding functionalist concepts and both produce sociological statements at the abstract level associated with such a mode of discourse within sociology.

Thirdly, both found it necessary to see society also as divorced from man. Each posited certain 'needs' not for men, but for societies. Certainly the needs seen were somewhat different. For Durkheim, the division of labour emerged as a response to the need for order in the face of competition for scarce resources. Renner's 'needs', as suited to a characterization of law as domination, included the requirements in society of orders of labour and of power. In both cases, however, man as subject was replaced by society as system, and theoretical statements were produced which failed to reach the level of social action.

CHAPTER IV

Law in Society

'Law in Society' refers to a myriad of research undertakings that cannot be regarded as a coherent or easily categorized corpus. The common links between them are simply that research is narrowly focused and that the correlates· of law investigated are of a less comprehensive order than 'society'.

We have chosen to discuss the work under the four topic headings of 'legislative studies', 'legal actors', 'legal profession' and 'legal services'. It should be clear that given the present state of the sociology of law, such topics could be investigated through a variety of theoretical or conceptual schemes. Further, such topics could be addressed with a self-consciously sociological intention and be expected to inform sociological understanding more generally. Sociology offers functionalism, conflict theory, interactionism and behaviourism as perspectives; it offers social order, social change, class, power and stratification as concepts; it offers professions and decision-making as topics. None of these are peculiar to the sociology of law, though all are open to adoption by the sub-discipline. But in fact, research has mainly been of the finding out variety—empirical work investigating particular legislative acts, legal settings or legal incidents, and reviewers have recognised these less sociological groupings by organizing their overviews according to certain 'central themes'. We can demonstrate this by reference to Schur and Treves.

Schur,[1] posits a number of recurring themes. First, we have the (reciprocal?) influence of the legal context on the social context, of legal change on social change. The sociologist is concerned with the effects of law and the 'realisation of purpose' of law. Secondly, the sociologist, saving himself from ethnocentricity, engages in cross-cultural research. Thirdly, the sociologist asks whether the use to which law is put in a particular society enhances individual freedom or whether it supports tyrannical rule. Fourthly, the sociologist analyses both procedural and substantive law, a distinction between those who go in quest of legality (procedural models) from those who investigate, say, change (substantive innovation). Fifthly, the sociologist questions the extent to which justice is a procedurally conceived notion and whether social science can advise the legal system as to the most felicitous path to substantive justice. Lastly, by 'bringing to light underlying causes and functions of behaviour and social arrangements, by specifying social costs and consequences of competing policies, and by developing a general understanding of how different kinds of legal systems work, the sociologist may be in a good position to provide policy makers with highly relevant information and perspectives'.[2]

Treves[3] also advocates a certain uniformity of themes. These are given as the relation between legal evolution and societal evolution; the evaluation of legislative and other legal reforms or innovations; the activities of legal personnel; and the opinions of the general public concerning either law in general or particular legal provisions.

Treves indicates two facets of these themes. First, he says that they are empirical topics with theoretic potential, and instances Aubert's use of the concept of 'function' and Podgorecki's generalizations with regard to public opinion on the law.

Secondly, Treves himself is mindful of the distinction between this level of theoretical potential and that achieved by Weber, Durkheim and those writers associated with the Marxist tradition in sociology. Such work may be of interest, but the themes are a response to a 'recent' recognition of the social transformations of past decades concomitant upon the progress of urbanization and industrialization. The sociology of law for Treves is not to generate knowledge of such processes but to view such processes as raising particular questions and problems concerning the role of law in society. Rather than looking back to its Weberian ancestry for instance, the modern sociology of law is given as 'an entirely new field of study with a basic objective of promoting and carrying out research in an empirical manner in order to satisfy the needs [of studying the profession, public opinion, etc.] in order to study and solve the problems to which they give rise'.[4] Our own four topic headings merely reflect the congeries of interests that have developed in recent years within which various authors have contributed to recognisable genres of output. We have consciously chosen both authors who have an explicit sociological purpose and those who have pursued the more prototypical style of research. We hope in this way to clarify the nature and variety of the sociological component in current work. However, certain writers have chosen to elevate two particular sociological concepts for especial attention. These concepts are social change and social stratification. Since such writings cannot be accommodated within the fourfold typic breakdown, spreading as they do across such boundaries, we have chosen to display the general character of the interest in the two concepts as part of the introduction to specific researches.

LAW AND SOCIAL CHANGE

'Law and Social Change' as a topic area is usually couched in the language of the law's potency to amelioriate the social context of individuals; to change the structure of society or to change the culture of society. This conception of law and social change takes the work of Sumner[5] as a point of departure. Sumner's influence was such that a view of law as dependent variable (the mores precede and have precedence over the law) became a major hypothesis behind a series of empirical studies. The converse of this dictum, couched in the question 'Can law affect social change?' is the keynote of a range of literature though not all of it is designed to provide a means of testing the Sumnerian doctrine. But it should also be apparent that the sociology of law has done more than draw blood from the stone of the nineteenth-century doctrine. Durkheim's analysis of the changing proportions of repressive and restitutive law according to emerging patterns of social solidarity; Renner's historical analysis of the transformations of the functions of legal rules; and Weber's depiction of substantive and procedural developments within the growth of legal formalism supporting changes in an emerging capitalistic mode of production, can all serve as a benchmark and corrective to the overly assertive renaissance of the topic of law and social change.

The terminological difficulties faced by the topic reflect the twinning of an undefined element—law—with a sociological concept itself open to multiple interpretation. In defining social change, Grossman and Grossman[6] refer to three possibilities:

(a) alterations in individual behaviour patterns;
(b) changes in group norms and/or changes in the relationships among groups;
(c) alterations in basic values or mores.

The typology would cover situations in which new group relationships developed; in which relationships between existing groups changed; in which interactional patterns between individuals changed; in which new forms of social organization rise and take hold; and in which individuals enjoy new behavioural opportunities even if these are not underpinned by any structural change or change in values or attitudes. Not all of these changes may be given the same importance but Grossman and Grossman argue that none should be ignored.

The concept of law utilized by studies also needs some scrutiny. Do we remain only with the state apparatus or do we include, as with Philip Selznick, 'incipient' law within organizations and elsewhere? Do we define law institutionally or via the use of some sociological peg such as the 'social functions' of law? Studies of both types are available and so further limit the comparability of results.

Finally, we may note that the twinning of a concept of law to that of social change does not indicate the type of relationship which is being searched out. Is it a causal connection which is being asserted or is it simply any connection which can help society to maximize the efficiency of legal innovations?

All these divergent strands are represented in the literature and an awareness of the distinctions being made should help an evaluation of the work as a whole.

Edwin Schur provides an opening gambit by stating that 'while there is little doubt that a legal system responds to broader patterns of normative and structural change there is a great deal of controversy as to whether law can induce, rather than simply reflect such change'.[7]

The division between normative and structural change allows Schur to subsume the legalization of both homosexuality and trade unions, for instance, under the umbrella of social change. The responsiveness of law to changing social conditions is illustrated by Schur by reference to three 'master trends' in American society, identified by Selznick, namely, the decline of fixed status; the ascendancy of large scale organizations; and the socialization of law. The declining emphasis 'on fixed status, together with the increased attention to furthering the general welfare, have tended to develop through the legal system in increasingly broad patterns of control over individual behaviour . . . similarly, the involvement of more and more people in the workings of large scale organisations has not only led to the expansion of certain kinds of legal problems, but has highlighted the potential disparity in power as between individuals and organisations, hence forcing further regulation in the public interest'.[8] Schur is seeing law and society as in a dialectical relationship, each side providing inputs for the other. As we have seen, the types of changes he is referring to are the changing status before the law of trade unions, racial minorities, women and so on, but equally those concerning business ethics and criminal sanctions. The substance of law is further seen as reflected in the overall organization and procedures of the legal institutions themselves. The Tribunal system and non-adversary proceedings, for instance, are seen in part as a response to the growing complexity of the relationship between state and citizen and between organizations and citizens, but also as a response to defects, including delay, expense and formalism, in the traditional court structure and the need for expert specialized tribunals for the resolution of certain legal conflicts.

Studies of law and social change can be seen as investigating two distinct questions: first, the potency of law to bring about desired change and, secondly, the genesis of those social currents represented by the desires for change. The majority of studies within the topic area 'law and social change' have in fact been concerned with the potency of law to affect the status and values, behaviour and relationships, of those not party to the social movement represented in the legal innovation or not party to the law's promulgation. What also is possible is the investigation of those factors which seem correlated to success, and many authors have confined their remarks to a roll-call of such factors. For instance, Evan suggests the following conditions for success: (1) an authoritative and prestigeful source of law, (2) sufficiently clear and justified law both in legal and socio-historical terms, (3) the availability of existing models of compliance for identification and publicization, (4) sufficient time allowed for the transition, (5) commitment on the part of enforcement agents, (6) the use of positive as well as negative sanction, (7) adequate protection for individuals who would suffer from violation.[9]

Drawn from studies on the legal promotion of racial harmony; the influence of law on business ethics; the efficacy of law in changing personal relationships; and so on, the tabulation by Evan includes considerable evidence on the relationship of legal innovations to behavioural and attitudinal change and the variables which affect the law's capacity in these respects. The published research, for instance, suggests that the legal recognition of rights has led to the enjoyment of facilities not previously accorded to sections of society (for example, public accommodation, services and employment). Such represents social change in at least one type of the Grossman and Grossman typology. Schur, further, argues that 'in the long run our attitudes are also affected, and this we would expect to the extent that attitudes depend on experience and the law affects the degree to which the experience of prejudice is prevalent in society'.[10] This would also be the case in the field of the efficacy of punishment. It is not clear that the law is capable of affecting criminal activity (special deterrence), but no study so far would lead one to believe that the law was not one institution which affected men's involvement in activity defined as criminal (general deterrence).

The empirical studies may then have revised Sumner's dictum to mean that laws cannot change feelings immediately, but men can perform acts prescribed by law. In addition, alterations in conduct are the most effective indices of change in thought and feeling. Research on the point remains equivocal. Mayhew concluded a study of a Boston anti-discrimination agency by saying that 'the commission has brought about only a "minimal" structural re-arrangement to combat passive discrimination'.[11] At least, however, the law was seen as providing other pressure groups with an institutional backing for further effort. We should perhaps not be surprised to find law being seen as both capable of forwarding change with a certain amount of autonomy (the potency of law to bring about desired change) and at the same time as dependent on social movements exist-ing independently of the law (the genesis of desires for change).

The question of whether law can bring about social change may be spurious and the studies can be seen as answering the two indepen-dent questions. In these terms, the studies of law and social change at least recognise that the law is a culmination of a social process itself dependent upon the experiences of men whose conduct represents that process. At the same time, it is only through experience that men come to develop certain values, exhibit certain patterns of behaviour and promote certain structural features of society. The studies simply throw up the law as a prime mechanism which asserts certain values over others, which defines and structures the relationships between men and which, in short, partly determines the type of experience possible in a given society.

By dividing the question in two, the studies could not only avoid the reification of law and the resulting logical difficulties but equally could accommodate interests wider than the instrumental dimension of law. Although studies have in the main concentrated on the effi-cacy of law to bring about normative or structural change (therefore having an instrumental value for those who are promoting such change) other studies have attempted to identify the symbolic value of law above and independent of instrumental success. Gusfield's[12]

study of the Temperance movement in America most closely subscribed to the distinction. In the battle between Protestantism and
Catholicism a legal enactment was achieved supporting the moral
code of the temperant Protestants. It may not have succeeded in
enforcing the values of those who promulgated the law, but it was clear
whose law it was; a moral code had been given political expression.

The sociology of law has yet to work out the relationship between
the various studies assimilated under the topic of 'law and social
change'. It may be that three distinct avenues will be followed in the
future, the first contributing knowledge of the way the law affects the
dimensions of change denoted by Grossman and Grossman; the
second the way the law becomes implicated in the routine activity of
men in actual legal arenas; and thirdly, the identification of those
variables related to the rationalization of law in the service of social
reform. The studies we have addressed do not really have the ability
or structure for contesting the Sumnerian thesis. The thesis itself is
perhaps too zealously regarded as significant. An evaluation of the
work at least requires a concern with problems of definition arising
from the use of sociological concepts and an awareness that the results
of 'competing' studies are not necessarily comparable. 'Law and
social change' remains a central motif of much empirical work but the
work retains a concern with providing a 'firmer base for future legislation' at the expense of a coherent sociological analysis of the legal
dimensions of social activity.

SOCIAL STRATIFICATION

It is axiomatic within general sociology that Western societies exhibit a particular form of stratification. Stratification is more than
differentiation, being a differentiation correlated to the exercise of
power; accumulation of material wealth; or ascription of status. This
is no place to document the various means by which sociology has
handled the concepts of class, status and power but we can note that
this general characterization of society is agreed upon. Differences
concern how we can explain such a characterization.

Schur claims that a relationship exists between law and stratification as evidenced by the 'overall differential legal standing of the
several social strata in American society'.[13] Although he finds much
support in empirical work for the relationship it is, he feels, not
possible to say more than that 'whatever patterns prevail or emerge in
society, they will importantly incorporate some degree of support
from legal institutions'.[14]

Certain writers see the concept of power as providing the link between law and stratification. 'The investment of a subject class with rights is a conferment of a degree of power on them, the power to pursue new opportunities, to seek new objectives, to give expression to their opinions.'[15] In these words MacIver suggests 'the ever present if subtle interplay among law, power and social class'. While law may then confer power and therefore change the relative position of social classes, for others law *represents* power. Whether called legal power, coercion or authority, this aspect of law has informed sociology from the time of Weber through contemporary empirical research up to the renewed interest in Marxist interpretations of law. While Weber built his concept of authority on a sociology that had, to his own satisfaction, settled the problems of a social science of human action, contemporary research has sought merely to demonstrate the fact that law is a vehicle for policy, that policy reflects interests and that once embedded in law such interests gain an authority above others. Alternatively, the renewed interest in Marxism removes power from its status as a variable of analysis into a concrete social reality. Law is not merely implicated in the stratification system but is domination itself. Changes in law are interpreted not as affecting such domination but merely as reflecting changes in the material base of society to which the law is organically linked.

The other two areas which have consciously developed from questions of stratification relate to the legal profession and its relation to the legal position of subordinate social classes. There is a tension in the work of particular relevance. On the one hand we are given a picture of lawyers as an elite group 'maintaining the legal order and shaping its development', while on the other hand, lawyers are portrayed as having an important role in alleviating the conditions of the under-privileged by strengthening the 'self-assertiveness' of the poor, 'their capacity for criticism and dissent, and their ability to affect the basic conditions of their existence'.[16] Either a lineal relation is suggested between the social order (unequal) and the legal order (lawyers help sustain the inequalities) or lawyers are asked to unshackle the chains of their class position and to join in the construction of a new society.

Dahrendorf,[17] in a more narrowly focused piece of research, contends that rather than primarily serving the needs of disseminating legal knowledge and skills, the subject of law in German law schools functions as an occasion for a more important social process. That process is the education of an elite. Whilst this is the core of

Dahrendorf's thesis he does draw out certain interesting suggestions concerning the nature of the German upper class and on the nature of the German legal profession. Dahrendorf says for instance that the function of legal education is to provide a unifying factor to an otherwise disparate upper class and further that it provides an upper class with a particularly well-developed conception of its own right and ability to rule. This special competence, he says, is justified by 'reference to the letter of the law'. Such authoritarian legalism is related to the nature of decisions in the business and political areas of German life. At the same time, however, this elite forming function of legal education has served to depreciate the legal profession itself, as evidenced by the low status of judges in Germany, and from this may flow certain characteristics of the whole legal process itself. 'Since the technical aspects of legal training occupy but a secondary place in the minds of many students, and since a majority do not enter the legal profession after their training, there is no distinct professional group which might be described as a guardian of legal institutions.'[18] If, however, concern is had with using a specific professional training 'as an instrument of selection and preparation for positions of power, none is more suited to this purpose than law'.[19]

Contemporary sociology of law, then, has accepted the implications of law in the class, power and status dimensions of society but has remained aloof from the more general sociological questions of the theories that generated such concepts. There is, for instance, no critical faculty brought to bear on the concepts themselves. They are treated as unproblematical. Further, once accepted, there is no feedback for general sociology of how we may account for the general features of a stratified society. Interpretations, to the extent they are used, are reported from particular perspectives but do not seem able to throw much light on the perspectives themselves. The extent to which the perspective throws light on the operation of the legal system in general and the legal profession in particular we will leave until later in this chapter.

STUDIES OF LEGISLATION

The emergence and implementation of legislation is a vast and heterogenous topic area. The work of most significance reflects a set of fairly traditional concerns but has potential for a radical reorientation of approach. Less convincing work we mention for the purposes of comparison. We can introduce the topic area at large by a brief outline of the analytic schemes most prevalent.

I. *The Emergence of Legislation*

(1) *Civil Law:* The area of civil law provides certain difficulties of encapsulation. Both Weber and Durkheim provided schemes for studying legislation but both were derived from a view of sociology in general rather than with regard to legislation itself. Perhaps for that reason their schemes are not found within contemporary work. Two specific areas of work that have been represented in the literature are property law and welfare law. To the extent that analytic schemes are employed in understanding the emergence of property law they refer to:

(a) the analysis of Marx (Karl Renner);[20] or
(b) the historical analysis of the political ascendency of property-owning classes (Chambliss and Seidman).[21]

For welfare law the schemes operate at the level of:

(a) the political structure of the welfare state (Mungham and Bankowski);[22] or
(b) the historical emergence of welfare law associated with identified prevailing social conditions (Abel-Smith and Stevens).[23]

As we should expect, analysis could be undertaken from the competing views offered by consensus and conflict theory on the source of societal norms, but the main emphasis in research has been an implicit reliance on a view of interest group politics. Legislation is the result of political pressure and debate trespasses on the interest of general sociology in the characterization of the political structure—that is the location of power in society, whether society is pluralist or has a ruling class mirrored in the legal context. The traditional sociological view of society is not questioned—order is provided by norms but norms (legislation) are the effect of political compromise, functional pre-requisites or use of power.

(2) *Criminal Law:* More work within the sociology of law as traditionally conceived has been done on criminal legislation, the works of importance being Carson on Factory Acts;[24] Aubert on Housemaid Laws;[25] Duster and Becker on Drugs Legislation;[26] Chambliss on Vagrancy;[27] and Gusfield on Prohibition.[28]

Carson[29] has argued that the dominant theme in the study of the emergence of criminal laws is a consensus that the concepts of conflict and power provide an acceptable frame of analysis. Chambliss in his study of vagrancy offers a reason when he says that 'the views of the groups in power will be expressed in criminal legislation simply because their perspective prevails among those who make the laws'.[30] The very existence of criminal laws is seen as marking the limit to which ideas of consensus can be taken. Durkheim would in part agree to the extent that crime marks the boundary of society, but he would further argue that criminal law represents a transcendental value consensus which can underpin a scheme of analysing legislation in competition with that offered by ideas of conflict in society. Given this alternative why has conflict and power remained as the dominant motif? First, perhaps it may appear as obviously applicable to others as it did to Chambliss. Secondly, and perhaps more importantly, the central motif has always remained ambiguous, an ambiguity deriving from open and alternative definitions of power. If power involves the ability of some individuals to impose their will on others, then law, within its organized apparatus of coercion, may be seen as a highly efficient mechanism for its existence. But 'power' no more implies coercion than does the concept of 'obligation' taken from consensus theory. Functionalism has had no difficulty in analysing power, it merely defines what it means by power in a different way. For conflict theory, power is a zero-sum, a constant. The amount of power in a society is fixed and so if one individual has it, another must be denied. For Parsons this is not the case; 'power' is a commodity to be introduced into social relationships and, like money, could be had by all and increase in amount. The analytic framework of consensus theory would remain even though the language of power were used to understand the emergence of criminal legislation. For their own part, the conflict theorists have recognised that coercion is an inefficient mechanism for maintaining order and that most people regard legal authority and resulting criminal legislation as legitimate. They defend their model of society by characterizing legitimacy as enforced acquiescence, in other words as contrived by the powers that be. The ambiguity of the central concepts may help to explain the dominance of the conflict model here in the face of a prevailing conservative orthodoxy.

Given the acceptance of the conflict power scheme, Carson offers three situations where empirical research may criticize and undermine the operating consensus. We can use his points to introduce certain of these empirical studies. First, there appear to be criminal laws that have been passed to the detriment of powerful interests. Carson's study of Factory Acts is one example but a situation which when explored showed the area of power to be contested by differing sections of the manufacturing class itself rather than between the manufacturing class and other sectors of society. Aubert's study turns attention to the possibility that barriers to efficient *enforcement* may have been built into the legislation at the *legislative* stage and that political expediency may force on powerful interest groups 'the necessity of pretending to do one thing while actually doing another'.

Secondly, there are criminal laws which appear irrelevant to power- ②
ful interests, for instance this may seem to be a salient feature of laws relating to morality. The work on the legislation relating to drink and drugs has attempted to show otherwise.

Gusfield in his study of the Temperance laws in America was concerned with the 'implications which the public designation of deviance may hold for the designator'.[31] Especially he was concerned to show that the very act of legislating can be symbolically significant and that deep-seated forms of social conflict can be relevant at this symbolic level. As Gusfield says with regard to the Temperance Movement; 'the political conflict lay in the efforts of an abstinent Protestant middle class to control the public affirmation of morality in drinking. Victory or defeat were consequently symbolic of the status or power of the cultures opposing each other. Legal affirmation or rejection is thus important in what it symbolises as well as or instead of what it controls. Even if the law was broken, it was clear whose law it was.'[32] So, according to this scheme, it is when consensus is least obtainable, when moral movements mirror a concern about threats to a way of life, that legislation relating to morality is perhaps most likely to be enacted.

A similar stance to that of Gusfield was taken by Troy Duster in his work on drugs legislation. His study reiterates that certain classes of persons are more susceptible to having the immorality of their behaviour legislatively underlined than are others. He says that it was when the addict population of America came to be perceived as young, male, working class and black that 'the bridge between law and morality was drawn'.[33] Becker took the issue a stage further. Divesting himself of any conceptual rubric he addressed the question of the essential features of deviant behaviour. The essential feature lay not in the behaviour itself but in the social rule outlawing such behaviour. The creation of such a rule (a legal enactment) became an issue not of supporting the concept of power, but of amplifying the concept of deviance. To the extent, however, that the concept of power remains unscathed by issues of morals legislation, we justify including in this chapter work drawn from general sociology on the concept of power itself.

Finally, Carson argues that the conflict-power model is not undermined by the widespread agreement on the virtue of laws protecting life and property. He argues only that such consensus requires refinements to the model; in particular the model must show how conflict and power are commensurate with the maintenance of social order. We would argue that the possibility of such refinements reflects a belief that law as an institution moulds the possible experiences of the world that man can enjoy, thereby underpinning social order.

The predominant theme then may be one of conflict, but not far beneath the surface is the theme of Durkheim's assertion that legal norms (in this case criminal laws) are an expression of social values which transcend the immediate interests of individuals or groups. Legal norms are still seen as emerging as a solution to certain needs and requirements essential for maintaining the fabric of society. The limits of the dominant theme reflect ambiguities in empirical analysis, apparent consensus in society and the principle that in the end 'any form of domination must be able to appeal to the principle of its own legitimation'.[34]

II. *Implementation of Legislation*

Within implementation studies certain interests have been carried over from work on the emergence of legislation, for instance the importance of understanding the way law is implemented to see the significance of power relations in the creation of law, but in the main the analytic schemes used have been of a different form, more concrete and easier to express. The two main variants are 'Intent-distortion' or 'Realization of Purpose' studies and 'Impact' studies. Both strive to achieve the experimental method, apprehending legislation as an objective fact of great specificity from which to make inferences of intent or impact. If legislation can be apprehended as a specific non-problematic variable, then comparative analysis is possible between the state of society pre-enactment and post-enactment. Work of both schemes shares a concern with the effectiveness of law and its effect on social structure or interactional patterns and both can be undertaken from within a functionalist framework (the functions of Marriage and Divorce laws within a changing social structure; the function and role of the family; etc.) or a conflict framework (in which case legislation may be understood in terms of those interactional patterns dominant in society which the legislation serves to sustain).

In the event, however, 'intent-distortion' and 'impact' studies remain motifs more applicable than 'functionalist' and 'conflict'. An intent-distortion study of Divorce Law for instance, would refer to the purposes said to be expressed in the Statute and the operational intent given to the law by those who have the task of implementation. There is a recognition that legislation is not a blueprint for a subsequent state of society, but rather than address the social processes involved in the translation, we are left with an input (intent) and an outcome (interpretation) and research seeks merely to measure the gap between the two. A good example of this line of work is available in Gorecki's study of Divorce Law in Poland.[35]

Impact studies of Divorce Law have been done on the impact of reform on family structure. But they could also have been studied for their impact on marriage guidance clinics, legal procedure; legal aid; etc. They differ from 'intent-distortion' studies by a more prevailing acquiescence in the facticity and non-problematic nature of law and a freer approach to the description of areas of research significant to the law's implementation. Both schemes could be contained within competing models of sociology and society, and empirical research may have the potential for deciding which sociological perspective is most suitable. The style of work undertaken, however, for reasons to be addressed in the conclusion of this chapter, makes this as yet a vain aspiration.

We have chosen to review briefly the work of three authors—Aubert, Carson and Lukes—the election relating to their standing within the traditions of studies of legislation given above. Aubert[36] pursued an intent-distortion and an impact study of the Norwegian Housemaid Law; Carson[37] the emergence and implementation of Factory Acts within a framework markedly different from that employed by Aubert; and Lukes[38] has introduced to sociology an important statement on the concept of 'power' which may, possibly should, be used to evaluate studies of legislation which either utilize the concept or are more generally indebted to a view of interest group politics.

AUBERT

Aubert, working in collaboration with Eckoff, Sven and Norseng, undertook an investigation of the Norwegian Housemaid Law of 1948. The primary concern was to study the impact of the law or the 'extent to which behaviour conformed to the rules laid down'.[39] Here then the particular process of law creation is not being scrutinized and interest is located at the point of social effects. To estimate the degree of conformity to the Housemaid Law a sample was drawn and a survey conducted. The results were summarized by Aubert as follows:

(a) ninety per cent of the sampled relationships exhibited contravention of the rules and half the cases showed deviations of great magnitude;

(b) deviations clustered in a certain number of households: 'occurrence of one type of violation increases the likelihood of other offences as well'.[40]

After quoting Sumner[41] on the impotence of legal innovation to change social mores, Aubert argues that mere lack of conformity is no evidence that law is without effect. He advocates a further stage of analysis: 'In order to understand the influence of a law it is necessary to study the variables which intervene between the promulgation of the law and the behaviour of the public.'[42] Two variables are seen by Aubert as particularly important; knowledge of the law and age. The intellectual depth of the work is not, however, particularly striking. We learn that:

(a) If legal norms are the same as custom then knowledge of the norms cannot be attributed to either *a priori*.

(b) If legal norms differ from custom, then knowledge of norms does reflect contact with the legislation.

(c) Where legal norms reflect custom there is wide knowledge of the law and great conformity in conduct.

(d) Where legal norms play a reformatory function there is less knowledge of the norms and greater contravention.

At this stage Aubert admits that the crucial question, 'Has the law influenced behaviour to any appreciable degree?' has remained unanswered. After a brief exposition of the scarcity value of housemaids; variation in levels of knowledge of legal conditions and intergenerational variations in defining 'good housekeeping conditions', Aubert concludes that 'at least for some years, the law was ineffective in the sense that actual conditions of work remained at variance with the norms laid down, and in the sense that even conformity to the legal norms was rarely due to influence from the law'.[43]

So far then, we have a study structured in terms of the investigation of law's effectiveness. Survey methodology has been adopted and shows widespread contravention. He is, however, left with one question: why was the law ineffective? Aubert gives two explanations both of which lie in the arena of the law's enactment. First, Aubert argues that the style in which the law was drafted was not conducive to the function the law should serve in communicating to housemaids and their employers the norms that were to govern their relationship. Secondly, Aubert bids us enter the arena of the 'latent functions' of the legislation and, quoting Arnold [44] to the effect that 'it is part of the function of law to give recognition to ideals representing the exact opposite of established conduct', suggests that the ineffectiveness of the Housemaids Law can be explained by the law's latent function of defusing an ideological split within the legislature. Framed in terms of compromise, the law was both enacted and at the same time enacted without effect.

CARSON

Carson stands both as a member of the fairly well-established body of British criminologists and as an advocate and forerunner of the sociology of law. The work with which we are primarily concerned spans these two disciplines and relates to the factory legislation of early nineteenth- and mid-twentieth-century England. Carson looked at this legislation both from an historical vantage point and from the platform of law implementation, administration and enforcement.

The Enforcement of Law

Carson investigated two hundred firms with regard to recorded offences against the Factories Act, 1961.[45] His concern was with how decisions were made about how to enforce the law and the primary research material was provided by the Inspectorate's own reports and other internal documents generated in the course of their dealings with the firms chosen for study. Although the Factories Acts provide an escape clause for management which exculpates them from prosecution in cases where due diligence has been used to enforce the legislative requirements, Carson's investigation was more concerned with decisions *not* to prosecute, which were less securely tied to the constituent parts of the legislation, especially with regard to the Inspectorate's use of conceptions of moral fault at the investigatory stage of their activities.

Smith and Pearson [46] had conducted a survey into the operation of the Food and Drugs Act, 1955, in which a clause allowed manufacturers to escape liability if they had shown 'due diligence'. From their data Smith and Pearson conclude that given, *inter alia*, the Inspectorate's concern with the previous record of offenders in deciding upon prosecution, such inspectors emphasized the actus reus rather than the mental element of the offence. Carson is concerned to ask, however, as to the accuracy of this statement in reflecting what actually happens in practice. As Carson says: 'An inspector might equally attach significance to the repetition of particular offences precisely because this seems to indicate a degree of negligence or even recklessness in the face of previous warnings or prosecutions.'[47]

Enforcement decisions studied by Carson comprised 663 departmental decisions about appropriate action. In ten cases decisions to prosecute were taken; in the other cases either no formal action was taken or enforcement 'consisted in the despatch of relatively standardized letters to offenders'.[48] These letters in a small percentage of cases threatened prosecutions; the remainder (87 per cent of the decisions) 'merely notified the occupier of "matters requiring attention"' with or without a rider of emergency.

Carson investigated how decisions were made to use one or other of these enforcement procedures by examining the internal documents of the Inspectorate. Of special interest is the way Carson interpreted the 'special reasons' which the documents provided as justification for recommending legal proceedings. From the documents it was evident that 'previous warnings' were a significant factor in decisions to prosecute; the converse also applied, and if prosecution was to be recommended in cases where the factory occupier had received no previous warning the inspectors provided reasons for so proceeding 'despite the lack of any previous instruction'.

This emphasis on 'previous warnings' could have been due to their procedural relevance but Carson questions this on grounds which reflect his 'action' approach. As Carson says: 'If such was the case, however, the reasoning must have remained at a very low level of consciousness for at no point did it find expression in the documents that were examined, a degree of reticence which would be surprising in view of the inspectors' forthrightness where similar procedural contingencies were involved.'[49]

Carson suggests that an alternative view is more attractive and more fitting the evidence. He suggests that previous warnings are taken by the Inspectorate as evidencing 'moral fault' on the part of the factory occupier—previous warnings then 'may have been regarded as the normal pre-requisite of prosecution precisely because they held this meaning for the Inspectorate'.[50] The evidence put forward by Carson in the form of quotations from Inspectorate reports support this view; for example one report states that '. . . it is clear that there has been considerable negligence on the part of the firm . . . there have been two previous accidents . . . with previous instructions following them'.

Carson is suggesting that the meaning of events for the Inspectorate is constructed in terms of knowledge of previous occurrences—in other words the Inspectorate takes a 'contextual approach to decision making'.

Previous warnings and instructions are, then, located with other aspects of the backcloth to decision making. Other factors are abstracted from the reports concerning, *inter alia*, a general knowledge of the firm and the firm's attitude towards the legislative requirements. For instance: '. . . my own impression of the place is that the management need gingering up. It is for this reason that I recommend proceedings . . .'; 'the firm seems to regard legal requirements as trivialities and therefore proceedings are proposed'. Such concerns could override the significance of the lack of previous warnings. With assorted extracts from the reports, Carson is able to give an account in fair detail of the manner in which conceptions of moral fault enter into the decision-making process and thereby highlights the significance of the constituent parts of the relevant legislation for the inspectors' own working-day tasks. The merit of such an analysis is its empirical adequacy; this in turn stems from a realization that sociology must recognise the necessity of making theoretical distinctions with 'operational sense to those who are being investigated'.[51] This emphasizes the usefulness of the Inspectorate's internal reports for the study in that these reports have been constructed for the purpose of 'making sense' to the inspectors and, therefore, indicate how the inspectors 'made sense of their own decisions at the time'.

The Inspectorate, in their enforcement of legislation, decided on procedures in terms of a conception of their job as being 'inspectors' rather than 'a factory police'. Prosecutions based on general impressions and previous conduct were a tool of inspection designed to make compliance more likely, rather than as a positive response to violation. Although Carson at times seems to suggest that the concern of the inspectors with questions of moral turpitude 'diverges from statutory definitions' his account remains less concerned with 'measuring the gap' between statutory intent and actual implementation, than with the logic-in-use of decision making especially with regard to operating conceptions of the efficacy of certain tools of inspection.

The Emergence of Legislation

Gusfield,[52] in his work on legislation, suggests that one avenue open to the sociologist who wishes to break away from the view of legislation as the reflection of power dimensions within society, is to analyse the law's symbolic character, but for Carson 'fails to portray symbolic meaning as an emergent property of the interactional sequences occurring in connection with particular pieces or types of legislation'.[53] Carson's substantive work can be seen, he suggests, as a remedy to such a defect, for with regard to the 1833 Factory Act we are to concentrate on an increasingly complex interplay between instrumental and symbolic elements and demonstrate how the 'legislative issue assumed symbolic significance in the course of an interactional sequence'.[54]

Carson accepts that the people who advocated reform in the industrial arena of early nineteenth-century England were indeed concerned with the instrumental effects of legislation. They did, he states, orient their thought to the actual impact of legislation upon the people's actions. This 'instrumental integrity' is allowed both to the reforming zealots of the time and also to those large manufacturers who supported the reformist measures. Rather than being trespassers on the ideology of another class, these manufacturers are shown to be aware of the instrumental effect of reform in weakening the position of small manufactureres whose competition in the now stabilized industry was a threat to entrenched economic strongholds.

Carson begins analysis of the symbolic dimension of factory legislation with a brief review of the dwindling traditionalism of early nineteenth-century industry.

As Carson puts it, 'if the ideology of traditionalism was suspect', a position for which he had already argued, 'then it followed that the political and economic hegemony which it had served to legitimate must be equally so'.[55] The stage is set, then, with an emerging middle class breaking down the traditional framework of industry and making demands on the political structure itself—a demand to have economic superiority translated into terms of legitimate authority.

If those who advocated reform were traditionalist in the economic sense, then it would be tempting to cast their role in terms of a symbolic crusade—'activated by a sense of imperilled prestige and aimed at the salvage of some self-esteem through the act of legislating'.[56] Certainly Carson gives evidence to show that the issue became a symbolic focus for emerging ideological and political divergencies and that in the narrower context of the penalties to be exacted for contravention, the proposed law came to stand, in the minds of the manufacturers, for their own moral debasement. For a time the battle became one concerned not so much over whose law this would be, but over whose knowledge and whose moral interpretation of the whole factory system would be 'publicly endorsed in the act of legislating'.

Carson continues the history of the struggle through the inauguration and report of the Royal Commission sought by the large manufacturers. The result of the Commission was to help to 'resolve the dissonance between desirable competitive effects and unpalatable symbolic connotations'. The manufacturing class succeeded in wrenching the legislation from the hands of the traditional reformists and made it their own. Triumph in the symbolic arena enabled the passage of the legislation not only to uphold the manufacturers' conception of capitalist enterprise but also to achieve for them the instrumental benefits of weakened competition.

Carson summarizes the points of analysis he takes to be central.[57] First, is the emphasis on the emergent nature of symbolic meanings: 'Symbolic meanings are not an intrinsic property of the attempt to make law, but an emergent property of the interaction which occurs along the way.' Secondly, is the critique of earlier studies of legislative passage in terms of a naive dichotomy drawn between symbolic and instrumental aspects of legislation: 'Particular emphasis was placed upon the fact that in the early thirties, instrumentally oriented support for further legislation existed, not only among the most vociferous advocates of factory-reform, but also among some of the manufacturers themselves. For the latter, however, the issue became increasingly infused with a symbolic significance which temporarily vitiated their instrumentally based acquiescence. This transformation was largely the result of interpretive possibilities opened up by the specific methods which the movement for reform chose to (or was forced to) adopt. Thus, the symbolic meaning of the struggle only emerged as the battle progressed.' It is this awareness of the complexity of the social process underpinning the emergence of legislation that Carson most clearly communicates.

POWER AND LEGISLATION

Within the 'schemes' available for studying legislation noted in the introduction was mentioned a reliance on interest group politics as a means of understanding the promulgation of laws in society. To an extent also, Aubert's discussion of compromise in the legislative arena and Carson's analysis of competing views of legislative protection afforded to factory workers, contained elements of this form of analysis. As Carson's own discussion of criminal law indicates, the concept of power has a strong influence on the ordering of legislative studies, but it is also true that the sociology of law has had only a marginal interest in sociological debates on how the concept of power is to be handled and applied. In this section we will discuss the concept of power in studies of policy making and the passing of ordinances in order that insight derived from such work should not be lost to the sociology of law. The type of work we are referring to is generally known as community power studies or societal power studies, depending on the breadth of focus employed.

C. Wright Mills's[58] account of the power elite formed the starting point and one side of a debate concerning the structure of power in American society. Mills regarded power as the capacity to make decisions having important consequences in society. He emphasized the decision making taking place outside of the formal arena of politics amongst the power elite comprising the leaderships of the economic, military and political spheres. The power of the elite was hidden in the sense of not being visible to observers of congressional political activity. Conversely, David Reisman's[59] analysis stressed the importance of those congressionally oriented veto groups so disparaged in *The Power Elite*. Reisman saw a large number of balanced and diversified interest groups initiating, challenging and vetoing a wide range of proposals, such groups having a limited range of interests restricted to a particular sphere of policy making.

Dissatisfaction with the generality of such approaches led to a substantial reorientation of power studies under the sponsorship of Polsby[60] and Dahl.[61] The focus shifted to analysis of concrete decision making in respect of important issues in communities, the purpose being to relate issue outcomes to the interests of possibly competing social groups. The operating concept of power stressed the observable activities of decision makers striving to obtain outcomes favourable to their own interests. In that such was not seen to occur, the findings of most decision making studies contradicted the 'elitist' conclusions of Mills and others.

An important change in the topography of the debate was ushered in when Bachrach and Baratz[62] broadened the 'power' framework to include a form of decision making directed at structuring the formal decision making arena to include only safe issues, e.g. by limiting the political agenda or manipulating the rules of the game. Using

Schatschneider's notion of 'mobilization of bias' they opened up the issue of the structuring of decision making itself and the impact of that structuring upon the nature of the issues contested and the outcomes of those issues which were contested. Their conceptual orientation allowed that decision-making outcomes might be biased whilst the formal arena retained a fictitious autonomy. Interests could be seen to be served disproportionately in contradiction to the findings of studies directed by a more limited conceptual scheme. Bachrach and Baratz thus saw a hidden face of power in non-decision making. Unlike Mills, however, this hidden aspect referred not to the serving of self interests by hidden decision makers deciding positive policy outcomes, but to decision makers confining the scope of positive policy making itself.

The relevant dimension of variance of these several views is the methodological, in the widest sense of that term. In 'societal' power discussions the notion of power is somewhat casually expressed. But more importantly, such discussions fail to explicate the crucial linkages between those who make decisions, and those who do not, and power thus remains as abstracted characteristic and cannot be expressed adequately as a relation between men. The power elite make decisions having important consequences; veto groups prevent one another from engaging in such undemocratic activity; but the conceptual apparatus of power employed cannot express the relations between such activity and the interests of men located elsewhere in the social structure. On the other hand the community power debate, with a more empirically attuned formulation of power, is limited in the classes of actions and actors to whom power can be attributed. Both debates have tended to run out of steam. In the first, the reliance on power has dissipated and discussion has shifted into more overarching debates of social theory and the re-emergence of Marxist theorizing in which power is subordinated as a concept to that of class. In the second, an impasse has been reached between the visionary conceptualization of Bachrach and Baratz, and the concretely empirical concerns of Dahl and Polsby. Research strategy feasibility varies with conceptual scope and in the ensuing impasse it is unsurprising that the choice of perspectives has rested as much on political preferences as anything else. Lukes proposes a radical alternative and without wishing to imply that his scheme developed in such a fashion, we can usefully trace through various elements in his argument.

(a) He has a concept of power which he claims to share with both Dahl et al. and Bachrach and Baratz. That concept is one 'according to which A exercises power over B when A affects B in a manner contrary to B's interests'.

(b) The exercise of power by A can be by way of:

(i) a decision which affects B;
(ii) a non-decision (itself a decision, e.g. to prevent discussion of an issue) which affects B's interests;
(iii) a situation in which although A does not positively act vis-à-vis B at all, the correlates of A's position in the social structure or role in social processes are such that B's interests are prevented from being realized.

The importance of point (iii) is that Lukes believes that it provides for the attribution of power on occasions in which the 'inactivity of leaders and the sheer weight of institutions' can affect outcomes. This in a sense is an extension of Bachrach and Baratz's 'hidden' face of power which for Lukes 'is not sustained simply by a series of individually chosen acts, but also, most importantly, by the socially structured and culturally patterned behaviour of groups and practices of institutions'.[63]

(c) Those interests of B prejudiced by A's activity (which includes inactivity) are not limited to those expressed by B either by intervention in the formal political process or as a less choate grievance. They are to be identified either (i) by B under conditions of relative autonomy, which means participation by B, or (ii) according to observer supplied criteria, empirically verified.

The specification of B's interests rests on the identification of a counter-factual to what happens when power is exercised. That is, since power is exercised when A gets B to do something he would not otherwise have done, the identification of a power exercise depends on the specification of what B would otherwise have done. For Lukes, this is 'one reason why so many thinkers (mistakenly) insist on actual observable conflict as essential to power . . . such conflict provides the relevant counter-factual, so to speak, ready made'.[64] For Lukes the point about interests is that men's wants may be provided in part by the society in which they live. Counter-factuals provide the tool for uncovering such situations.

Lukes himself considers that his framework allows the superseding of earlier formulations in three ways. First, it moves beyond behaviour, overt and observable and displayed only in decision making, as a source of data. Both inaction and unconscious action are brought within the rubric. Secondly, power may be exercised by collectivities, for instance social groups and institutions. Thirdly, it supplies a criterion, in the appreciation of the importance of specifying the relevant counter-factual, for identification of a power exercise.

The framework raises a number of issues, certain of which await exposition in the conclusion. One central problem, however, concerns a lack of complementarity between two important parts of the argument. The notion of power is used to refer to two or more actors whose interests conflict in a latent or overt manner. We can contemplate that both parties exercise power albeit that one party's interests will dominate, and although Lukes does not appear to appreciate the point, the notion of counter-factuals can be utilized not only in the analysis of the party on the receiving end, but also in describing how the victor might have preferred a more substantial victory. Now the benefit of Lukes's scheme is supposed to be that it affords analysis in power terms even where there is no setting in which the depictions 'victor' and 'vanquished' are obviously suitable, because an observable conflict played to the rules of the game does not take place. And this in turn confirms the need to utilize the method of 'counter-factuals'. But if we can identify counter-factuals for both parties, how are we to establish their relative power? The problem goes unrecognized because Lukes's conceptual starting point does not contemplate mutual power exercise—thus A has power over B, etc., but there is nothing of B's (defeated) power. For Dahl et al. there is no issue because the power exerciser must have won out in a situation of overt conflict. In winning out, for instance by the legislature enacting part of his programme, he can be declared the powerful. The utility of conflict for siting analysis is not only that it provides ready made the relevant counter-factual—it also provides a winner. Under Lukes's scheme, however, there is a strong likelihood of identifying a counter-factual for *both* parties, without the discriminating criteria of who won.

In the current context the importance of his self-labelled 'radical' view is both the affinity it possesses for study directed at law making in society (and non-law making) and the linkages established between such study and wider social theory. To the extent that law is required to be an item of study in the sociology of law, law making tends to invite power analysis in the behaviourial terms of a Dahlian framework. Lukes's view would have the advantages of widening the focus. Under Dahl the requirement would be to relate participants' activity in the law making process itself to the explicated interests of relevant actors and groups. Under Lukes the conceptual net could embrace a wider set of actors and would invite the examination of power relations between disparately related actors, rather than simply those in which the connection was overt and observable. Such analysis could then be fed back into more general analyses of power structures and group relations, and this would mark the integration of studies firmly based in the sociology of law. What must, however, be added is that the promise will remain undelivered unless certain aspects of Lukes's position receive greater clarification.

Whether the provision of a 'winner' by the legislative assembly, say, could limit difficulties in the identification of counter-factuals must remain an open question. The scheme provided by Lukes would certainly have the merit of denying a place within the sociology of law to the type of *superficial* use of functionalist terminology, concepts of power and so on, presently prevailing. It may also provide a means out of the impasse reached by the juxtaposition of consensus and conflict models. The success to be attained, however, will remain dependent upon the sociological commitment of research and the extent to which the scheme can satisfy the demands of research for a clearly denoted subject and acceptable conceptual framework.

THE LEGAL PROFESSION

Studies of the legal profession possess an intrinsic interest for the sociology of law. First, the legal has invariably been regarded as one of the professions which displays the quintessential characteristics of that designation. Lawyers have often acted as both an empirical and theoretical bench mark in the study of occupations. Secondly, lawyers have been the object of research at a number of levels—their role as legal actors generally; in the provision of legal services; or more general research aimed at generating 'relevant' knowledge. But as the legal *profession*, lawyers have been studied within a sociological framework. Studies of the profession have been called upon to witness the veracity or applicability of available social theories. It is these latter studies with which we are primarily concerned as they represent a sociological toe-hold in the sociology of law. Fully understood, the studies also serve to provide a sociological means of evaluating the more widely prevalent work on the ethnography and structure of the profession to which we shall refer.

Sociology has provided two dominant modes of analysing professions. For both, professions are seen as a product of the division of labour in industrializing societies and as performing specialized roles in the social order, especially as the bulwark of individual freedom and democratic values. The first, 'trait' theory, sets down the definitive characteristics of collective orientation; skill based on theoretical knowledge; actions relevant to a central societal value; and a code of professional conduct to control and guide such action; the second, 'functionalist' theory, extrapolates from the above characteristics their necessity and inter-dependence.

Trait Theories of the Profession

Trait theories according to Johnson,[65] refer to a distinguishable manner of studying professions such that the characteristics identified are either utilized for the purposes of adjudicating claims to professional status among a range of occupations or serve to operationalize the concept of professionalization. In providing characteristics of professions; determining the process of professionalization; and describing the relative degree of professionalism achieved by a given occupation, the law, along with medicine, stands as an accepted frame of reference. If occupations are regarded as achieving the transition to a profession, the law usually serves to point the way for less-developed brethren of the professional community.

Johnson himself provides a useful summary critique of this approach. First, he regards 'trait' theory as over-evaluative and as too readily accepting the public image promoted by the professions themselves. The legal profession is accused of self-interest as frequently as it is credited with public service, but the former is not to be found in the constitutions of professional associations nor in the catalogues of trait theorists. Secondly, the approach is ethnocentric and neglects to address the specific historical, political and cultural context of the acquisition by an occupation of 'professional' attributes. Thirdly, many of the traits are empirically vague. What is to be regarded as 'altruistic' service, and is this to be seen as attaching to the occupational role itself, the motivations of individual members or both? Finally, Johnson regards trait theory as atheoretical and lacking a framework according to which a sense of discipline might be injected into the cataloguing of 'professional' characteristics.

Functionalist Theory of Professions

As proposed by Talcott Parsons,[66] functionalist theory views the professions as standing between two major aspects of the social structure—political authority and the individual. The theory seeks to show

how professions function on behalf of the social structure and to explain the characteristics of the profession by reference to what is required for it to fulfill those functions. Within the functionalist treatment of professions are two central propositions. First, that professions apply 'systematic bodies of knowledge' to problems and, secondly, that these problems are closely related to a central value of society. For medicine, the body of knowledge can be seen to be more or less theoretical and removed from the knowledge of lay members, and the central value can be taken to be 'health'. The legal profession, Parsons maintains, is manned by trained members who have a fiduciary responsibility for the maintenance and development of the law; they provide a service to the public without regard to self-interest; and the complexity of legal knowledge precludes lay evaluation and so generates a strong emphasis on individual self-control, expertise and powerful socialization procedures. Many of the elements catalogued by the 'trait' theories are present but are now theoretically ordered. The characteristics are not the result of empirical inquiry, but result from the place held by professions in the Parsonian model of society.

Parsons is attempting to show that the legal profession can be analysed in the same way as other professions by reference to the functional interdependence of the 'professional' characteristics, such analysis being asked to explain not only the normal operation of the profession but deviance, and strains to deviance, within the profession as well. Functionalism is not simply a disciplinary device for professional traits, it seeks to explain the interdependence of such traits by reference to the place of professions in the social structure and to explain other features by reference to the strains put on the profession by its location in the social structure.

For present purposes, criticism of the functionalist treatment of the legal profession can be taken from Rueschmeyer's[67] comparison of lawyers and doctors on the functionalist doctrines of 'central values' and 'theoretical knowledge'. The doctrines are central to Parsons's account of the relationship of professions to social control and underpins the assertion that professions depend on strong internal control and professional ethics. Rueschmeyer argues that while doctors have a science of medicine to serve the universal value of health, lawyers can be distinguished from Parsons's theoretical model. The value of 'justice' is problematic, open to competing interpretations and incapable of providing a sure frame of reference for guiding professional behaviour. Further, he argues that the legal profession's working knowledge is not theoretical and scientific, but is pragmatic to a degree that allows for client evaluation of the service offered.

Clients are able to exert pressure on lawyers and lawyers have no central and unambiguous value to fall back on. The lawyer finds it difficult to resist pressure exerted by clients most of whom for any particular lawyer, are drawn from a particular economic strata. The internal differentiation within the profession[68] means that lawyers work within different client milieux which partially determines the attitudes and values of practitioners. This differentiation undermines professional solidarity and questions the extent to which professional status achieves strong internal control of professional conduct.

We can see that if functionalism itself is unacceptable, its use by Rueschmeyer as a model against which to compare the legal profession in a more empirically attuned fashion, does provide some potentially useful insight into the inner workings of lawyers as a social group.

The Client in the Study of the Legal Profession

We continue this section on the profession by giving consideration to two more recent approaches which seek an understanding through an appreciation of the client in professional dealings. In this respect Rueschmeyer constitutes an advance on trait and pure functionalist theories insofar as the client is recognized as contributing in some way both to the orientations adopted by legal practitioners and also to conceptions of justice. However, in Johnson[69] and in Bankowski and Mungham[70] the client becomes a fully fledged participant in the theories about, though not necessarily the practices of, the professions.

Johnson's scheme is directed at professions and to an extent occupations, writ large. Law then takes its place within the scheme. He suggests that the key issue for an occupation lies in both the degree of dependence of clients and the social distance between provider and recipient. Social distance creates a 'structure of uncertainty' and power relationships, in particular, the resources of power available to the occupational group, will determine both to whose advantage the level of uncertainty is reduced and also the possibility for 'professional' control. Hence in this scheme a profession is not an occupation as such, but a means of controlling it.

Johnson's method is to categorize occupations and the history of occupations according to varieties of the key notion of control. Three are identified. First, collegiate control, in which the producer defines the needs of the consumer and the manner in which these will be met. Consumers have diverse interests and are exploitable, and engage producers on a fiduciary and one to one basis. These are the hallmarks of the 'professions', and, for all that lawyers depict their clients as sovereign, law is taken as the 'extreme expression' of such a form of control. Secondly, patronage control, in which consumers dominate and define their own needs. Modally, Johnson refers to aristocratic patrons as the major consumers of various artisan crafts and to oligarchies of corporations who control the market-place for occupations such as accountancy. Thirdly, mediative control in which a third party, Johnson cites the state as an example, intercedes between producer and consumer and determines needs and the conditions for servicing them.

By the light of this categorization, Johnson is able to describe the development and characteristics of the legal profession according to the levers utilized to secure and retain advantage. Thus the 'major collegiate functions of the occupational group are carried out by a practitioner association or guild which bestows status and identity and attempts to sustain uniform interests among the members and promote uniform policies by imposing a monopoly on practice in the field and regulating entry to it'.[71] Johnson thus achieves a framework for reinterpreting the ideology of the profession according to the nature of control of the structure of uncertainty.

A central problem in Johnson's work is in fact the locus of this motivation to control. On occasion it appears to reside in lawyers themselves, and reflect base and materialist considerations on their part. Elsewhere the profession seems to take on a life of its own. Compare for instance '. . . the function of a ban on advertising . . . is an attempt to minimise such a threat (of pressures towards diversity within the profession) . . . by limiting the degree to which the wealthy and influential members of the occupational community can take advantage of their already favoured position'.[72]

Bankowski and Mungham attempt to avoid any such confusion by demarcating the intentions of men from the consequences of their action. In a study which relates solely to the profession of law they argue that their assessment is directed 'to trace the outcomes of the actions and the ideologies of earnest and honourable men . . . many of the consequences of good intentions have the effect . . . not of widening the area of men's freedom, but of compounding their domination'.[73]

The focus is upon the manner in which the law oppresses, even in the actions of 'liberal' lawyers, because it is the form of law, not its content or degree of humanity, which strips men of their dignity and deprives them of the capacity to resolve their own problems. Law stands above men and so cannot be of them. An expert in poor man's law is still an expert who removes both the problem and its resolution beyond the reach of the experiential world of the victim.

The client, therefore, is significant because of his lack of importance. Johnson would see the significance of the client for a lawyer in two ways. Either a client exercises minimal control by way of paying for a service dominated by the power of the profession or, where Legal Aid is available, control is mediated for the client (though not necessarily in his interests) by the state. Both authors, therefore, perceive minimal client control. But whereas for Johnson this is an issue of unequal resources and interests, Bankowski and Mungham emphasize the experiental sovereignty of the client. In the former, the state may define a client's needs for Legal Aid purposes, but they can still be real needs for the client, and still be met. In the latter, a client who resolves a problem perceived by him through the use of a lawyer's services merely contributes to his own experiential debasement, however the lawyer's fee is paid.

The Ethnography and Structure of the Legal Profession

Some interest has been shown by the sociology of law in collating material on the social background of lawyers, of depicting forms of training, describing professional ideologies and relating these to career patterns and styles of legal work. In comparing work on English and American lawyers certain features of organizational structure also have to be borne in mind, especially when relating the empirical work to the models of professions.

Whereas research in England has mainly been concerned with the structure of the profession, American studies have been more interested in the wider question of the relationship of professional behaviour to social characteristics. In both countries, however, it has been asserted that the term 'lawyer' has very little meaning given their bewildering variety of tasks, from court work to advice and preventative channelling. Nor are these non-litigatory tasks treated as unimportant. They are seen as prime means by which the profession acts to re-orient expectation and conduct within society. The ability of the profession to define situations and have their definition prevail, an ability endorsed by their capacity to re-orient client expectations, is not only a significant topic of analysis for the sociology of the profession but is also, as we shall see, important in legal services research.

The studies of Smigel and Carlin[74] in America raise the issue of what stratification within the legal profession means for the professional experience of lawyers. In studying how professional competence is affected by organizational surroundings (Smigel) and socio-economic background (Carlin) research did develop a picture of the dominant patterns of legal work—a more or less adequate ethnography of lawyers and their occupational dealings. Smigel draws a sketch of large law firms wielding considerable influence and providing prudential and technical assistance to the management of the private sector of the economy. In return for serving high socio-economic clients the firm gains the status to employ prestigeful lawyers from the big-league law schools. The transactions within the firm support an ideology not available to the individual practitioners studied by Carlin, but the large-firm lawyer also has to face the problems of working within a restrictive setting, achieving only a narrow work experience and the danger of a strong identification between lawyer and client. The individual practitioner of Carlin, a lower-class member of the Metropolitan bar, is distinguishable by reference both to the social background of practitioners and clients and to the types of legal work routinely handled. There is more litigation but limited to matrimonial and criminal proceedings. The individual practitioner has a precarious foothold in the profession. The continuous battle to find work, the low level of remuneration and involvement in the seamier side of legal practice leads to a style of legal work that owes little to the standards of the profession. They are themselves captive of a particular client milieu which not only promotes a particular commitment to professional ethics, but by also restricting types and volume of work, leads to the use of political channels and an undermining of professional status.

The lawyer who does matrimonial work and the Wall Street lawyer are in many respects in different professions, and the research points to several instances of incompatibility between trait and functionalist theories of professions and the ethnography of legal work. The same is true of those studies more concerned with the structure of the legal profession.

If the above works reflect the style of research on the legal profession at an empirical level, can we draw any points of contrast between ethnographic and theoretical work?

Skolnick[75] claims that the concepts of 'role', 'self-image', 'recruitment' and 'socialization' provide the rubrics for organizing empirical data about the lawyer's world. Certainly patterns of legal work depicted in the studies do depend for their interpretation on such concepts, and we can note a similarity between these concepts and the 'characteristics' of professions offered by trait and functionalist theories. The use to which the concepts are put, however, differs.

Patterns of recruitment and socialization are, for trait and functionalist theories, to be explained either by the status of the particular occupation as a profession or by reference to the function of recruitment and socialization patterns in allowing the profession to fulfil the role in society claimed for it by the theory. In the empirical work the thrust is rather different. For instance, from evidence on socialization and recruitment patterns, Landinsky concludes that the effect has been to elaborate 'legal procedures to handle the problems of corporate enterprise as opposed to those concerned with the problems of private citizens'.[76]

Similarly, with regard to legal ethics, models of the profession take ethics to be a characteristic of professions at the same time safeguarded by the internal control allowed by professionalization. Carlin's study of legal ethics attempted to show that the particular structure of the legal profession in America made it difficult to accommodate to demands brought to the lower levels of the profession without violating those ethics. There was a moral division of labour reflecting the stratification within the profession itself. Ethical commitments were conditioned more by organizational context than professional status.

Such studies may give support to Rueschmeyer's[77] argument that client identification can capture lawyers within an organizational context not well pictured by the theoretical models. It may be the case, however, that the models are significant in providing a range of issues to be reflected upon in any discussion of professional organization. For instance, departure from the characteristic of internal control towards client identification or from scientific to pragmatic knowledge, may affect the role the profession can be expected to play in developing the legal order. The isolation of the English Bar, for instance, may generate restrictive practices, but it may also enable the Bar to retain its independence from client pressures, leaving the solicitors to respond and accommodate to the variety of demands that are made on the legal system. To the extent that the models uphold certain forms of professional organization and to the extent that empirical work seeks out the existence or otherwise of such forms of organization, contact between the two forms of work can be maintained and certain possible developments indicated should changes in professional structure be proposed.

The particular structure of a profession (for instance, formal stratification as against socio-economic stratification) may offset the extent to which occupational groupings display features of professionalization, and empirical work may have questioned the extent to which theoretical models can be used to relate professional conduct to professional status rather than socio-economic—organizational constraints. But both theoretical and empirical work allow a more cynical appraisal of the legal profession than that often encountered in texts on the sociology of law. Nonet and Carlin for instance, assert that when law becomes seen as 'the embodiment of values rather than as a sheer social technique' the legal profession assumes the 'critical mission of maintaining the legal order and shaping its development'.[78] The relationship offered would neither be expected by the theoretical models nor supported by the empirical work. The profession, whether seen via theory or empirical work, is not autonomous, but firmly placed within the structure of advanced societies by which it was given birth.

LEGAL ACTORS

This section refers to a somewhat residual category within the subdiscipline—work which neither, for instance, crouches under the umbrella of legal services; commits itself to sociological themes such as social change or stratification; or refers to legislative enactments; and has not already been assembled under the particular sociological banner of 'professions'.

Legal actors as a category, however, does have a rationale in being of a certain style of work. Most importantly it is work which pursues an investigation through empirical field research with the object of collating specific data on a topic of interest. And if it is permissible to define by negatives, the general lack of concern with issues of wider sociological significance also helps to mark the boundaries.

We have assembled 'legal actors' studies under three heads which reflect varying complexity in the treatment of the 'social'. In ascending order the three categories pay greater attention in both topic and method to the intricacy of social behaviour as it relates to law. Since studies have been eclectic they have sometimes touched on more than one level at different points in their analyses. Also, those wide-ranging investigations such as the Chicago Jury Project concerned more with the substantive topic than with issues of sociological propriety, encounter the 'social' in different ways at different times. The greater or lesser attention paid to the 'social' revolves around issues of sociology to be taken up in Chapter V. For now we are concerned to display the character of work along this dimension.

Legal Behaviour as related to Social Factors

Work under this head is geared to the discovery of relationships between items of behaviour and a variety of social factors. The data collected, often with a minimum of analysis per se, tells the story—the material is the message. Examples include relating judge's decisions to their political affiliations, jurors' participation to their socio-economic backgrounds, and citizens' opinions of law to a range of sociological variables. The tenor of the work is to exhaust limited propositions relating aspects of social and legal behaviour rather than to engage in more speculative analysis, but it is important to note that limiting the range of data collection means neither that the investigation is uncontentious, nor that considerable opportunities for choice do not still exist.

Thus, the techniques of small group research were utilized at one point in the Chicago Jury Project[79] which allowed certain variables to be associated with participation in jury work. For instance, males and those of higher socio-economic status were found to participate in, influence and have greater satisfaction with jury decision making. Patterns of participation suggested that the majority of jurors were neither coerced nor dominated but worked 'responsibly and with democratic recognition of available competence'. Note first, however, that the material was also compatible with a judgement that the jury merely reflects the stratification and inequality prevalent in the wider social system.

We can also see that the variables utilized to explain behaviour possess differing character and necessitate great selectivity in those to be investigated. Gender may have social consequences but it is essentially a biological category. Social class, often used though less frequently properly used, can be employed as a mere reflection of material inequality or as a full-blooded theoretical construct. Where theoretically loaded terminology is used the quantitative bent of legal actors research often militates against sophistication (because of the simplification required for numerical treatment) but it is perhaps the range of choice of variables which deserves the greatest emphasis.

It is not only the explanatory variables to which a lack of precision attaches. Whilst 'jury participation' may appear an unproblematic category it continues to require the close attention of the researcher. 'Participation' may be related to the frequency and duration of utterances by jurors in the deliberations, but research would need at a minimum to reduce this category to include only 'significant' utterances. The boundaries of the data to which variables refer are not always as clear cut as may appear to be the case.

Fuller[80] expresses this critical theme when faulting studies of judicial decision making on the grounds of their inability to represent accurately the social reality they purport to display. For example, many researchers have documented the social background and political affiliations of judges and have related such variables to judicial decisions. It has been suggested, for instance, that Democratic and Republican judges differ in the tendencies of their decision in a range of legal areas including criminal and constitutional cases; labour/ management disputes; tax and personal injury cases; and others. But even if such studies provide a framework for relatively accurate prediction as to future decisions this in no way stakes a claim to having revealed the nature of the social processes involved nor an ability to equate predictive with causal significance. Prediction does not allow us to attribute causal weight to the predictive factors (e.g. that pro-Labour decisions are 'caused' by Democratic affiliation) and little is learnt regarding the actual nature of judicial decision making.

Fuller gives an example of a judge declaring invalid some exercise of power of a labour union. Does this prove the judge to be anti-Labour/union? Fuller says that it does not. First, the judge may not see the issue in those terms but rather in terms of his professional role in applying established legal principles. Secondly, it may be that the decision is forced on the judge by a procedural technicality. Thirdly, it is possible that without such constraints the judicial vote 'against' the union reflects in fact 'a deep faith in the labour movement' and a conviction that 'the greatest threat to it lies in irresponsible actions by unions'.

Studies of judicial decision-making[81] identify and classify legal decisions but of the social processes which result in decisions, and give them the character of particular types of decisions, we are told nothing. The assumption that 'variables' work their way through into other 'variables' in some sort of mechanical way led to inaccuracies in the conceptualization of the legal process.

Similarly, by conceptualizing the composition of courts as small groups representing voting blocs, a number of studies[82] have tried to investigate aspects of judicial leadership as well as to provide yet more refined techniques for predicting judicial voting behaviour. Here again, however, the method may radically misconstrue the nature of the legal process and, especially, judicial conceptions of the professional role of judges. As Fuller says studies using game theory as a means of studying decision making are 'concerned with the "pay-off" and not with the rewards itself . . . judges may derive rewards from collaborative efforts which transcend individual "pay-offs" '.[83]

The studies of the legal behaviour of the judiciary in relation to social factors have been augmented by studies designed to ascertain the opinions and attitudes of the general public towards law and particular legal enactments.

However, as Fuller questions the manner of conceptualization of 'decisions', so have both the status of 'opinions' as building blocks for sociology and the appropriateness of the questionnaire as an instrument for displaying 'opinions' been made subject to scrutiny. Blumer[84] has directed attention to the assumptions contained in any attempt to elicit opinions via the administration of questionnaires. He denies that 'an opinion' is a simple entity that can be treated as a fundamental unit for analysing the relationship of actors to, *inter alia*, the legal system. The assumption that they can be so used, locks research into a particular view not only of sociology but also of the social world itself. The point can best be made by way of the example of knowledge and opinion of law studies. Knowledge and opinion studies have a theoretical intent, which we consider under the second head of the section, but we can see that they seek to develop that intent through the collection of survey material about citizen opinions of law writ large, the morality and punishment which should attach to individual laws, the extent to which legal enactments find popular support and so on. Thus Van Houtte and Vinke[85] inquired of 1500 people in Holland and Belgium their views as to the degree of punishment and moral disapprobation which should attach to acts contravening the legal code. Respondents indicated their opinion by selecting a point on a five-point scale (severe, very severe, etc.). The material collected included base-line information on the respondents themselves (age, sex, etc.), and provided explanatory variables relating to both structural (class, occupation), cultural (religion, education) and psychological (severity; authoritarianism) factors. So broken down, the new data comprised the responses of subjects to a variety of questions.

But consider what we are asked to understand by a response that evading a small income-tax liability should be punished severely and the relation it bears to another respondent's view that *very* severe punishment is appropriate. Common sense suggests that designations of 'severe' and 'very severe' do not reflect fixed quantums of punishment from a respondent's point of view and that the meaning of the designations will vary between respondents, as will the significance of the question—think about a motorist being asked two questions about fishing without a licence and about avoiding payment of motor-vehicle tax. The election for the questionnaire, however, commits the study to standardized responses. Such standardization strips a response of its meaning, significance and context and yet it is only in the light of such aspects that the response makes sense at all. It is the sheer impossibility of reproducing human beings and human action as computerizable characteristics and questionnaire responses that Blumer places in doubt.

Whilst the detailed methodological arguments await exposition in Chapter V, there is enough here to witness Blumer's contention that the techniques of attitude and opinion polling pay insufficient regard to the fundamental question of 'What is an opinion?' or the related question of how such entities, once identified, enter into the operation of society. Attitudes must be regarded in the absence of such attention, as merely the 'things that attitude scales scale', and opinions as merely the 'things that opinion polls poll'. Without working through both the social nature of opinions to be investigated and also the relationship between such a nature and the instruments for displaying and recording them, the concrete expression of opinions in rates and percentages is a mere façade serving to conceal the complexity and intricacy of how social life is held together.

Actors' Relationships to Law

The sociology of law in general has adopted as a major issue the discrepancy between formal legal structures and social behaviour as in, for instance, studies of incomplete compliance to legislation, and research focused at the level of legal actors has frequently reflected such an approach. The work expresses an attempt to distinguish and display the orientations of actors to some legal enactment, process or institution.

To this extent the treatment of the 'social' is taken a level higher than in the earlier work reviewed. The best available example is the Chicago Jury Project which, in addition to accumulating material such as has already been mentioned, selected and investigated a

range of topics relating to the 'quality' and character of jury
decisions. The Project concerned the injection by juries of substantive
'justice into what might otherwise be a coldly efficient system of
rules'.[86]

Such considerations necessitated inquiry into the processes of
reasoning engaged in by actors in decision making and this represents a
clear shift in topic from, say, the judges decision-making studies
criticized earlier by Fuller. Implications for methodology also follow
and in many respects the use of quantified data is inhibited. Whilst
the desire for quantification is often apparent, the requirement for a
qualitative assessment of actors' reasoning can create ambivalence
within the work.

Such ambivalence is well displayed by Kalven and Zeisel[87] when
they discuss discrepant determinations of cases by judge and jury. It is
quite clear that measuring the extent of disagreement is, for them, an
important endeavour and one which they sought to accomplish by
statistical analysis of data drawn from both real and simulated legal
decisions. From such analysis, Kalven and Zeisel assess the magnitude
of disagreement in both civil and criminal cases to be of the order of
twenty-two per cent. The jury is 'less lenient than the judge' in three
per cent of criminal cases, and 'more lenient than the judge' in nine-
teen per cent of criminal cases. This was based on the number of
convictions or acquittals. Further the jury was shown to be more
lenient in criminal cases in terms of the specific charges to be made
against the defendant and also in those cases where the jury can
disagree with the judge on the penalty to be exacted from the defendant. If in civil cases the total disagreement between judge and jury
was approximately the same as for criminal proceedings, the direction
of disagreement was substantially changed. On the civil side the 'disagreement is distributed evenly in the two directions. In 12 percent of
the cases it is the jury that will be more favourable to the plaintiff,
and in 10 percent of the cases it is the judge who would be more
favourable to the plaintiff.'[88] As Kalvin and Zeisel express the point,
this finding 'is in the teeth of the popular expectation that the jury in
personal injury cases favours the plaintiff, at least if that expectation is
taken to mean that the jury is more likely to favour the plaintiff than
is the judge'.[89]

The position of the jury, then, does display a marked contrast and
one which Kalven and Zeisel wish to see as indicating 'something
profound about the values, attitudes and functions of the jury in its
criminal and civil sphere'.[90]

Having established the area and direction of disagreement, Kalven and Zeisel attempt an explanation of the variance in criminal trials in terms of five factors. These factors are constituted by 'evidence'; 'facts only the judge knew'; 'disparity of counsel'; 'jury sentiments about the individual defendant'; and 'jury sentiments about the law'. Summarizing, Kalven and Zeisel say that 'slightly over half the job of explanation falls to the evidence category'. Apart from evidential factors, the explanation for disagreements resides principally in jury sentiments on the law or jury sentiments about the defendant. Perhaps the most interesting aspect is 'the salient role played by jury sentiments on the law causing disagreements; jury equity looms as a significant factor'.[91] In other words, the fact-finding role of the jury is given the lie because in nearly half of the cases in which judge and jury disagree the jury 'is giving expression to values and sentiments under the guise of answering questions of fact'. If, however, 'the factual leeway is not present, the sentiments and values as a rule have to be particularly strong to move the jury to disagree. Conversely, if only ambiguity in the facts is present, and the directionality of the sentiment is absent, the jury will be less likely to disagree with the judge. The decision-making patterns we are pursuing are subtle ones.'[92] Along these lines Kalven and Zeisel assert that factors of 'sentiments concerning individual defendants' and 'disparity of counsel' will rarely be sufficient standing alone to cause judge/jury disagreement, 'rather they gain their effectiveness only in partnership with some other factor in the case'.[93]

To the extent that the Chicago researchers showed an interest in actors' orientation to elements of the trial, this engagement of the social at a moderate level of complexity is further exemplified by Broeder's treatment of the jury. Broeder[94] sets out evidence of jury departures from strict substantive law arguing that implicit in his research findings is the fact that in increasing or decreasing damages according to whether the injured party is required to support or is instead entitled to be supported by his spouse and/or children, the jury was repudiating 'the fundamental tort concept that a negligent defendant's duty is to pay strictly according to the pecuniary value of the interest he directly injures'.[95]

We are not saying that the study is significant because it showed the jurors to be cognisant of tort doctrines—this was not necessarily the case. The point is that Broeder looked at elements of cases to which jurors *did* give attention in order to build up his conclusion.

Skolnick in commenting on the jury project praises its documentary value and no doubt he is correct to do so. Certainly the study provided a wealth of data in the form of the relation of certain social and economic variables to participation in the legal order, and if the methodology was inadequate to generate explanations of legal behaviour, a low-key profile of the legal process was achieved. Skolnick does, however, find fault with the project, and presumably with similar projects conducted elsewhere, in terms of their lack of 'theoretic or philosophic' interest, most notably the lack of any analysis 'of the administration of justice as a social system' or 'higher order concepts for interpreting the findings'.[96]

But for our own part the sociological contribution was more related to the recognition in certain of the studies that investigation of, say, discrepant determination of cases could not be exhausted by reference to computerizable variables but had to rely on categories of analysis developed at least in part from the actors' own understandings of the factors at issue in their decisions. The quest for quantification of such categories created tensions within the work. But at least the tension was not resolved at the expense only of the qualitative material.

The importance of this temperance becomes apparent if we look at work on knowledge and opinion of law, where the concerns prompting inquiry also related to actors' relationships and orientations to law. In the example given earlier, for instance, Vinke and Van Houtte collected data in order to throw light on the conundrum set by observers such as Dicey and Sumner as to whether conviction was a necessary basis for the efficacy of legal rules. Their concern was to identify and describe the extent of a sense of justice amongst the Belgian and Dutch populations. Such issues relate to the orientation of the citizenry as legal actors to the legal system and, prima facie, appear to favour qualitative data which might more adequately reflect the hermeneutic quality of such a relationship. However, the determination of the researchers to pursue a particular, scientistic mode of inquiry led them away from an appreciation of qualitative data and the alternative of a numerical treatment of qualitative material. Instead they chose to operationalize the issue of the existence of a 'sense of justice' into a questionnaire via a recognition of the significance for such a question of how the citizenry perceive and accept law and, further, hypothesizing that attitudes to law are likely to vary according both to different laws and also to the characteristics of the respondent. Vinke and Van Houtte therefore eliminate any possible tension between the issue and the data by a strict behaviourist treatment through which the issue is reduced to standardized questionnaire responses.

The ability to operationalize subtle conundrums is methodologically problematic but for now we can simply throw a question mark around whether research of this nature can properly contemplate the complexity of the issue.

Take the example of 'a sense of justice'. We may all be convinced of the need for the incarceration of murderers, and at this level share a view of what constitutes justice as applied to acts of homicide.[97] But does tolerance for fishing without a licence (one of the questionnaire items) by a majority of the population undermine the consensus of respect for law's major prohibitions? The rights and wrongs here are less important to establish than that the ways of operationalizing the conundrums are multifarious, and any particular avenue must be argued for—in much knowledge and opinion work the availability of multiple operationalizations is not even made apparent, let alone explored.

Undoubtedly the problem of linkage between theoretical issues and research findings arises partly from the purposes for which the work is designed. Explicitly, studies seek to contribute to more efficacious social engineering. After all, if the unpopularity of a law can be discerned, or a disjuncture between the sanctions it invites and the sentiments of the population uncovered, then the legislature can perhaps better calculate the costs of enforcing conformity and avoid the erosion of its own legitimacy.

The resulting concern for precision induces over enthusiasm for quantification of intricate issues. Such problems have been forcefully taken up by Bankowski and Mungham[98] for whom such studies are an example of 'taking law to the people'. They put law in touch with the needs and feelings of the populace, thus serving to bridge the communication gap and to lodge the regulation of an increasingly complex society in the 'reality' of questionnaire elicited attitudes to the rules. The authors' objection is that such an approach reflects a profound commitment to social democracy and is an attempt to shore up the system. In so doing the work finds it impossible to question the institutions it seeks to enlighten, and the power relations which sustain them. Since the legal machinery of capitalism is to be oiled, the law itself remains bracketed and hence arcane. Knowledge and opinion studies can tell society how to frame laws, but nothing about the role of the legal system in maintaining that society.

If we have seen that knowledge and opinion studies resolve any tension in favour of the numbers game, and that certain of the jury studies merely pass on the contradictions to their audience, brief mention of Macaulay's[99] analysis of businessmen's orientations to contract law will reflect the alternative stance of resolving tension so as to keep faith with the subjective point of view of the actor. At one level Macaulay treads the ground of his contemporaries in pitching his study in terms of discrepancies between the formal structures available in the legal machinery for identifying and resolving disputes and the actual behaviour which occurred when disputes arose.

Macaulay found that businessmen did not use the formal machinery, a finding that was the more remarkable for the apparent commitment to detailed contractual arrangements as represented in the exhaustive and specific conditions of sale and purchase printed on the documents of exchange. More important, however, in the current context was that he uncovered the basis for the discrepancy in the orientations which businessmen brought to their transactions and to the disputes which arose through an elicitation of the reasoning processes of the participants—and this material he communicated in his analysis without rendering it devoid of its context by assembling it into a spurious numeracy (of the order of 'the amount of discrepancy is X%'). Basically businessmen avoided the courts in order to maintain cordial, or at least continued, relations with their clients and suppliers, and the technical detail specified on invoices and other documents was to be interpreted as a routinized procedure somewhat lacking in relevance to the transaction, despite its apparent confirmation of the transaction as legally binding and as subject to specified conditions of sale and purchase.

Legal Action and Social Process

The third head of legal actors research is characterized by studies which identify the social process and social practices which constitute action relating to law. This is not a dominant tendency in the sociology of law. However there are some examples, and where they do exist they exhibit a reliance on an interpretive understanding of social action, and describe such action as illustrative of the conditions under which action is constructed or as a depiction of a type of relationship between participants.

Garfinkel provided an early example in his analysis of courtroom interaction and of the way participants managed the transformation of public identities.[100] He also attended to the lay methods and theories constructed and utilized by jurors in the jury room for determining questions of guilt, amounts of compensation and so on. From transcripts of jury deliberations Garfinkel was able to analyse such things as 'jurors' uses of some kind of knowledge of the way in which the organized affairs of society operated', jurors' concern with 'adequate accounts' and 'being legal', and more generally 'how jurors knew what they were doing in doing the work of jurors'. The concern was a low-level analysis of procedures used to get the work of being a jury done in a manner which the jurymen felt met the requirements of that office.

McBarnett[101] in a recently published piece of research, was concerned with pre-trial procedures and their effect on both rates of conviction and decisions to convict. The issue of social processes is paramount at the level of ordering data, but an attempt is made to straddle two diverging trends in the sociology of law, identified by the author as 'why the substance of law takes the shape it does and how the routine outcomes are achieved'. Taking the primary concern to be 'how does the judge or jury become *convinced* of guilt or innocence', a level of analysis closely geared to the analysis of social processes, McBarnett claims that the analysis of pre-trial procedures shows how those processes are underpinned by structures of power, with society being reproduced in the legal arena.

It is very significant for the sociology of law that analysis at the level of societal structure should be twinned with analysis of the routine interactions within legal settings. It is a feature displayed also in the work of Carlen on Magistrates Courts.[102] Concerned to explore the interplay between abstract rules (the formal structure) and situational rules (patterns of action which exemplify the means by which actors handle social situations), Carlen sought to describe how these two types of rules are systematically and routinely orchestrated in the accomplishment of judicial acts and how such orchestration can result in a series of 'remedial routines' for reasserting control over the proceedings if repudiation by the defendant of the socially constructed reality of the court process occurs.

One such routine relates to the means by which defendants are separated from their commonsense world and required to participate in the very special reality of the court. At one level the simple ability to ask questions can be significant, for as Carlen points out with reference to studies of language use, the failure to answer to a question is itself an event liable to permit inferences as to the reasons for such a failure. When defendants participate, as they do normally, then they are required to forego the assumption that other actors will proceed so long as it is 'obvious' as to what they say or mean. Defendants must play their part in sustaining those features which symbolize the court setting as the arena for meting out justice.

Carlen gives an example of a woman accused of stealing, and the following interchange is recounted.

Clerk: Do you plead guilty or not guilty?
Defendant: Yes, I did it. I said I did it.
C: No. Do you plead guilty or not guilty?
D: Yes, I did it. I just want to get it over.
Magistrate: (to probation officer). Can you be of help here?

The probation officer goes over to the defendant and eventually goes out of court with her. Later in the morning the case is 'called on' again.

M: Do you plead guilty or not guilty?
D: Yes, I did it.
M: No, I'm asking you whether you plead guilty or not guilty. You must use the words not guilty or guilty.
D: (Looking towards probation officer) She said 'say guilty'.
M: No. You must say what you *want* to say.
D: Yes, I'll say what you like. I did it.
M: No. You must use the language of the court.

We can see that the commitment to eliciting the actors' part in the social processes at work may extend, as in this instance and in McBarnett's research, to reporting actual sequences of interaction. The final analyses are, however, achieved by reference to structural features (McBarnett) or to procedural features which are held to reproduce the structure of social order of society (Carlen).

Such issues are seen as important by Carlen in a collection of articles possessing a self-consciously Marxist and politically critical approach to law. Carlen offers the work as mapping out new themes for the sociology of law ready and able to compete with those set up by such as Treves and Schur. The new themes are, *inter alia*, materialist approaches to law and law as a mode of reproduction of the social order. The latter, exemplified by the work of Carlen and McBarnett, is taken a stage further in an article by Burton[103] on the relationship between the Irish Republican Army and its community, a piece which, while displaying a critique of the legal ideology which tries to depoliticize the I.R.A.'s involvement in the community, is based essentially on empirical data of strategies used by the I.R.A. to resist 'criminalization' and to gain and maintain political authority within the community. Thus he cites an instance of counter-information bulletins issued by the I.R.A. which designated the British forces as 'troops of occupation' and themselves as 'troops for the defence of the community'.

It is important to note, not necessarily critically, that the studies offered depend very little on a Marxist analysis as such—and, 'critical' or not, they do not necessarily require to be evaluated as to their sociological contribution on grounds any different from those we would apply to other work.

This section has addressed work which has treated social processes as significant in the understanding of legal activity; of how the law enters into the construction of routine lines of action; and how participants use knowledge, theories and so on, to produce such routine action. This level, most clearly hit by Garfinkel, was continued, albeit in different form, into those newer studies self-prophesying a commitment to the structural interpretation of data. How convincing are the latter studies, however, is an issue which we would see as resolved by the adequacy of the methodology used rather than, say, the availability of a critical mind to display a congruence between the data so collected and the wider political structure. The congruence may exist but its exposition can only be as significant as the date is convincing. In Burton's article for instance, he has selected a topic area of great controversy within the political arena, but the choice of topic cannot undermine the conditions on which sociology evaluates such study. Burton limits himself to the collection of evidence in the form of actual interactional sequences which undermine alternative accounts of the relationship between the I.R.A. and its community. In this he is convincing. But the study at that level owes little to critical sociological theory. Carlen's article again uses interactional sequences to show how a disruption in court on the basis of a commonsense rejection by the defendant of modes of legal procedure is managed by magistrates. Again nothing is owed to conflict theory. McBarnett's study of pre-trial procedures is convincing because of the quality of data generated—not her desire to pursue a 'critical' analysis.

By treating the 'social' in a more or less sophisticated manner, by appreciating issues of sociological method, the studies separate themselves from those of the ilk of knowledge and opinion of law—they set themselves up as significant contributions to the understanding of legal activity, and legal settings. They do not, however, establish their 'themes' as obviously meritorious, nor do they establish a critical self-consciousness as a necessary or sufficient condition for the production of good sociology. Good sociology remains an issue both of an adequate methodology and a recognition of the complexity of the 'social'. Within sociology, that must come from the analysis of empirically acquired data which treats social activity as a subject-matter of study rather than from the imposition onto the social world of *a priori* categories, be they from commonsense, radical or orthodox sources. Such, to use the authors' own term, have as much ability to reproduce the social world ready for its discovery by sociologists as ever did have the law.

LEGAL SERVICES

The traditional sociological concern with material and social deprivation finds an expression also within the sociology of law. The twinning of sociological notions of class and power with the stated goals of the legal system has been the primary objective of a substantial portion of research in the sociology of law. For convenience it can be considered under the heading of legal services.

The main direction of work has been to examine the self-image of impartiality, neutrality and objectivity professed by the legal system and to overlay this self-image with a sociologically generated picture of the class-ridden society. The result has been a series of telling indictments of the legal system's complicity in the 'sociological subordination of the poor'.

The work can be broken into four broad categories, distinguishable in terms of a particular orientation to the topic. The most substantial in terms of output assesses the reality of the maxim 'equality before the law'. The style is discursive, the work emphasizing the need for social reform in the face of description and analysis of the difficulties facing the poor relative to other sections of the population. Secondly, are a number of studies which aspire to an empirical baseline for their observations and employ the research techniques of sociology to collect evidence to refine and sharpen particular analyses. Thirdly, greater sophistication has been attempted through the adoption of definite perspectives on such issues as 'unmet legal need', 'legal problems' and the concept of 'rights'. Finally are to be found self-consciously radical views which question the totality of the endeavour to reorganize the practices of an 'inherently dominatory' legal system. Each of these will be reviewed in turn.

Legal Services as a Social Problem: Mainstream Interpretations

There are three aspects of this most prolific category: observations on the legal subordination of the poor; explanations of this subordination; proposals for reform.

Carlin and Howard[104] provide a useful summary view of the treatment of the poor. First they argue that the legal system contains inherent prejudices in so far as biases operate through what they term the dual system of law. They suggest that whether one looks at 'the poor' and the law that is applied to them, or at 'roles' (such as 'consumer', 'father', 'husband') the incumbent of which may be either a poor man or a rich man, one finds that the law applied to the poor is of a differential quality. This dual-law argument is generally taken to refer to the fact that for certain problems common to both rich and poor, the rich have redress through private law whereas redress for the poor is provided through the avenue of public law. This dualism is self-evident in areas such as family law, because both rich and poor alike resort to court adjudication, but it is also reflected throughout the legal system in the form of the quasi-judicial tribunal system which is the deliberation machinery for those problems especially affecting poor people. The law itself, then, is seen as structured so as to take account of differential social position and to mete out justice less in accordance with timeless stone-carved enactments than in relation to the social position of the recipient. By establishing a machinery for processing the poor, the formal framework of justice fails to justify the mythology of equal treatment.

Beyond this 'de jure' bias of the law, Carlin and Howard also detect a 'de facto' bias, said to occur when the law treats rich and poor alike but where the correlates of poverty deny the possibility of equal treatment. This entails the recognition that realizing the protections and benefits provided by law depends upon factors which do not necessarily attend those protections and benefits. Legal representation in particular, as a gateway through which access to legally prescribed benefits can be attained, is seen to be an important element in winning available advantages. Carlin and Howard assert, not without justification, that the poor are less likely to seek a lawyer's help; less likely to receive competent help when lawyers are consulted; more likely to receive help from lawyers whose ethical standing will not bear too close scrutiny; and that help is likely to be remedial rather than preventative. Nor is the relatively low use of lawyers to be accounted in terms of a lack of legal problems. It is certainly the case that instances of tax, company and conveyancing law will have a remoteness to the poor bordering on irrelevance. These are traditional legal problems but the situation of the poor is such that their economic and social problems are, first, not well represented by the legal system and secondly, when the legal system does provide an avenue of redress, not defined by the poor as legal problems.

In terms of explaining the occurrence of such injustices the tendency is to rely on a description of the post-war rise of the welfare state and increasing state intervention. Thus in Carlin and Howard the development of dualistic legal machinery is seen as an outgrowth of government in people's lives. The welfare state marked a phenomenal increase in both the scope and scale of government intervention with the extension of social and welfare benefits creating areas of contention involving the poor in which government was the 'other side'. However, such matters were not seen by and large as between parties with complementary rights and obligations but rather as a relationship between recipient and donor in which social need was being met. That conception of government/welfare beneficiary found expression in the powers given to administering agencies to vary benefit in certain respects according to social need. Similarly the appellate machinery of quasi-judicial tribunals were seen as eschewing due process and formal application of law in favour of, in certain cases, an attempt to get a second opinion on the 'merits of the case' and the extent of social need and, in others, an attempt to ascertain the 'real facts' as a basis for applying either legal rules or, more usually, rules constructed outside of the formal law-making arena. This less than equal treatment of the poor was seen as replicated in nominally judicial bodies to the extent that, for instance, courts were dealing with social problems likely to involve the poor. In particular Carlin and Howard cite the practice of juvenile courts in acting as benevolent administrators solving the social problems of delinquency rather than resolving a legal dispute by impartial adjudication. The poor are treated as having problems, not grievances, and in need of treatment, not justice.

The implications are that justice is discarded in the name of fairness; procedural standards are weakened; adversariness is replaced with 'agreed' decisions; and, with responsibility diffused throughout bureaucratic administrative agencies, the poor are confronted by an opponent holding most of the cards and using the ideology of the welfare state to mask the exact nature of the rules of the game. Unsurprisingly, the poor are unable to take advantage of the process by which more powerful groups capture the agencies set up to regulate their activities. Whereas in the fields of commerce and industry, regulating agencies often identify with the object of regulation, mediating and softening government policy and even acting as advocates on behalf of sectional interests, the poor constitute inefficient constituents. Their own passivity reinforces the reluctance of welfare agencies to serve the needs and protect the interests of poor people.

While such analysis accounts for the gross features of the current position of the poor, issues such as the failure to achieve representation are explained in more limited terms. One might expect an account couched in terms of recent historical changes in the structure and activity of the profession but Carlin and Howard[105] emphasise the 'complex social process' entailed in achieving representation. The discrepancy in levels of explanation throws doubt on both levels but the authors commit themselves to arguing that whilst financial barriers are important, any of the following may also prevent successful contact between lawyer and client. A person may fail to perceive a problem as one on which lawyers could assist; be reluctant to seek help, even having overcome the barrier of perception, because of a general condition of dependency and insecurity or some previous unsatisfactory experience; be constrained by problems of geographical access; be screened out after gaining entry to the lawyer's outer office as a result of poor financial standing or lawyer distaste for issues of which he lacks experience and for clients who are at a considerable social distance. Such problems facing the poor client have the effect already mentioned of steering clients to low-status lawyers who may adopt the client as a good case for exploitation—the lack of legal competence makes poor clients especially vulnerable to sharp practice.

The relation of such description and analysis to issues of social reform is strong and explicit. Whilst it is not part of our brief to examine particular proposals it is open to remark both that authors addressing legal services from a disciplinary point of view have felt able to contribute to debates on social reform, and that social reformers per se have borrowed analyses for supporting pressure for reform. Beyond this we can note, first, that social scientific analysis is generally linked to the more far-reaching proposals for reform which are mooted—presumably a reflection of the questioning stance taken towards public justifications of the current nature and level of legal services provision. Secondly, accounts tend to be lodged at

the particular level suitable for inclusion within a reform prospectus.

The Empirical Refinement of Mainstream Interpretations

Although clearly sharing the social and political commitment of
those with a wider purview, researchers such as Mayhew and Reiss [106]
represent a different style of investigation. Their work is an example
of attempts to document the problems and effectiveness of legal services in some empirical detail in the hope of refining both the available data and the mainstream interpretations.

Their contribution was to provide a demography of citizen contacts
with lawyers on the basis of 1000 or so interviews. Their inquiries
charted certain background information about the respondents and
then located the prevalence with which help was sought from lawyers
and for what purposes. The greater part of the contact of higher
socio-economic groups with lawyers was based on property ownership
and this led them to suggest that resources and income were less a key
to understanding the use of legal services than aspects of social organization, and in particular the socially organized character of property
ownership.

In similar vein, Morris [107] and associates investigated the subjective
assessments of 112 residents of two London boroughs by asking questions about problems experienced, whether advice was sought and so
on. To the extent that many of the problems elicited did not tally
with patterns of legal practitioners work, and included such items as
difficulties with government, income, maintenance, agencies and
housing problems, a gap in services was noted. But this was less
important for the researchers than their assessment that the problems
uncovered could be seen as originating in the social and economic
structure. It was seen as important that whilst such problems may be
experienced at and be manifested in individual instances, their character was essentially collective, and stemmed from wider societal
issues.

In both studies we can see a purpose which goes somewhat beyond
immediate considerations of reform. Each of them utilizes empirical
material to aid the identification of pegs on which to hang a good
deal of work on legal services, pegs which are less in the nature of
theory per se than of general propositions which help to contextualize
the debates. Mayhew and Reiss do not explore fully the position at
which they arrive—it is left unstated, for instance, whether the
dominant property motif subordinates the profession totally in its

service—nor do Morris et al., make it clear whether they regard the problems experienced by their respondents as arising in the *structure* of society writ large or in the *structures* of which society is composed. But they represent none the less a distinct avenue by which sociologists of law have sought to grapple with legal services issues.

Perspectives on Key Concepts in Legal Services

A number of authors have sought to clarify issues and re-orient analysis through reconceptualizations of certain basic terms and concepts employed. The object is to seek new frameworks of interpretation for a range of data and by illuminating problems from new angles to throw into relief the taken for granted terminology of analysis. The added verve is not immune from relevance considerations—all of the most significant attempts serve to direct attention more cogently at the problems of the disadvantaged—but the sophistication achieved is not to be faulted for that.

We can begin with a brief mention of Philip Lewis's[108] reworking of the notion 'legal problem'. His particular slant is to point out that such a depiction of a person's difficulty carries above all the suggestion not so much that the problem per se has a definite 'legal' character but that it can best be resolved through legal means. In many cases an equally apt depiction might be that the difficulty was a political problem, political means holding out at least equivalent capacity for resolution. Lewis shows that whichever adjective be allied to the problem, this represents a definite attitude to its nature and source, and carries implications as to the appropriate remedy.

Whilst Lewis limits his analysis in the most part to such clarificatory matters, Reich[109] and Morris[110] have made vigorous efforts to establish a terminology for legal services which is suitable for analysis of the problems of the poor.

On the face of it their efforts run almost counter to one another. Reich asserts the concept of legal rights as relevant to welfare benefits and other forms of state largesse through an analogy with the concept of property. Legal categories are paramount. Morris wants to break the hold of the law on poor people's problems and, accordingly revises the notion of unmet legal need in a manner which emphasizes its social character and hence denies primacy to the 'legal'. But if the issue is one of differential social advantage with regard to the use of legal machinery, both authors display clearly whose side they are on. The similarity extends to complementarity for whilst Morris shows that unmet legal need is socially defined and hence non-absolute and

subject to disagreement, Reich tries to show how a particular definition, grounded in the enduring legal category of property, throws new
light on the need which is taken to exist.

Reich's focus is upon the general category of government largesse.
Jobs, franchises, contracts, subsidies and state benefits are seen as
growing facets of governmental distribution of wealth in the form of
rights and statuses. In terms of their function in people's lives,
such rights and statuses are akin to property, yet their legal status
depends less on the legal relations obtaining between property and its
owner than upon a distinct system of law for adjudicating disputes
arising from the distribution of largesse. Having created wealth in this
way government is reluctant to underpin its gifts with legal rights and
to entrust adjudication to the formal legal order. Government retains
many of the prerogatives of a donor and hedges largesse with conditions; fealty oaths may be a pre-requisite for receiving benefit; benefits
may be suspendable or revocable without compensation; the claimant
must forgo due process when applying for benefits and accept the
mysteries of administrative discretion.

The picture being built up is familiar, displaying many similarities
with that of Carlin and Howard. Likewise, his remedy, that the 'concept of rights is most urgently needed with respect to benefits like
unemployment compensation, public assistance and old age insur-
ance' has a by now familiar ring. Some of Reich's criticisms have
been superseded by legal reforms, but his importance lies in the
method he used to achieve the concept of rights. Government largesse
he terms the 'New Property' and by demonstrating its equivalence to
that most ancient and revered social and legal institution he invites
his audience to adopt a radically new framework for looking at the
whole issue. Once the property perspective is taken on, the
inadequacy of the legal protection afforded welfare recipients
becomes unjustified not only in 'objective' terms, but within the terms
of the accepted correlates of property. Received assumptions about
the nature of welfare provision lose sensibility and have to be
regarded as a mask for a fundamental refusal to grant the poor dignity and justice. Viewed as property, how can welfare benefits be
revoked without compensation; appealed against without due process;
and decided according to administrative discretion without reasoned
argument and without explicit reference to specific rules available to
the claimant? Reich's challenge to his readership is to reorient the
frame of reference used to consider the legal and quasi-legal interests
of the poor.

Where Reich attempts to assert the primacy of the legal category of property, and bring poor people's rights into that category, Morris aims to subordinate legal definition to social definition. The main claim of Morris is that need has to be seen as *socially* defined in contradistinction to the definitions of lawyers and the legal system generally. This appears to mean that competing definitions to the 'legal' can be offered; the act of defining need is a social process; need cannot be defined in any absolute sense. These three elements provide in turn for (a) making poor people's problems a suitable object of legal attention; (b) a series of potential research projects; and (c) an awareness that certain definitions prevail over others and thus we are dealing with 'questions of values, not scientific objectivity'. The idea seems to be that with a 'relative' notion of need and with competing definitions, it ought to be possible to investigate why definitions of problems as having to do with issues located deep in the social structure are not given more credence.

If state benefits can properly be regarded as a form of property, and if the way legal need is defined is a matter of values, then we might legitimately ask why the notion of property as understood legally has restricted its ambit and excluded state largesse, and if values are at issue, whose values and in which direction they operate. In both cases the authors' views are muted and for that the analyses have a curiously incomplete air. But both have been responsible for welcome breaths of analytic fresh air in a topic which lends itself to polemic more frequently than most.

The Radical Critique

Finally, we will refer to a piece of work which represents a view taken in a number of works in progress that law is inherently dominatory and that even apparently progressive reforms in legal services provision merely serve to substantiate such domination and, perhaps, coopt more effective strategies for confronting the law's oppression. Bankowski and Mungham,[111] in analysing both a duty solicitor scheme and neighbourhood law centres, represent this radical stance and stand at one end of a progression of critiques of legal services provision. As the authors of earlier polemics see their arguments accepted by the authorities, and their programmes for reform implemented, at least in part, so a new critique has arisen to feed upon the vision of the old. It is no mere coincidence that two of the authors of *Social Needs and Legal Action*,[112] one of the first of a wave of academic analyses of legal services in Great Britain, subsequently worked for government on legal services provision; that reforms such as duty solicitor schemes and law centres were important elements of the programmes on which they advised; and that such elements are now themselves under fire from sociologists of law. We have no remit to explain this progression, perhaps by reference to a Gouldnerian thesis of the academic's radical self-image, but a brief review should help the reader keep tabs on the unfolding sequence of arguments with regard to legal services.

Duty solicitor schemes and neighbourhood law centres represent two substantial innovations in legal services and in many lines of analysis are regarded as standing within competing traditions of legal service. Whatever the benefits of the increased representation created through duty solicitor schemes (whereby solicitors are available on a rota basis for contact by defendants in Magistrates courts) they operate under the auspices and with the personnel of the private profession. Duty solicitor schemes are constructed to resolve the problem of access to lawyers and the law, but within the confines of an unquestioning stance to law, individualized representation and private profit. Neighbourhood law centres are public agencies in the voluntary sector, employing salaried legal and non-legal staff, which provide legal resources within a defined geographical catchment area, with a self-conscious stance not only to offer free legal representation but to pursue test cases of relevance to disadvantaged people; undertake educational work; act for *groups* of working-class people affected by common problems; generally to exploit the opportunities and benefits afforded poor people by law; and to contribute to law reform where existing case and statute law disadvantage poor people. Law centres themselves have often been regarded as reflecting disturbing and radical tendencies by establishment bodies and it is quite clear that the self-conscious commitment to the interests of poor and working-class people, combined with radical work practices (lawyers work alongside community workers and others, rather than above them; a commitment to parity of salaries within law centres) serves to distinguish them from both corporate lawyers and the pristine neutrality, coupled with private profit, of the private profession.

In Bankowski and Mungham's analysis, however, the two services are not distinguished along these dimensions. A difference is drawn in terms of motives of personnel but not in terms of their effects and consequencies. For the duty solicitor scheme motives are seen to operate at two levels—economic and altruistic. Only the latter are regarded as being shared by law-centre operatives.

Economic motives are located in those solicitors who joined the duty solicitor scheme in order to try and break the monopoly of the 'Big Five' firms on lucrative criminal legal-aided work in Cardiff, a monopoly buttressed by collusion between the firms and certain sections of the local police force. Rather than the duty solicitor scheme emerging for reasons of the clients' interests, it was born of a political struggle within the local profession about differential and unfairly achieved economic advantages through 'privileged' access to certain types of work.

Bankowski and Mungham then turn to consider the effects and consequences of such services as duty solicitor schemes and law centres. Altruistic motives are recognized by the authors in the personnel of law centres and in certain participants of the duty solicitor scheme, and are regarded as instances of a desire to 'take law to the people', and to satisfy unmet legal need. In terms of the consequences of such honourable designs, duty solicitor schemes and law centres are treated alike. Satisfying unmet legal need may have propelled law centres into existence and supplied the motive force for altruistic private practitioners, but this is seen as problematic in so far as the notion of unmet legal need is held to contain a basic assumption as to its own absolute character (i.e. objective standards for identifying 'legal need' are available) for it speaks to problems for which there are currently available legal solutions. Bankowski and Mungham suggest to the contrary that legal need cannot be discussed without reference to the distribution of power in society and to the class structure; and that the emergence of phenomena such as law centres presupposes that legal solutions to the problems[113] of the poor are the most suitable and satisfactory.

That law centres give credence to legal remedies is regarded as implicating their work within the framework of repressive law itself. To widen the dominion of law, to 'take it to the people', is to widen the domination of law. One might be forgiven for imagining that to a person evicted illegally, or a recipient of welfare whose benefit is revoked, the assistance of an agency which can help to reverse such decisions would be regarded as anything but domination. But such service, and the efforts of law centres to help the poor mobilize themselves to promote their interests through law, is not regarded as a change of sufficient significance by Bankowski and Mungham. In their view it may have the effect of diverting or coopting more effective forms of action. The poor must instead wait upon the creation of 'institutions, forums and ways for people to air their grievances, in which welfare officials can be held accountable. In other words to create the possibilities whereby people can function without lawyers to create and to realize their own potential.'[114]

Doubtless the legions of the poor who will read the book will be pleased to learn that the authors refrain from foisting on them the form that such institutions should take. The responsibility for their creation lies firmly on the shoulders of the disadvantaged themselves —'we do not give a description of what is to be, for that denies what this book affirms, that men create their own future'[115]—the authors' role as a vanguard is limited strictly to the realm of ideas. However, certain lines of action are suggested as of potential effectiveness, lines which mainly revolve around making the trial an overtly political event. Men are exhorted to seize their lives in the manner of the (poor and working class?) defendants of the Angry Brigade and Chicago Trials, and to confront the court with the knowledge of its inherently dominatory character.

The arguments are stimulating but it is at this stage that the faulty logic becomes most apparent. Law centres are berated for their superficial analysis of their own role as community leaders and as professional advisers. Such is seen as leading to dependence rather than emancipation of the clientele. But the only assistance the poor are to receive under the rubric offered is the example of sophisticated and self-proclaimed political activists who have had the necessary courage and possessed a developed political awareness sufficient to turn the ideology of the court on its head. Political consciousness, and consciousness of law's domination, is prior to such courtroom confrontation, not a result of them. In the main, law centres' personnel are doubtless poor only by virtue of relatively low salaries, and neither that nor a commitment to working with and for poor people can dissipate totally the distance which the possession of legal and other skills creates. But neither were the defendants of the Angry Brigade and Chicago Trials poor people, and nor can their commitment to confronting the legal system dissipate the distance between their symbolic example and the life experiences of the poor.

CONCLUSION

The work on law and society comprises numerous threads of argument and approach, and displays overall a fragmentation of topics, orientations and methods. In this conclusion we will separate the issues displayed according to the categories of 'Use of Theory', 'Categorization and Concepts' and 'Explanation'. The intention is to ascertain the sociological basis of work undertaken. As a preliminary it will be useful to address in general the rationale for the type of research portrayed especially with regard to the issues of relevance and the degree of sociological commitment obtaining within the research. There can be found three alternative rationales for research undertaken.

First, research may satisfy an issue of theoretical concern. The theory may be questioned as a whole; a gap in the theory filled in; or a conundrum resolved. Such work does not necessarily take any definite form. Parsons, for instance, argues for the utility of functionalism in situating the role of the legal profession in society; Rueschmeyer, while not openly criticizing the framework of functionalism, seeks to undermine its applicability to the legal profession; Johnson reviews a range of existing theories and in the light of criticisms made erects a competing framework of analysis; Bankowski and Mungham reject consensus theory as a legitimate mode of analysing the profession in society and propose a conceptual framework as different from Parsons as it is from Johnson. Theoretical issues are prominent in all the above works, but the approach varies as does the type and level of theory encountered.

Secondly, work is undertaken for no better or worse reason than that the topic has an inherent interest for the practitioner and his presumed audience. Again the work need not take any definite form. The interest may be connected to a desire to provide a 'theoretical' or 'empirical' cover for an issue not yet so treated and so will take on the colour of the researcher's own commitment to issues of theory and methodology. Or the interest may stand alone and receive the treatment gleaned by the researcher from manuals on 'good research practice'. The acquisition and interpretation of data is often pursued with no guide and even in studies which have a guide (for instance works as different as Carlen's study of Magistrates Courts, and Nagel's [116] of judicial voting behaviour), the research remains strongly indebted to a concern to provide data to an audience on issues which may have no explicit relevance for sociology in general.

Finally, an issue of 'relevance' can provide its own rationale for study. Relevance as a rationale does not necessarily condition the method or theory but instead conditions the topic. Theory can be tested across a range of substantive situations—this is entailed in the notion of theory as genealization—but relevance work implies a topic.

Of the three rationales, 'relevance' is the most popular in law and society research.

We need not, however, be fatalistic with regard to relevance. There are examples of relevance and non-relevance work co-existing even within the same topic division. Both Aubert and Carson share a concern with legislation and its implementation but the level of inquiry pursued by the former is conditioned by an interest in issues of relevance (how better to transmit legislation to an affected public) not given in the implementation of law itself. That Carson avoided the trap of relevance indicates that there is nothing inherent within legislative studies that negates a sociological commitment.

The range of 'relevance' work within the subdiscipline can be seen by assembling together studies geared to clarifying the language used to discuss a relevance issue (Lewis); confirming or refuting arguments as to the nature of a social issue (Jury Project); or implying a particular path of reform (Reich). Certain areas of work carry a particular predeliction for relevance. Legal services research is one such area, lending itself to relevance whether the approach is conceptual (Reich and Morris); empirical (Morris et al.); or pitched at the middle range (Carlin and Howard). But the influence of relevance is wide enough to justify certain general comments. First, 'relevance' work does not exclude a reliance on theory or conceptual apparatus but it does seem to sidetrack research away from those issues within sociology around which particular theories developed, and away from debates concerning the legitimacy and applicability of theories and theoretical models. Not having a commitment to furthering sociological knowledge in a way conscious of the limitations and potentials of social science, relevance invites eclecticism. Theories and concepts are chosen for use and fed into empirical work rather than empirical work being used to develop, refine or defeat theories. Since 'topic' is given pride of place above scientific discipline, relevance work is not self-consciously aware of any commitment to address the legitimacy of tools and methods of research used when bringing a theory to bear on a relevance issue nor, more commonly, when used directly on the topic without the intervention of a theoretical scheme. The important point is not whether relevance work is theoretically aware but whether it is aware that social science, like any other science, requires its practitioner to be cognisant of the limitations placed on research by science itself.

For instance, Zeisel and Kalven state the five factors regarding judge and jury disagreement as a 'theory'.[117] There is, however, no way that those propositions constitute a theory. They simply provide a bounded set of arguments on the issue which may or may not be acceptable within a forum of public debate. As an inductive theory—the only type to which the propositions might lay claim—there is no means of moving upwards to any general theoretical proposition on legal behaviour. This should not be surprising; 'relevance' provides its own rationale and one which perforce takes precedence over theory construction and use.

But as we said, the issue is not theoretical awareness but sociological commitment. Studies within the 'relevance' genre that aspire to sociology can be compared to non-relevance work on the issues of subject-matter and dialectic as outlined in Chapter I.

Subject-matter: If we take Parsons's analysis of the legal profession we can see that the analysis may provide arguments for or against certain proposed lines of reform in professional organization. But this does not make Parsons's 'relevance' inclined. His analysis is provided by a sociological theory (functionalism) which (whether we agree with it or not) has an easily identifiable subject-matter independent of particular topic choice. The theory is built up from an idea of social action translated into the language of functional processes and these remain the subject-matter approached by the theory whatever particular topic selection be made. With relevance work this is not the case. Relevance work in fact does not have a subject-matter as such and ultimately the subject-matter approached will be a consequence of methods used to gather data. If Zeisel and Kalven are interested in judge and jury disagreements there is no point in looking behind the study for a sociological subject-matter as was possible with Parsons. 'Disagreement' may be the subject but only as affected by the methods chosen for use. Only when a method is employed do you begin to attack a subject-matter at all.

Dialectic: The importance of a dialectical relationship between research within a sub-discipline and the discipline itself is, as we have seen, closely related to the idea of a unified science, and the very possibility of doing sociology. By work having a common subject-matter it is possible to build up knowledge; to have studies accrue to one another; criticize one another concerning the nature of that subject-matter; learn from one another; and represent the boundaries of a social science. Within contemporary empirical and theoretical work there are studies which allow this form of progression if only in part.

Rueschmeyer and Parsons are to some extent talking the same language; Parsons's work on the profession, by being undertaken with reference to the same subject-matter as his theoretical model of society, can talk back to that model, support or refine it. The dialectic may not be complete, the work on the profession may not be able to refute the basic conceptual hardware of the model, but some form of discussion concerning sociology is possible. With relevance work, because of the lack of any sociological commitment, this form of debate is not generated. Debate is aimed elsewhere and it is hard to conceive of any feedback from Kalven and Zeisel's study for the discipline of sociology in general. To deny that feedback is necessary can only be for a more overriding concern (relevance) or because sociology is itself unproblematic. The latter must be denied as a possibility as an unproblematic science would be a finished science, a closed book and of interest only to historians.

THE USE OF THEORY

There are a variety of levels at which 'theory' has entered into contemporary sociology of law and a variety of meanings attributed to theory. For the purposes of discussion we can break the authors down into three groups; those that rely on a meta-theory to guide the acquisition of data; those that rely on a substantive theory to interpret data and which may also guide the collection of data; and, finally, those that elect to use the language of theory within essentially descriptive pieces of work. This latter group, which show most signs of eclecticism, usually introduce theory by way of conceptual usage. Concepts can generally be taken to mean those concrete expressions which locate a particular piece of the empirical work within the framework of an existing theory.

Meta-Theory: Meta-theories are series of propositions about the social world, what it is like and the fundamental units of which it is composed. They include specified procedures for sociological investigation into the world but do not contain statements concerning the substance of, nor operation of, society. The postulate that 'social behaviour is meaningful to the actor and can only be understood by reference to that meaning' and the postulate that 'social life can be analysed by cause and effect' could both participate in their respective meta-theories. A proposition that 'the division of labour in society causes the development of specialized institutions and procedures of restitutive law' could not be party to a meta-theory for it speaks of the substance of actual specified events and phenomena.

There are three meta-theories operating in the reviewed work; functionalism (a meta-theory, though one associated closely with the substantive theory of Talcott Parsons); behaviourism (not associated with any particular substantive theory); and interpretive sociology (again not identified with any particular substantive theory). The particular significance of these avenues of sociological inquiry is the topic for Chapter V but we can briefly indicate certain points here.

Functionalism as a meta-theory proposes that social phenomena are sociologically significant in so far as they contribute to the orderly operation of a social system. They can be explained by reference to their 'functions', a concept which is able to refer to any particular piece of the substance of social life. Behaviourism proposes that social life can be studied in the language of cause and effect. Each social item is a cause of some other later item and the effect of some other earlier item. The causes and effects can be specified to provide a substantive theory able to explain the existence of a phenomena by way of the meta-theory. Interpretive sociology proposes that behaviour is meaningful to the actor and that to understand social action, sociology must also be able to understand the meaning it has for the actors involved. The meta-theories, thus, engage respectively in teleological, causal and interpretive explanation. Meta-theories provide a means of guiding the acquisition of data, their contradictory postulates remaining at a level abstracted from empirical adequacy.

It is possible to look at the meta-theories in terms of the subject-matter reached and the potential displayed for allowing the dialectic between study and subject-matter to which we earlier referred.

There is nothing within the meta-theories which would deny that the subject-matter of sociology is social action or that such action was meaningful to participants. But there the level of agreement ends. In their actual operation, functionalism replaces social action as a base unit with functions; behaviourism replaces social action with indices of behaviour identifiable by external observation; and interpretive sociology alone retains social action as the key reference for work.

The functionalist meta-theory is employed by Parsons in his work on the legal profession. His comments on that profession are provided by a substantive theory built up by procedures indicated in the meta-theory of functionalism; behaviourist work is best exemplified by

Nagel and interpretive work by Carson. Each avenue of work has a distinct capacity to throw light on the nature of social action. Parsons's work and other work pursued under the same framework (e.g. Rueschmeyer) can only speak back to the meta-theory via the substantive theory. The substantive theory on professions can be faulted and refined but the meta-theory could not be breached. Behaviourism, similarly, allows no questioning of its major tenets. Investigation by cause and effect is possible but research could only throw up substantive theories rather than question the use of cause and effect as adequate tools for sociological investigation. Interpretive meta-theory, however, has a particular structure which ought, if fully understood, to be able to question its own tenets. By using meta-theory for empirical analysis without leaving the base line of 'social action as meaningful' should enable that work to throw light on the significance of meaning and its significance in the construction of those lines of action studied.

Substantive Theory: Substantive theories comprise propositions of substance about the social world. Two main variants were identified in Chapter III namely the functionalist theory of Parsons and the conflict theory of Chambliss and Seidman. Both worked as models of the world to be used to interpret empirical data. It is the substantive theory which provides the spectacles for viewing social items (for example Parsons on the legal profession). The application of a substantive theory to a phenomenon is itself the act of interpreting that phenomenon. This is important because it implies that studies performed under the banner of a particular substantive theory can only talk back to the theory itself because empirical material has no life other than that given to it by the theory. If, then, the theory is constructed to exclude certain possibilities (for instance the denial by functionalist substantive theory that the meaning of an event is critical to our ability to understand that event), then work done under that banner cannot contemplate the reverse possibility. The availability of substantive theory to empirical test does not refute this. Substantive statements concerning phenomena can be changed, modified or supported but the meta-theory, with its own conceptions of the nature of the sociological subject, cannot be reached unless that subject-matter partakes in the construction of substantive theory.

It is, of course, possible that one may find difficulty in recognizing the application of substantive theory within the literature of Chapter IV. To the extent that conflict and functionalism are the two theories most well known they operate on the level of law and society and were discussed in Chapter III. Functionalism via the profession operates in Chapter IV, but for the rest of the work no substantive theory is particularly applicable. Work has progressed either direct from a meta-theory; by an eclectic use of the concepts of substantive theory; or by an eclectic use of methods which successfully capture the unwitting researcher within the particular meta-theory whose ascriptions regarding the social world are built into the particular method chosen for use. This problem is also encountered when research 'operationalizes' a particular theory, a necessary process for empirical work, especially that associated with theories of the 'middle range'. Such theories, neither simple empirical statements nor explanatory systems but rather propositions containing relationships between identified phenomena, are very common in the sociology of law. These theories are not as abstract as say, Parsons's functionalist model, but yet still contain propositions which require 'operationalizing' prior to use in empirical settings. Once operationalized the proposition containing a relationship can be tested—the methods used are paramount though not especially designed around a particular meta-theory.

The Language of Theory: We can introduce the empirical work into the discussion by reference to the study by Aubert and this can also stand as an introduction to the eclectic use of theory.

At various points in his exposition 'Some social functions of legislation', Aubert[118] offers the following:

'The new law had a reformatory function.'

'The . . . law . . . is written in a language shaped by an entirely different function.'

'The function of this law . . . is a question of its influence and its ability to communicate a message.'

'. . . because they are shaped by the traditional function of facilitating precise communications with the legal profession many clauses of the law are unable to fill the more pressing function of communication to housemaids'.

The use of the term 'functions' can be excluded and leave a proposition merely to state that:

Lawyers, judges, legislators and other legal personnel communicate in a certain way; they do so for purposes of exactitude. Lay men do not communicate in this manner. Therefore lay men often do not understand the language of legislation. This prevents legislation from working as it should or was intended.

Without a commitment to the meta-theory of functionalism, a commitment explicitly eschewed by Aubert in a head note to one edition of the work, it remains unclear why the terminology is used as a frame of reference in which to lodge the data. The frame of reference, having no rationale, still succeeds in making itself felt by the exclusion of certain possibilities, for instance that the empirical data could fit some other model in which reference to 'functions' would be wholly inappropriate or misleading.

Not all 'law in society' work suffers in this way, but even those pieces of research aligned to a particular meta-theory do not thereby deserve acceptance. We need to investigate their use of methods and the relationship of such methods to the subject-matter.

The work of behaviourism exemplifies a failure through commitment to a particular meta-theory. We can see this in two examples. First, the work on judges: the criticisms made by Fuller express how behaviourism can easily destroy the subject-matter of study by incorrect assumptions about the construction of patterns of social interaction. The predictive factors identified were not only incapable of standing as 'explanations' but, further, served to blind sociology to anything significant about legal behaviour or legal reasoning. Secondly, knowledge and opinion of law studies present a similar problem via the 'operationalization' of hypotheses. Operationalizing 'human conviction as the basis of legal rules', Van Houtte and Vinke finish with responses to a set of questions. Not only does this tie them to a meta-theory which denies the significance of situational interaction for comprehending people's relationship to specific legal ideals, arenas or events, but in the final analysis we do not have any idea of what 'human conviction' is, save that it is incompatible with the responses to questions posed by Van Houtte and Vinke. At least that much is evident, but the problem remains that the linking of particular data to the proposition through a particular avenue of operationalization leaves the reader no means of interpreting the data or the proposition in any other way. The study seeks to make a generalization, and for that we need something above and beyond the data, but all one is left with is the data and an assertion that it is incompatible with 'human conviction'.

If we compare the work of Aubert with Parsons we have on the one hand a use of functionalist terminology which bears no reference to any functionalist meta-theory, and on the other hand we have interpretation of data by reference to a substantive theory built up from a meta-theory. The latter has to be more acceptable. With Aubert, we find a cacophony of levels of approach from methods of communication to political structure; with Parsons at least we know where we are. Parsons's work can talk back to the substantive functionalist theory even if not to the assumptions located at the level of meta-theory, but Aubert's study remains as an island. Compare also Rueschmeyer with Carson. Rueschmeyer seeks to deny the applicability of Parsons's substantive theory to the professions but would appear to allow the possibility of the theory's applicability. The theory is criticized for its lack of empirical validity but that validity is not challenged at the level of the legitimacy of the functionalist approach to the social world. Carson, on the other hand, would appear to challenge the availability of the social world to interpretation by substantive schemes. This is implicit in his attempt to eradicate certain analytic schemes from the study of the implementation of legislation replacing them by a method of approach compatible with the meta-theory of interpretive sociology, *and which could challenge the tenets of that meta-theory.*

Issues of theory, then, have arisen in various guises. Each carries its own conception of the subject-matter of sociology and each to varying extents allows the dialectic to operate between individual studies and conceptions of the subject-matter inherent within particular meta-theories.

To close this section we can note that the operating meta-theories appear to contain incompatible guides for study—to find more than one meta-theory behind a particular study (for instance cause and effect, and motive) becomes sociologically alarming. Substantive theories, both from competing meta-theory and from the same meta-theory, can be erected, especially at the middle range, in a way that makes data common ground and open to multiple interpretation. Data ceases to adjudicate between theories. Handled with precision these problems are probably intractable, but handled in an eclectic fashion the problems become supreme and remain the most conspicuous feature of contemporary work. We are not being alarmist in saying that the failure to handle problems of theory is an important feature in the contemporary creation of sociological holograms—a believable appearance with a total lack of substance.

Categorization and Concepts

A number of the authors reviewed pursued their studies by developing categories and concepts as a means of handling data. Here the categories generally are developed during the research or elected for use because of their ability to highlight features of the data seen by the researcher as particularly significant. They are not, in this instance, the result of the application of a particular substantive theory.

Reich, Morris and Lewis are represented here from the legal services research: Johnson from professions along with trait theorists, and Lukes from the section on legislation. Such authors do not merely categorize, but such is an important feature of their work.

Whilst we would not wish to draw the line too firmly, there is a difference between categorization and conceptualization in so far as the former refers to the ordering of data into typologies and the latter to the use of concrete expressions which represent the data within any ensuing analysis. Thus there is a distinction between the concept of power which can be represented by a particular empirical index and the category of 'profession'. Johnson operates at both levels; his 'structure of uncertainty' is a conceptualization of a central issue in the activity of professionals, but he also uses a typology of forms of control (mediative, collegiate and patronage) which organizes data on the profession according to the way the 'structure of uncertainty' has been handled by occupational groups.

The issue of significance for sociology is the extent to which categorization and conceptualization within empirical work has addressed a subject-matter which itself has been seen as able to guide the processes of categorization and conceptualization. We saw in Chapter II that both Durkheim and Weber engaged in such processes and that both did so in a manner which each felt was consistent with their respective conceptions of social action, this base conceptualizaion standing as meta-theory guiding successive stages of the research act.

The work in the sociology of law has been heavily one sided and the side followed has closer proximity to Durkheim than to Weber. It is rare to find a typology or system of concepts which is consciously constructed from an understanding of social action as meaningful. Take the approach of the 'trait' theories of professions. Here the categories are organized around items which may or may not have significance to the actors concerned. Presented as observer-identified universals they belong not to men but to the 'profession' writ large. Functionalist categories can be similarly faulted, though they are sustained by the justification that they are not created solely by the observer but by reference to a developed theory. The problem is not circumvented but is relocated.

Johnson, himself, stands mid-way; the 'structure of uncertainty' is very much an action oriented concept though no commitment to an interpretive meta-theory tying concepts to social action is apparent. In the hands of Reich, conceptualization gives its closest commitment to the purpose of persuasion. Conceptualizing state largesse as property invites a change of perspective and alters the significance of particular features of the provision of welfare. Since this use of conceptualization is made explicit it does not necessarily need to satisfy the demands of any meta-theory—it seeks merely to invite a political judgement. In the main, however, conceptualization is used *within* the research; not merely to write a judgement, but to organize the interpretation of the *sociological* significance of data.

The main issues concern the way concepts arise and the use to which they are put. Concepts can either be brought to bear on data or can arise out of data—the concept of 'power' could be taken from Lukes and brought to empirical data on legal settings just as the concept of 'white-collar crime' could have been used by Carson; compare the 'structure of uncertainty', which as a concept appears more to arise out of Johnson's studies on professions rather than pre-dating the work. In either case, the concepts can remain as descriptions or an attempt made to elevate them as explanations. And in each case the concept is linked, usually only implicitly, with a particular meta-theory.

Take for example the discussion of power given by Lukes. He disparages competing conceptualizations as behaviourist but he never in fact tells us where he himself stands. The intimation is that a form of social-action perspective is being employed—the language of action rather than behaviour is used and the intentionality of the actor is regarded as important. Clearly he goes beyond behaviourism. If we look to certain of the dimensions of social reality held by Schutz to be excluded by pure behaviourism [these include: variance in the meaning attributable by actors to the same overt behaviour; intentional refraining from action; the importance of non-face to face interaction], arguably all could be accommodated within the scheme provided by Lukes. But Lukes gives no expression to the need for the *use* of his concept to pay attention to these interpretive postulates and so the scheme itself does not provide a sure avenue for progress.

Knowledge and Opinion of Law studies illustrate problems in the use of concepts as explanation. This is also a feature of other studies, as was made evident in Chapter I when we saw the use of the concept 'social control' by Black within a tautology in the guise of explanation. But similarly in KOL studies, concepts purporting to be explanatory variables are brought to bear on a range of data. In Kaupen's[119] study, 'authoritarianism' towards the legal system is such a concept though in fact its causal connection with the other features of the relationship of respondents to the legal system is not argued for and remains unclear.

Explanation

Finally, we need to consider the manner in which 'law in society' studies handle the problem of explanation. We have of necessity already covered part of the ground. We have seen briefly how meta-theories are in part identified by particular ways of explaining social phenomena; substantive theories explain in the instant that the phenomena acquire a place within the theory—the application of the theory stands as an explanation; conceptualization can be the mark of explanation either by being tied to a causal proposition or more simply by ordering data in a way by which it is made more comprehensible. Not all such 'explanations' are comparable and we have no wish here to treat them all in the way the general issue of explanation was introduced in Chapter I. We can say, however, that if explanation is a method of shedding light on a phenomenon, then sociologists have chosen to shed light in a number of ways—inevitably explanation takes on a different cast under each.

Within the work reviewed it is possible to identify the various levels of explanation as associated with various meta-theories: functional explanation is represented by Parsons; causal explanation by Nagel; interpretive approaches to meaning by Carlen and Carson. Most significant for our purposes, however, is the extent to which the various levels co-exist within single pieces of work despite the incompatibility between the relevant meta-theories.

Mungham and Bankowski for example explain the instigation of the duty solicitor scheme by reference to the economic *motives* of participants, but the *effect* of the scheme by reference to the *unintended consequences* of participants' actions, which themselves are interpreted by reference to a theory of law and the state. Lawyers' attitudes are seen as caused by professional socialization but lawyers' involvement in welfare movements by economic and material forces. Similarly, Zeisel and Kalven explain disagreement between judge and jury by reference to a series of factors which, if analysed, contain references both to motives and 'objective' characteristics; Carlin and Howard pin together geographical dimensions of habitation with the mental dimension of client fear as two key reasons why the poor do not use lawyers.

Before it is claimed that either we are being unfair or indeed pointing to a situation which poses no problems, we stress that the issue is not one of compatibility between levels of explanation alone but one of the relations of particular levels to an understanding of social action. Different types of explanation are not free-floating agents to be employed at will but linked inextricably with quite definite and distinct stances towards the study of the social world. If economic and material forces determine the structure of patterns of interaction then explanation belongs at that level; if meaning is critical to our ability to understand patterns of interaction then explanation belongs at that level. If both levels are to be used then the linkages between the two have to be shown or reasons given for limiting the range of applicability of either. Simple explanatory eclecticism merely deprives the audience of the ability properly to assess the explanation being offered.

We do not have here the wish to progress further into a full evaluation either of competing theories, conceptualizations or levels of explanation. We wish to stress both the structure of contemporary empirical work as ill-disciplined on these issues and also the necessity of the sociology of law to embed itself into general sociology by a conscious appraisal of the current debates between various theories and levels of explanation available. Sociology of law is sociology and it is to certain dimensions of sociology that we turn in the next chapter.

PART III
INTRODUCTION

Should we be in mind to seek a maxim for this final section, as likely as not Max Weber would be the source. The choice would rest on Weber's composure at the realization that, whatever the potential of sociology writ large, the lot of any one sociologist or particular sociological perspective was to be able to claim no more than partial knowledge. The discipline with which he conducted all of his inquiry was ultimately tempered by the root appreciation that dogma in any form was alien to science and that only the fractious, incompetent or insecure made claims to having found the true path of sociological piety.

For sociology, there is only one core principle: to recognize the unitary character of its subject-matter and the need to allow science to pursue the subject-matter whatever the substantive object of sociological investigation and whatever aspect of sociology be employed. Beyond this we can both expect and hope for lively debate and a degree of partisan polemic, for those are features of vigorous inquiry. As long as the nature of social phenomena is not ignored, then perhaps entrenchment can be avoided and sociology allowed to display to the full its collaborative potential.

This mixture of a clear conception of disciplinary purpose with a willingness to accept the limitations of inevitably partial researches best conveys Weber's integrity of purpose. It is the position we try to adopt in these final chapters.

The importance of guiding the concluding section with a principle of toleration and moderation lies in the ambitious task being attempted. Given the attention at present being addressed to the sociology of law, growth is inevitable and we feel that development should be spurred by considerations other than those of 'relevance' and inter-disciplinary study, the two most vociferous current contenders. Sociology alone should be the touchstone. This means that the sociology of law must establish social action as an ongoing referent. The path of development implied would constitute a reorientation of the sub-discipline, and, since that is a far from modest aim, circum-spection as to the form that sociology should take will provide a safeguard against an overly narrow view of the reconstituted sociology of law.

In Chapter V we try first to clear away sociological approaches which through choice or consequence fail to reach the base line of social action. This inability we find in functionalism and positivism, the two main styles of analysis within the normative paradigm. The second part is an enunciation of the tenets of sociological schemes committed to an interpretive understanding of social action.

Any chapter, however long, would be too brief to exhaust the twin objects set and so the discussion must be seen as indicative and as a forerunner to Chapter VI. There, we aim to spell out in detail the implications for the study of law of normative conceptions in sociology and of other misdirections founded on a functionalist or positivist commitment, and to juxtapose these with a full account of what it looks like to dispense with such conceptions yet retain the possibility of doing research.

CHAPTER V

Sociology in the
Presence of Law

The journey through the sociology of law completed in the previous section has allowed us to reaffirm that obstacles to development faced by the sub-discipline reside not in the imperatives of relevance, nor in inter-disciplinary study, but within sociology itself. But whilst there is sufficient evidence that sociology needs to be regarded as the mother discipline, contentment cannot be expressed at such a finding without further contemplation of what that sociological component contains.

Apart from relatively few exceptions, the component identified displays the theories, methods and structures of explanation characteristic of functionalist and positivist sociology, and it is here that obstacles to progress can best be located. That done, we will be in a position to base a claim for the reorientation of the sociology of law along non-positivist lines.

In order to convey a keen sense of the bifurcation existing between popular contemporary approaches and the under-utilized alternatives, we can best begin by representing Durkheim and Weber as standard-bearers of the respective traditions. For the first, meaning had to be eradicated before any sociological science was possible; for the other, the elimination of meaning was a denial of the possibility of ever having a sociological science. Hence, it is the place of meaning in sociology that will constitute the organizing framework for this chapter.

POSITIVISM AND FUNCTIONALISM

Put simply, positivism in sociology refers to that doctrine stipulating the absence of any significant differences between the natural and social sciences. Multiple formulations are available but the following will suffice as a depiction:[1]

(1) Social phenomena are, for all analytical purposes, qualitatively the same as natural phenomena;

(2) The techniques of analysis developed in the natural sciences are applicable to sociological investigation; and

(3) The aim of sociology is to produce a system of high level, empirically grounded theoretical propositions which would provide the basis for predictive statements about social phenomena.

The earlier review of Durkheim demonstrates clearly his endorsement of such tenets. Whatever we take to be his view of the nature of the underlying social reality, *for analytical purposes* his strictures were emphatic: the social world comprises social facts which must be treated as things. Sociology not only can utilize the methods and techniques of natural science in explaining social phenomena; it must so use them.

It is a little less easy to arrange the functionalist albatross around Durkheim's neck but more than one author has argued convincingly that 'his influence served to establish a functionalist/holistic school of sociology'.[2] The difficulty in making the charge stick arises in that, overtly at any rate, Durkheim tried to avoid functionalist theorizing. He rejected in particular the idea that the cause of a social item could be located in its effects on other items and the part it played in sustaining their social existence. Causes, for Durkheim, came before effects and were not to be confused with functions. Yet, as Cohen has shown, when Durkheim came to give his account of the division of labour in society he does seem 'wedded to the view that the division of labour emerges because it is needed to restore order where unbridled competition might otherwise destroy social life'.[3] Again, in his work on religion we find an ultimate reliance on an imported notion of the 'social need' for religion. For all the commitment to causality, Durkheim is left with the assumption that 'the beneficial consequences of religion partly account for its existence'.[4]

Since, then, quite apart from any other similarities displayed by the two approaches under review, both can be traced to Durkheim, it is hardly surprising that they have been treated together in certain of the discussions of the various types of available theory. Both Wilson and Dawe, for instance, do just this.

For Wilson,[5] both operate under what he terms the normative paradigm, the notion of a paradigm being drawn from Kuhn's[6] influential formulation and referring to the pre-theoretical notions which underlie scientific statements and the matrix of assumptions, beliefs, practices and maxims which serve to orient a given corpus of work along a selective path. Wilson identifies two major orienting ideas of the normative paradigm: interaction as essentially rule governed; explanation as deduction (as per natural science). The first he sees as resting on the unwarranted assumption of cognitive consensus, that is that actors 'discriminate situations and actions in very nearly the same way'.[7] The second unjustifiably requires settling, *a priori*, the empirical features of social phenomena, and has to assume the established and non-problematic character of such features in order that explanation can have a fixed background from which to deduce.

Dawe's[8] compass is somewhat broader. Noting the apparent agreement within sociology, including functionalism and positivism, that the central concern is with the problem of social order, Dawe sets out to show that such a concern inevitably orders sociological discourse around the core concept of system. The implications of that core are that the actor becomes merely an adjunct 'on the receiving end of the system' and that subjective meanings are reduced through the postulate of the central value system and become 'external conditions of the actor's situation: essentially, objects of the environment'.[9]

Our own predilection at this stage, however, is to keep the two strands of positivism and functionalism separate. There are good pragmatic reasons for this, in that their modes of discourse, reasoning and inquiry look on the face of it quite different. For the relatively uninitiated, grouping them together may have the virtue of simplicity but comprehension of their respective problematics would thereby be reduced. There is, moreover, a less directly pedagogic justification. We wish to emphasize meaning as a central concern of sociology, and in this respect functionalism and positivism do vary somewhat. We agree with Dawe and Wilson that both at some stage eliminate subjective meaning, but whereas for positivism this occurs early on as a more or less direct result of the election for natural scientific methods, for functionalism (at least in its most sophisticated form) meaning only becomes logically and empirically excluded during the development of the edifice, the initial premises being related firmly to social action as inherently meaningful. Clearly, the elimination of meaning would not have occurred had the construction of the theory remained tied to the subjective nature of action in its empirical context. The failure of functionalism in this respect establishes the link with positivism, but the important difference can none the less be seen and is one we do not wish to obscure simply for the purposes of a clinical presentation.

FUNCTIONALISM

The student seeking arguments to pit against functionalism has a wide range from which to choose. He can select what is in effect a celebration of the doctrine in the claim of Kingsley Davis[10] that functional analysis is not merely good sociology, nor simply one among many sociologies but is *the* method of sociological analysis. Those inclined to the more polemical may be attracted by the charge that functionalism is inherently politically conservative and therefore ideologically tainted.[11] Humanists may be tempted by Homans's[12] arguments that all functionalists desert their 'systems' in the breach and rely finally upon social psychological propositions about human beings. Wherever the choice finally rests, the conscientious student will learn a great deal from such and other critiques. Two points however, must be borne in mind.

First, it is tempting to take on board all available criticisms without due regard being paid to the logical, empirical and theoretical contradictions being subsumed in the process. There is more than one way to skin the functionalist rabbit, but many may be mutually exclusive.

Secondly there is a necessary distinction to be drawn between:

(a) criticisms which fail to get to grips with functionalism at all;

(b) criticisms which question functionalist doctrine, that is, its substantive theorizing, but leave the method (i.e. the meta-theory) untouched;

(c) criticisms of functionalism as a method, that is as an inquisitive device underpinned by a series of assumptions and base propositions about the social world.

'Function' in sociology refers to the interdependence of social phenomena by which the effect of a social item constitutes an important or indispensable item (or input) for other items to exist as relatively smoothly working congeries of social roles and statuses, sufficiently internally connected to merit depiction as a social system. The function of an item, however, is not simply its effects or consequences in general, and if the designation of 'function' is claimed for particular effects or consequences then it should be possible to relate that function to a finite and specifiable list of the functional processes required to maintain or improve the system receiving the input. Similar lines of argument apply to negative or dys-functions. With this in mind we can more easily identify the three levels of criticism.

(a) *Criticisms which fail to get to grips with Functionalism:* It is particularly important to deal with this level because, where sociologists of law have aspired to sociology, they sometimes leave the false impression that a critique of functionalism can consist merely of placing a few question marks around points made by Bredemeier or Parsons. Schur is a good example.

Having identified a series of problem areas in Bredemeier's discussion of law as an integrative mechanism, problem areas pointed to by Bredemeier himself, Schur uses these as a point of departure for some general criticisms of the functionalist approach to law. He asks rhetorically if there is a monolithic set of values in a society and replies that the consensus is far from complete ('the continuing struggle between competing interests' suggests 'the inadequacy of an exclusive emphasis on law's integrative function'.) [13] But this is prefaced by '. . . certainly, a reasonable amount of broad value consensus is necessary if a society is to continue as a going concern',[14] which is all that Bredemeier requires! Again, Schur wants to undermine the extent of the claim to integration, but predates this with '. . . it is true that in a very general sense a legal system does tend to contribute to the orderly workings of society' [15]—again Schur provides the only entry that functionalism needs!

(b) *Criticisms of Functionalism as Doctrine:* Sklair has shown that it is possible to penetrate much deeper into functionalist theory than Schur was able to do, yet still respect the assumptions made by functionalists that society is made up of systems, with needs to be met for the systems to persist, and so on. Sklair draws a distinction between functionalist method and functionalist doctrine, the first referring to the general lines of approach taken by analysing social phenomena (the meta-theory) and the second to the major substantive doctrines which have thus emerged (e.g. Parsons's work). The problem he identifies in at least one field of functionalist inquiry, that of deviance, is that major authors 'violate the methodological norm of functionalism—system specificity'.[16] By this he means that there is an identifiable failure to spell out whose and which values underpin the various patterns of behaviour and expectations comprising the social system and its sub-systems. There is insufficient specification of which systems are involved when functionalists engage in analysis, and too little separating out of the various functional and dysfunctional consequences. Like many other authors, Sklair locates the problem mainly in the functionalists' doctrinal assumption of cognitive consensus, an assumption which he feels is gratuitous to functionalist method as such. As a method, functionalism merely 'indicates not that there can be no necessary solution to the problem of standards, but that the solution will be an empirical one. The functionalist doctrine, on the other hand, in the form of consensus theory, stipulates the solution *a priori*.'[17]

For Sklair, a return to the principle of system specifity would open up the issue of the nature of and supports for the level of conformity required for systems to persist; whether for instance conformity reflected genuine consensus or imposed constraint. This would allow sufficient attention to be given to power in social systems, a dimension which is 'systematically underplayed' in functionalist inquiry.

(c) *Criticisms of the Functionalist Core:* The points made by Sklair reflect criticisms levelled by many others that functionalism has not handled either power or conflict adequately. But while he argues that functionalism *has not* handled power, for many the line has been that it *cannot* handle power. In reply to these, Cohen takes the view, echoed later in Sklair, that 'there is nothing in functionalism itself which encourages an emphasis on unity and solidarity as opposed to conflict'.[18] For Cohen functionalism can recognize and cope with conflict both within and between various systems. He also takes a similar line to Sklair in arguing that the complaint that 'functionalism over-emphasises the harmonious inter-relatedness of parts of a social system',[19] must be seen against Merton's point that 'items may be functional for some groups, or for some features of social life, and dysfunctional for others'.[20] That is, if sufficient specification is given, then the substantive trap of overharmony can be avoided.

This imaginative defence of functionalism is of course a covert attempt to deny the validity of Marxist-based refutations of functionalism's substantive conclusion about the nature of social order, and is best seen as a drive to by-pass or reformulate the evergreen debate between conflict and consensus perspectives in sociology. As such it usefully elevates for scrutiny the distinction between functionalism as a theoretical edifice making certain substantive claims about society and on the other hand as a set of meta-theoretical ('methodological' in Sklair's terminology) assumptions capable of producing a range of substantive conclusions.

Cohen's stance, however, can deflect only (a) those hesitant critiques claiming that conflict is not given sufficient weight in functionalist accounts, and (b) those of people such as Chambliss who, though claiming to reject functionalism, fail to replace it with a genuinely alternative conflict method. Chambliss differentiates his position only from functionalist *doctrine* and at the level of method, as we showed earlier, the bulk of his assumptions are indistinguishable from those of his functionalist opponents. The full-blooded and more thorough-going conflict critique opposes functionalism with an authentically different set of theoretical assumptions and places conflict at the centre of any theory of society, in the traditional formulation the conflict being that between the forces and the relations of production. In such a scheme conformity is at least as handleable as is conflict within functionalism. It may be a result of compulsion or of false consciousness, but this is not central. What is important is that structural conflict between social classes is the root assumption that can provide for a variety of substantive analyses—as with functionalism there is a distinction to be made between the general lines of approach and the substantive analyses, between in Sklair's terms, method and doctrine.

The inability of heralds of the functionalist revival to meet this fundamental challenge is well demonstrated by Cohen when he tries to show that functionalism cannot provide an adequate account of social change only 'because they have not produced adequate theories of social persistence'.[21]

For Cohen 'if functionalism could really state the conditions under which social systems persist then it could also explain change simply by showing that some of these conditions are sometimes absent'.[22] This may or may not be true, but it clearly does not meet the point made by the conflict perspective that understanding class conflict is to grasp the core truth about the development and nature of societies. Cohen's arguments cannot stand as refutation of that which it never confronts. Yet Cohen does give a useful insight into the reasons for the failure of both functional and conflict theories when stressing the importance of social theory being able to explicate its *own* assumptions. As he says of functionalists, 'their ideas do not explain why it is that functional interrelationships exist in all social life . . . if it could do this then there would be no difficulty in showing that the explanation of both social persistence and of social change makes use of the same theories and models of social life. *This explanation must proceed by way of some notion of social action and interaction*'[23] (our italics). This we take to mean that one *can* order the empirical world according to the dictates of theory and method, but what is necessary is to show how theories and methods are linked with an ongoing subject world. With that we have no disagreement, and we can in fact start to understand why a functionalist view could never offer a warrantable account of, for instance, the social nature of law, by tracing the path by which subjectivity and meaning are excluded by being rendered unproblematic in the building of the functionalist perspective.

The loss, and the subsequent closure of functional theory from the empirical world, occurs at that point of construction when the necessary assumptions about action are introduced to make 'system' a viable sociological entity. It is not that action is deliberately excluded, but that the analysis of action as such is taken as complete for all practical purposes in so far as it is constituted through the notions of role and status into functioning systemic items of the social universe. In the initial stage, action and its defining property of meaningfulness, comprise the ordering framework for a series of postulates about the nature of social behaviour. As Devereux has said, 'Parsonian theory . . . is based upon an action frame of reference. Where others talk of organisms and environment Parsons talks of action and situation. Where others talk of behaviour as response, Parsons talks of action.'[24] Talk of action is talk of subjectivity. For the actor-in-situation what is important is whatever is meaningfully organized in his orientation. Even the situation itself cannot be defined without reference to the actor's definition of it. (Parsons: 'One cannot speak of action except as a relation between both action and situation.)[25] Subjective processes are also central in the initial Parsonian analysis of interaction. The definition by an actor of what is going on, of how the situation relates to his own goal choices and what he construes as relevant to the practical concerns of an unfolding interaction sequence, constitutes the key to understanding the action matrix. (Parsons: 'Underlying (the scheme) . . . is the conception of the relevance of the cultural level of categorization in terms of meanings. This implies that an essential point of reference must be a postulated "knowing" and "feeling" unit of reference, an actor *for whom* the objects of his situation have meaning. This is the famous Weberian "subjective" point of view (Verstehen) which has always been essential to the scheme.')[26] So far, so good. But at this point a pincer movement develops which successfully establishes the claim of 'system' and concurrently severs meaning from action.

One arm refers to the exigencies of stable interaction. For Parsons there are three possibilities when actors come together: random orientations of one actor to another, in which case stable interaction is either not possible or not recognizable as such; conflicting orientations and expectations of such an order as to be incompatible with the continuance of interaction; a certain degree of complementary expectations about the course, nature and conduct of the interaction. Two actors brought together, then, each capable of providing definitions of and inputing meaning to the situation will either come to share in some sort of basic consensus or they will be unable to interact. Should they succeed then they will have created an emergent collective reality partaken of by both but belonging to neither. Ownership instead is vested in the incipient social system which they produce but cannot possess.

The second arm consists of the recognition that action in society occurs after this stage, when emergent social systems are already in existence. The network of social relationships which are prior to any one course of social interaction is already constituted of those emergent realities generated in the hypothetical account of inter-actional settings, emergent realities which combine and recombine by being taken account of by successive generations of actors until they represent the social system writ large. Such a system, and its subsystems, exist as ongoing entities comprising actions but by now above them. Standardized expectations, derived from a central value system, pervade action at all levels and the actor, by virtue of his socialization and the requirement that he attend carefully to the goals and standards of the socio-cultural nexus, is assured of finding matching expectations among others with whom he interacts.

The personal biography of the socialized actor during which the internalization of goals, needs and dispositions has occurred, combines with the dictates of stable interaction to be the pincers for the encirclement of subjective meaning. Meaning is less deliberately excluded than incorporated. It is not written from existence by philosophical or methodological fiat, rather its analysis is completed and subsumed in a fashion which makes of it a derivation from properties of the emergent level of system and in particular from the cognitive consensus underlying each system.

With clean hands the analyst is able to switch attention to system properties of equilibrium; functional interdependence with other systems; the various functional prerequisites necessary for system maintenance; system adaptation to a changing environment; and so on—in short the characteristic terms of functional theory—without the vexatious intrusion of subjective meaning.

It is, then, possible to see how functionalism makes certain claims in moving beyond the level of action which make meaning redundant at the systems level, the level where functionalism undertakes substantive inquiries. The objection which has to be made to this rests not on the elevation of meaning to a sociological dogma, but simply on the grounds that the act of making meaning redundant separates any theory from the empirical context. As Blumer has said of theory, it 'is of value in empirical science only to the extent to which it connects fruitfully with the empirical world'.[27] Blumer indicates three major lines of deficiency in social theory, each of which is applicable to functionalism.

First, theory is glaringly separated from the social world; it is 'compartmentalized into a world of its own'. When it is applied to the social world, it orders that world into given conceptual and theoretical devices such that 'in terms of both origin and use social theory seems in general not to be geared into its empirical world'.[28]

Secondly, theory does not guide social research. Its implications are generally untestable. 'Its divorcement from research is as great as its divorcement from the empirical world.'[29]

Thirdly, theory appears not to benefit from the growing accumulation of data and findings of research. 'While this may be due to an intrinsic uselessness of such facts for theoretic purposes, it also may be due to deficiency in theory.'[30]

Expelling subjective meaning prepares the ground for all these deficiencies to prosper. With meaning written out of the plot the author can supply increasingly rarefied scenarios. Without the massive prescience of the empirical world to contradict and talk back to them, theories can talk only to themselves and to each other.

POSITIVISM

Earlier, we established the paternity of positivism in the work of Émile Durkheim. To the extent that such was a proper judgement, an air of paradox can be created by his vehement statements that subjectivity played a full part in his sociology. He expressly stated that social life is constituted of '*representation collective*' (collective orientations). At the same time, of course, sociology was to address a body of data independent of subjective orientations. Legal regulations were given a central place mainly because they are what they are and 'there are no two ways of looking at (them)'.

For Durkheim there was no paradox. No matter how widespread the *representation* or how pervasive its subjective character, science demanded that it be studied objectively. If this stipulation were followed then the proposition that social facts be treated as things could only coexist with the notion that, essentially, social life consists of *representation* if a demarcation were accepted between the nature of social life and the methods that had to be employed if it were ever to be understood. Durkheim did in fact accept the division between the *subject* and the *method* of study and, although the polemical character of his methodological writings tended to obscure this point, he did not do so in any wanton fashion. Understanding the social world was conceived of as a vast project and therefore 'we must approach the social realm where it offers the easiest access to scientific investigation. Only subsequently will it be possible . . . to encompass . . . this fleeting reality, which the human mind will never perhaps be able to grasp completely.'[31]

This brief look at Durkheim's reasoning will assist in understanding the rationale for the use of positivist methods but in the main they are adopted as a necessary stance in the pursuit of verifiable knowledge, such pursuit being thought to entail the use of procedures based on natural scientific modes of inquiry. Many proponents of positivism go along with non-positivists in seeing a subjective world, the point of disagreement being how to handle that world scientifically. Granted, one or two brands of positivism do not see a subject world, seeing instead only conditioned organisms, but these are idiosyncratic and uninteresting variants that we do not intend to cover.

Giddens[22] has identified three suppositions in positivist sociology:

(a) that the methodological procedures of natural science can be directly adapted for sociology;

(b) that the outcome of sociological investigations can be formulated, as per natural science in terms of 'laws and law-like' generalizations about social phenomena; and

(c) that sociology is neutral in respect of values and, as in natural science, the findings of sociological research do not carry any logically given implications for value positions.

Of the three, methodology is most central. As Giddens himself says, positivism in sociology 'may be broadly represented as depending upon the assertion that the concepts and methods as employed in natural science can be applied to form a science of man'.[33]

Certain authors, however, do place greater emphasis upon suppositions (b) and (c). Methodology in some lines of argument is made subservient either to the sociological purpose of discovering law-like generalizations or to the need for a value-free sociology. We will therefore discuss positivism in the latter two guises before turning to methodology, but we do so only on the basis that approaches which make method a derivative of either of the other suppositions are unpersuasive invitations to reorder our priorities, and are so for two reasons. First, in a pragmatic vein, we note that the divide, on either side of which stand the two camps of positivist and interpretive sociology, is generally recognized as splitting the 'methodological' from the 'outcome' and 'neutrality' tenets of positivism. Authors such as Weber and Schutz reject the first and accept at least one and arguably both of the latter, but only the unhelpful assertion that we are all positivist could lead to the reassignment of these two scholars from the interpretive to the positivist camp. Secondly, and more constructively, the methodological level seems to us to deserve pre-eminence on the grounds that the initial collection and ordering of data, if defective, somewhat defuses reflection as to both the sociological purpose and the purposes to which sociology is put. In what aspires to be an empirical science, defective data can serve no values and can generate no laws.

Finally, a brief word must be said on the manner of presentation of the three sub-sections following. They reflect the issues taken by us to be important for the potential of sociology of law as it relates to each of the three suppositions. The issue of values we see as a relatively unexplored area in the sub-discipline and the section focuses on problems arising as a result of this. In terms of law-like generalizations, the sub-disciplinary literature displays a lack of appreciation of (1) the implications of such a pursuit, (2) the necessary distinctions between that objective and the aim of producing deductive systems, and (3) the relations of both of the latter to *sociologically* distinguishable propositions. Discussion addresses these problem areas. Positivist methods, the core of positivism, we see as pervasive and as adopted unreflectively. They are here addressed in vigorous fashion in keeping with the need to achieve a successful refutation.

Value Neutrality

Within the sociology of law there is something of a mainstream to be discerned in respect of values. It consists of fairly passive acceptance of numerous of the major statements available, coupled with an absence of their lucid appreciation. The existence of a mainstream, however, does not indicate much of a consensus amongst practitioners since over the last few yards of its course that mainstream is deflected with the purpose either of flooding arid pastures with the likes of Gouldner and Becker, or of saving unsound sociological structures from the threat of refutation. Against this judgement can be placed the odd tributary, representing all too infrequent struggles to think out seriously how debates on values could inform the pursuit of a viable sociology of law—Selznick is one example—but overall the sub-discipline has opted for a policy of meandering around the issues rather than for confrontation.

The rather complacent mainstream can be briefly designated as one in which values are seen as pervasive in sociological inquiry without infringing sociologists' ability to identify and juxtapose 'facts'. Value intrusion into the act of choosing a problem to analyse and research is regarded as inevitable and most agree with Black in extending this Weberian insight to 'grant that these value orientations may bias the analysis of the problem as well as its selection'.[34] Disengagement, it is recognized, requires effort. One cannot simply strip off values for a purified plunge into research proper. In addition to their acceptance of these points, sociologists of law frequently join in the general celebration of Gouldner[35] for his demonstration that value neutrality as a doctrine is as open to sociological analysis as any other set of beliefs or ideology. Further, although Gouldner's relativism in this is very different from Becker's, the latter's relativist argument that one can choose to serve the masters or the underdogs but that willy-nilly one's research cannot serve neither also usually gets a ritual genuflect.

This matronly clasp of all arguments to an ample and uncritical bosom, gives rise to numerous difficulties. For example, even a cursory reading of Gouldner makes clear that his analysis is not available for appending to that of Weber. The demonstration he gives that Weber's formulation of value neutrality can be seen as a peculiarly apposite and morally conscious stance given the context of German Universities at the turn of the century, cannot be an amendment or supplement to Weber's formulation. It is rather an invitation to rethink the problem of values anew for the post-war American context.

Placing this and similar contradictions to one side, the insubstantial and ineffective treatment which values receive in the sociology of law has helped to sustain two important obstacles to development in the sub-discipline, those of relevance and of positivist methods. The first concerns the displacement which occurs in those studies which tread too far in the direction of relevance; the second refers to the unwarranted confusion which obtains between (i) value intrusion in research and (ii) the (subjective) interpretation which researchers have to make at different points in the research process, and the use of arguments based on such confusion to support claims for positivist methods.

(a) *Displacement:* The too easy acceptance of the idea that values inevitably play a part in the choice of topic for investigation has encouraged workers not to worry overmuch if they move too far in the direction of relevance. The displacement which then takes place is achieved quite naturally and effortlessly, and without any abrogation of the ethics of integrity and lack of prejudice. When relevance is held too dearly, questions get framed in such a way as to negate the possibility of making contact with human action in its social context. Data are gathered in terms of questions which require them to be prised more or less gently from the only context which makes them sociologically comprehensible. Social action as an object of study is side-stepped to facilitate and speed up inquiry of what are seen as more central issues.

Take for example questioning as it might relate to child care. Such a focus could give rise to numerous studies with an overly relevance bent with the object of investigating why children were taken into care, the background characteristics of affected children, the part played by various organizational actors and the organizations themselves in contributing to a high or low incidence of children in care and so on. But, as long as data are collected *in terms of* the relevance issues of reducing, increasing, improving or finding substitutes for the taking of children into care, then human action as such is not addressed but only that part of actors' behaviour as it impinges on those issues. Activity is abstracted from its context and displacement occurs from action itself to action as-it-pertains-to-the-relevance issue. This is not to say that sociology is incapable of addressing the social processes which collectively constitute 'taking into care', but simply that serious risks are run if an understandable concern with child care in the guise of a social problem is not disengaged when it comes to formulating and investigating researchable issues. The research act becomes in danger of being short-circuited and the merit of the contribution reduced accordingly.

(b) *Value Intrusion and Subjective Interpretation of Data in Research:* Lack of clarity as to the issue of values in sociology also serves to promote the cause of positivist methods within the sociology of law. This arises as a result of the assumed coterminity between the stages of research at which one is called upon to interpret (i.e. do more than mechanically record unproblematic 'facts') and stages at which values are thought to intrude into the research, either actually or potentially. Whenever a researcher's own subjectivity is called upon, value-intrusion is thought to be an imminent threat. Subjectivity is equated with the possibility of bias. However, not only is this a trivialization of both the problem of values and of the problem of the interpretation of data but it also provides a smokescreen under which to advance the claims of 'neutral' statistical techniques, a smokescreen which hides the fact that data do not speak but have to be interpreted. The highly moral issue of values and the appreciation that, in Popper's language, observations are theory impregnated, becomes reduced to the vulgar issue of how best to control bias. Instead of sociology being put on trial and the issue of how to validate knowledge receiving due attention, the integrity of researchers is called into question. The invidious character of that questioning is not reduced by the forgiving afterword that such biases 'cannot be helped'.

It is a short step only from the argument that occasions of subjective interpretation are invitations to distort the evidence to the idea that if sociologists cannot control their own value impulses then technique and methodology must be made to do it for them. It is thought necessary to lock research into a methodology which has the potential, for instance, to show up correlations against our will, correlations that we would find distasteful from a value standpoint. If the logic of statistics, and variables whose influence is not predictable, can be made to be a mechanism for processing hypotheses without sociologists' constant intervention, then maybe we can protect research from bias, subjectivity, interpretation and values in one glorious act of insulation. The difficulty is that such an act would effectively insulate the sociologist from the social world and the feature of meaningfulness which underpins the designation 'social'. We will have constructed a methodological padded cell in which, if he is prepared to submit to it, the sociologist can be saved from himself and can do himself no harm. The only price he will have to pay is to have little idea of what is going on outside.

Law-Like Generalizations and Deductive Theory
The title of this section refers to topics within philosophy and the sociology of knowledge awesome in their complexity, but the reader will by now be unsurprised to learn how little of an idea of that is conveyed in contemporary sociology of law. All of the language of

natural science—deduction, law, hypothesis, concept, etc.—is present but with only a pale reflection of the clarity which its employment generally occasions in the natural scientific context. It is our purpose here to clarify issues in scientific language which arise from comparison of the two formulations of positivism given by Walsh[36] (see the introduction to this chapter) and Giddens[37] (see the introduction to *Positivism*). The context of the discussion will be the types of statements which are given in the sociology of law or which base sociological approaches open to use in the sub-discipline.

It will help to demonstrate certain difficulties which are consequent on an acceptance of the validity of a positivistic purpose for sociology if statements which appear in sociology and in the sociology of law are compared with each other and with natural scientific statements, such comparison being undertaken with the potential differences between law-like statements (Giddens) and predictive statements (Walsh) kept in mind. Prediction as explanation in positivism is prediction based on an ability to engage in deductive theorizing rather than say mere prediction from simple repetition. Since it is the nature of positivist explanation that we wish to place at issue, deductive theorizing will provide our explicit point of reference.

Consider the following four sets of paired statements:

(1a) Every body near the earth and freely falling towards it falls with an acceleration of 32 feet per second per second.

(1b) Every body starting from rest and freely falling towards the earth falls $16t^2$ feet in t seconds, whatever value t may have.

(2a) Law tends to become implicated in social life to the degree that other forms of social control are weak or unavailable.

(2b) The police relatively infrequently make arrests when some other form of social control is available in the situation.

(3a) Social systems function interdependently.

(3b) Law serves the function of integration for the wider social system.

(4a) Action proceeds on the basis of the meaning of the situation for the actor.

(4b) The Factory Inspectorate tend to see their job as one of regulation and not enforcement.

Each of these statements is a law-like generalization. This is self-evidently true for most of them, but is also the case for (3a) and (4a).

(1a) and (1b). This pair consists of (1a), the first-level proposition of the Galilean system of mechanics, and (1b), a hypothesis which is deducible from that proposition according to the principles of integral calculus. It is easily recognizable as the form to which natural scientific statements aspire.

(2a) and (2b). These are provided by Black in his discussion of how the sociology of law can and should ape the natural sciences and aim for a general theory of law, the idea being to explain the behaviour of the police by predicting and deducing it from a more general proposition about law. According to Black the first- and second-level propositions he gives can lead to third-order hypotheses. Thus, if 'the likelihood of legal control is greater where other forms of social control are absent, it follows that the police are more likely to arrest a stranger who, let us say, assaults a stranger than a son who assaults his father'.[38]

In an earlier discussion of Black we indicated certain of the difficulties in his scheme. Here we can immediately note that as the propositions stand they are not directly deducible. To make (2a) and (2b) stand in a deductive relation would require the addition of some statement expressing a determinate relation between the police and the law, and it would also be necessary to make explicit what is implicit in the two statements, namely that (1) law is a form of social control, and (2) the police making an arrest is an instance of social control. Were Black to explicate in this fashion, there would remain at least two types of question to be asked of his deductive scheme.

First would be a series of issues concerning the relationship of the empirical world to certain key aspects of his terminology and to his first-order proposition. Evidence for the construction of (2a) requires the identification of analogues of certain patterns of police behaviour. Such identification is given in terms of the category of 'social control', but that concept itself remains opaque and insufficiently connected with the social world. This is true both in Black's work and, in the literature more generally. Opacity is not in our view the result of incompetence as such but is related to the manner of generation of concepts, the purposes to which they are put in such schemes as that of Black and the procedures utilized for ordering data into their environs. These issues are taken up in Chapter VI.

Secondly, if we give him his head on these matters of not inconsiderable contention, what do we get in return? Do we understand any more about the social processes involved in making an arrest by being able to predict that arrest is more likely in certain settings rather than others? At one level there seems to be an improvement in our understanding for, in accepting Black's line of argument, we would have accepted that cases potentially involving arrest are classifiable according to the status of the parties to the case. But reflection suggests that any understanding achieved is mainly supplied by the reader of Black's assertions. We, the reader, automatically 'fill in' his account with understandings of why police might come to see an assault case as one of intra-familial dispute and why they might view the implications and ramifications consequent upon such identification as excluding the need for, or desirability of, an arrest. We do all the work. Understanding is supplied as much by common sense as by deduction from the 'general theory' and the understanding is only of sociological value if it expresses the relationship of police behaviour to certain types of situations in terms which relate to the meaning of actions and events as established by the police in deciding upon courses of action. Even if Black's general theory of law had produced a rule of police behaviour operative at the level of the construction of courses of action, and it is difficult to see how it could, we would still need to inquire as to how that rule is recognized and brought into play in specific social instances. What Black's objective of a general theory of law would leave out seems at least as interesting as what it would incorporate.

Pair (3a) and (3b) manifest similar problems at the points of, first, concept formation and, secondly, the exclusion of issues of the social processes indexed by the statements. We discussed the first under functionalism as it relates to the notion of system, and as the lines of argument for the second point follow those in respect of pair (2a) and (2b), it only remains to make one or two remarks on the status of the two propositions.

Proposition (3b) is not strictly deducible from (3a) at all. This is not because a little supplementary information is required, as for (2a) and (2b), but because whilst (3a) and (3b) share similar conceptual elements and are therefore empirically related, (3a) (that social systems function interdependently) specifies a general property of social life. This does not mean that it constitutes necessarily an *a priori* assumption, since its adherents would claim that it is founded on experience and open to empirical test. But its level of generality separates it off from (3b) (law serves the function of integration), which is not just a *specific* instance of the general property, although it is that, but also a *substantive* instance. New concepts, again claiming an empirical basis, are introduced in (3b) which must rely on empirical establishment, since the general property of functional interpendence is incapable of stipulating the concepts of integration and legal system. However, it would be possible to create a deductive system involving propositions of the order of (3b) and derivative propositions about, say, the place of judges within the legal system, in order to produce lower level propositions concerning judges' behaviour in specific situations in much the same manner as Black 'deduces' police behaviour. Such would still face the problems of concept and method as faced by (2a) and (2b) but the system *could* in principle be established. Again, however, the claim would have to be made that something called integration could be positively identified independently of any actors involved in the process.

In some respects the pair (4a) and (4b) are similar to (3a) and (3b). Here also we find a second-order proposition not deducible from the first. The notion that 'action proceeds by way of meaning' cannot stipulate the notions of regulation and enforcement contained in the second. Although (4a) is a law-like generalization, predicated on experience and open to empirical test, it is stated as a property of action and cannot stoop to make substantive claims as represented in (4b), even with the assistance of principles of translation (as are given in (1a) and (1b) by integral calculus and would be given in (2a) and (2b) by supplying a formula for relating the law to the police).

Differences do start to appear between pairs (3) and (4) when we try to move to the level of creating a deductive system for pair (4) out of additional imported elements. We can in fact, establish the procedures for creating such a theory working with propositions (4a) and (4b), but must emphasize that we have chosen the example of Factory Inspectors for the purposes of exposition and are not following Carson's analysis. Presumably one would start the construction by working from research findings of the order of (4b) (the Factory Inspectorate see their job as regulation not enforcement) until an identifiable characteristic of enforcement agencies was found to be present when the view of regulation was taken, and absent when the enforcement view was upheld, or vice versa. Such a characteristic (two candidates for which might be the size of the penalties attached to the enforced legislation or the nature of the setting to which the legislation referred, e.g. a business setting) would then be set up in a first-level proposition relating it to the views taken by members of that organizational type, e.g. 'Members of enforcement agencies enforcing low-penalty legislation will tend to see their job as one of regulation.' A particular instance could then be deduced for organization X as long as X was directly relatable to low-penalty type legislation. The system would be established.

At this point we can stop and ask what gains have been made by successfully establishing a deductive scheme. On the basis of the research needed to be undertaken for the first-level proposition to be formulated and the research required to assess the deduced instances concerning organization X, we can expect to have achieved a level of understanding enforcement agencies and how their members see their tasks. But little appears to be added to such understanding by ordering the propositions according to deductive logic.

Quite a different reply must be given if we ask what is lost. The very attempt to test a specific predicted statement against empirical social settings is likely to be an exercise in moulding data to the statement rather than vice versa. We do not have to be dishonest selectively to collect that data to which we have been sensitized by prior possession of a specific hypothesis. Instead of studying social processes with a view to grasping their complex, intricate and inner-moving character, the task will tend to be one of collecting evidence. Openness to the wholesome, contextual features of instances of social action, will be put to one side, for that is not a requirement of testing hypotheses. Attention will be focused and narrow. Items, in the form of behaviour, talk, 'attitudes', will be given their meaning and significance by the theory and hypothesis, not by their context. Such dangers are real and ever present and, perhaps, unavoidable within the positivist method.

In the end, however, it may be unnecessary to force this issue. After all, consider again the hypothesis that is being put to the test in this current context. We began with a proposition about the Factory Inspectorate and their understandings of the purpose of their task, and showed how it might be possible to build up a deductive system using similar empirically derived propositions to identify a characteristic of enforcing agencies. This characteristic then formed the backbone of the first-level proposition in the deductive system.

From the first-level proposition, combined with principles of translation, we aimed to deduce the nature of mens' understandings of their tasks at hand. To the extent that such understandings are bound up with the particular social universe in which they arise, and, being dependent on an active subject, are open to change, there is doubt as to whether they allow of the determinate relations implied by deducing hypotheses—this indicates that the language of action and understanding may be fundamentally incompatible with that of deduction and prediction. Even were this not the case, however, the question would still need to be asked as to how we can best study and make inferences about mens' understandings. If we cannot talk of understanding without also talking about subjectivity and the meanings attributed by actors to items in their social universe, then we must consider which methods of inquiry can best elicit the data we seek. In particular we need to think about whether the methodological correlate of deductive theorizing, positivist methods, are the most suitable for inquiries which give pre-eminence to the investigation of meaningful behaviour.

Methodology

In this final section on positivism, the methodological tenet will be reviewed. That tenet can be put to the test by criticisms operating at different levels, but they can be synoptically regarded as attempts either to repair positivist methods with the aim of eliminating or reducing the impact of identifiable gremlins or to refute entirely the potential for use of such methods. Repair critiques can be further divided according to the facet seen as constituting the weak link, such as failures in statistical methods, difficulties in obtaining true data, the careless choice of variables and so on. Refutation critiques also vary and, although neat sub-divisions are more difficult to establish, the variance appears to lie in whether the implication of the attack is (a) that positivist methods leave many areas of social life untouched or are incompetent to examine such areas, or (b) that such methods are wholly unacceptable in sociology.

Here the focus will be at the refutational level, without regard to subsequent implications, though it may not be a matter of chance that the authors relied upon to spearhead the assault (Schutz, Cicourel and Blumer) represent major figures in the three brands of interpretive sociology given in the second half of this chapter as alternatives to positivist sociology.

Against the positivist principle that the methods of natural science can be adopted for studying social life, is put a denial based on two premises:

(a) Social life is intrinsically meaningful; and

(b) Methodology must be compatible with this meaningful component, i.e. the subject-matter contains imperatives for study.

According to Schutz, avoidance of these premises vitiates positivism because, first, such study takes for granted the social reality which is the object of attention for social science ('Intersubjectivity, interaction, intercommunication and language are simply presupposed.')[39] and secondly, the identification of social experience with the observation of behaviour excludes several dimensions of social reality from inquiry. Here, Schutz cites the inability of positivism to explain the behaviour of the observer himself; the different meanings attributable to 'objectively' the same piece of behaviour; how social reality can depend on the definition of the actor; cases where actors *intentionally* refrain from acting; and, non-face-to-face settings in which actors, without guidance from direct sensory experience, none the less 'understand' many of the unseen background features of what people say and do.

Schutz's argument is here being directed at exponents of that style of positivism identified with the behaviourist school of sociological research. Although sociological research is undertaken more by eclectics than behaviourist purists, researchers embrace positivist methods to the extent that they subscribe to one or more of the various components of that school, and if we address those components we can feel confident of addressing positivism in a sufficiently comprehensive fashion for our purposes. Nagel has conveniently provided a synopsis of the methodological tenets of the behaviourist orientation. The main emphasis lies in 'the quantitative testing of generalizations about the relations between various legal phenomena and other phenomena'.[40] In procedural terms the quest for quantification usually involves determining:

(1) some hypotheses to test;

(2) a sample of persons, places or things on which to make the test;

(3) measurements for the relevant characteristics of the entities; and

(4) a tabulation of the relations between the measured characteristics.

The objective is to frame generalizations in the language of cause and effect with reference to investigated items.

The framework, constituted as principles of methodology, can be questioned at a number of overlapping levels.

(a) Is the importation of natural scientific approaches logically permissible?

(b) On what basis is it possible, proper or helpful to measure social phenomena?

(c) What is the status of the 'entities' and the 'measure characteristics'?

(d) Is the language of cause and effect admissible within sociological discourse?

Although given in a slightly different context, the discussion of causality and social phenomena in Chapter I exhausts all that is necessary to say to meet the purposes here. Used in its strict natural scientific guise causality was seen to be an inappropriate mode of discourse. When transmogrified by authors such as MacIntyre, in an attempt to retain for it a relevance for investigation of social phenomena, it was seen to have a forced character and to add little to what could be conveyed by alternative modes of discourse. This topic will not therefore be covered here. To answer the other three levels of questioning we will adopt the arguments of Schutz, Cicourel and Blumer.

(a) *The Logic of Positivist Methods in Sociology:* The arguments used by Schutz to demonstrate the illogicality of positivist methods in sociology are deeply rooted in the Husserlian phenomenology which was the proximate basis of his attempt to reconstitute the premises of interpretive sociology. The commonsense knowledge of everyday life is seen as the background against which all inquiry starts, is carried out and is irretrievably imbedded. Such a background can never be escaped, for to escape it is to be no longer either of, or in, society. With specific purposes in mind, it is possible to abstract out of this *Lebenswelt* the existant background which, being inescapable, is the originating source of all scientific concepts, but it is only possible to do this if the act of abstraction is related to the purposes for which it is undertaken. On these grounds natural science is seen as inquiry founded on the idealized abstraction of Nature, an abstraction which 'on principle and of course legitimately excludes persons with their personal life and all objects of culture which originate as such in practical human activity'.[41] Natural science then, imposes an order on the natural world for the purposes of facilitating an understanding of the relations between those aspects of the *Lebenswelt* abstracted into the concept of Nature and which relate to tangible, non-meaningful objects.

Schutz, however, sees the task of social science as inquiring into the *Lebenswelt* itself, since that is the layer of social reality at which sociality itself operates. Sociology, therefore, studies the *Lebenswelt* from which Nature can be abstracted and idealized by natural science. Since natural-science methods have been devised to facilitate analysis of the idealized abstraction, then *ipso facto* they must be inappropriate for analysis of the base level itself. When natural scientific methods are used, the result is abstract and remote theorizing which 'will not tell us anything about social life as experienced by men in everyday life'.[42]

(b) *Measurement of Social Phenomena:* A major problem in positivist methods lies in the capacity claimed to assign numerical properties to social phenomena and subsequently to manipulate them through the use of statistical techniques. As Cicourel has shown, such a claim must be withheld until successful analysis has been completed as to the basis on which quantification is possible. For social events to be amenable to measurement requires, in Cicourel's view, that 'the events of interest to the sociologist have the same properties mathematically that physical properties have, and, therefore, that social events are amenable to the same kinds of measurement theories . . .'[43] This has yet to be demonstrated. The character of the social world as meaningful and as comprised of active, understanding subjects gives a picture of the social world that cannot be painted by numbers. Sociological methods must be able to grasp the shifting and context-bound character of meaning and the processes involved in meaning-construction rather than be comprised of measurement systems having a forced and arbitrary correspondence to the social phenomena they are trying to grasp. The social processes of group life are ongoing and unfolding with actors making sense together amongst the intricacies and intimacies of action settings. Social processes are set against a background of commonsense knowledge and taken-for-granted assumptions upon which actors rely to make sense of what is going on. Assigning numbers to the properties of social processes is impossible to achieve without a leap of faith which no researcher has yet been able to explicate satisfactorily or to explain with reference to specified procedures. Since the stuff of social life is not arranged discretely, the use of numerical scales and statistics can only lead to measurement by fiat.

The importance of Cicourel's analysis is to reveal that any completed piece of sociological work relying on an ability to measure social phenomena is but the tip of an iceberg in at least two respects.

(a) It is the tip of the social processes to which measurement is applied. The assignment of numbers is an indexing of social life but, being achieved by fiat, those numbers cannot display social life itself nor can their manipulation constitute a proper analysis of it.

(b) It is the tip of the social processes which are constitutive of the research act itself. The interpretive work done by the researcher is hidden under principles of statistics.

If confirmation of the relevance of Cicourel's observations of quantification and measurement for the sociology of law is wanted then Nagel can provide all the necessary evidence. Taking at random any one of the twenty or so studies in his collected articles on the legal process from a behavioural perspective is to be struck at once by what is *not* talked about. We are given correlations between the characteristics of lawyers and their rates of success in the courtroom but the assignment of characteristics and their involvement in the analysis is achieved in a manner which fails to retain the integrity of the lawyer's role and his relation to other persons in the courtroom setting. Further, no idea is given of how such characteristics manifest themselves in the courtroom, or whether there might be important (from the point of view of lawyers and others) ways of winning a case without obtaining a formal victory, and, if so, of how actors themselves recognise and assign the categories of victory and defeat. To count the number of formal 'successes' is not to elucidate the meaning of a legal pronouncement for those involved. Further we saw in the works on legal actors undertaken from a behaviourist perspective that discussions relating the characteristics of judges (such as political affiliation) to judicial decisions were responsible for gross inaccuracies in the conceptualization of the nature of legal processes, especially of legal decision making. Nagel claims the right to identify, categorize and classify judicial decisions but of the social processes included in making a decision we hear nothing. The concern with tabulations ruptures behaviourist analysis from the area of social life under consideration and the assumption that 'characteristics' work their way through into social activity in a totally mechanical and measurable fashion severs the analysis from the processes of social life.

Nagel, unsurprisingly, supports the use of his method of research in terms of its disciplined, logical style. But what does this style consist of? Nagel makes an embarrassing attempt to demonstrate and explicate the testing of empirical generalizations in legal research. Several steps are involved in such testing, the first of which are choosing a topic and reviewing the literature. The guidance given by Nagel is of the order 'the better topic, of course, is also the one that is more controversial and that has been less adequately researched'[44] or the one that has 'greater theoretical significance'. No assistance, however, is given for assessing controversiality, adequacy or significance. The next stage is the formulation of a hypotheses, the most interesting being 'those that indicate a relationship between two or more variables'. What are these variables to consist of? Nagel tells us that 'the variables can refer to almost anything, although in order to keep the hypothesis within the field of law, at least one of the variables must refer to some legal phenomena'.[45] After this we must 'sample the entities' choosing those 'on which data is accessible' and which are 'relevant to the hypothesis'.[46] Nagel, however, provides no suggestions as to how we are to decide which variables are 'relevant'. We are forced to an implicit reliance on common sense. The ascription of relevance to variables, then, can stand as a final affront to Cicourel and a final example of the deficiencies in Nagel's account. It is clear throughout Nagel, but perhaps most clear in relation to ascriptions of relevance to variables, that the 'disciplined' method advocated is heavily indebted at all stages to the commonsensical reasoning of the researcher. The researcher's reliance on common sense provides the working part of the method but it is a part of such low profile that Nagel fails to recognize it. This 'worst form of subjectivity', so necessary to the positivist method portrayed, is an indictment of positivism, and Nagel's total inability to explain what actually goes on in testing generalizations is compelling testimony to Cicourel's charges.

As Blumer has pointed out, and in this he agrees with Nagel, there 'seems to be little limit to what may be chosen or designated as a variable'[47] in sociology. But whereas this represents for Nagel freedom of action, for Blumer it is a licence for sloppy research. To avoid debilitating laxity in the use of variables, Blumer advocates that preceeding the application of the techniques of variable analysis there should be a familiarity with the social phenomena under investigation, and a consideration of the various theoretical schemes which might be available to subsume the particular relationship under test. Such would, it is hoped, provide not only for coherence between different pieces of variable analysis but would facilitate the choice of variables meaningful to the area of social life being studied.

Now it is possible that Nagel, for instance, might wish to claim that this is precisely what his own vague injunctions were meant to imply. Should he accept Blumer's formulation, however, then Cicourel invites us to inquire why knowledge acquired prior to variable analysis is permitted to base that analysis. First it can be asked that if prior knowledge is required to ensure the adequacy of variable analysis—in other words if it has somehow a greater validity than the variables—why not debunk variable analysis and concentrate on producing valid methods for acquiring such 'prior' knowledge of action settings. Secondly, we can ask that, within the positivist programme of research, prior learning of situations and settings be formally admitted to that programme. Without such admittance, the knowledge gained is given no academic standing, is without means of validation and is without an explicit method for its acquisition. In such a state, the knowledge is problematic and what seems at first sight to be a defence of positivism only serves to underline its shortcomings.

A major point of criticism of the use of variables in the positivist method is the image it portrays of a social world in which the interpretation of meaning is irrelevant to the explanation of social phenomena. Encapsulated by fiat within a variable, meaning can be ignored and explanation can proceed by way of analysing action as the product of the mechanical association of variables. A possible defence of the positivist method could propose that interpretive processes be included within the analytic scheme of positivism. Interpretation, however, implies a formative process of action construction, a process involving an active subject making judgements, constructing and assigning meaning and reaching understandings. Such a process cannot be held within the scheme of positivism. Further, interpretation is context bound and hence only contextually comprehensive. As such, what value could it receive within the positivist scheme? How could instances of interpretation be classified? Since variable analysis 'seeks necessarily to achieve a clear identification of the relation between two (or more) variables'[48] the logic of its structure could only include interpretive processes if such were viewed as a mere neutral intervening medium for the translation of variable into variable, for instance background characteristics of judges into decision-making outcomes.

Positivism fails because the social world is not available in the form of discrete, unproblematic entities. It does not comprise neat packages independent of the interpretive work of its members. Attempts to treat the social world as so available for the purposes of 'refined techniques' simply *impose* an order on to that world and treat meaning either as irrelevant (background characteristics *themselves* 'explain' behaviour observed) or as derivative of observable categories (independent variables determine interpretation) or as unproblematic (responses to questionnaires index meaning perfectly). The meaningful nature of objects, events and actions within the social world is never properly addressed. Within the sociology of law this has led both to the undermining of law (explanations are inconsistent with the particular character of legal processes and decision making) and to the undermining of sociology (the interpretive processes which exist as recognizable core features of human activity are ignored).

INTERPRETIVE SOCIOLOGY

So far in this chapter we have identified the major perspectives employed in the study of law. In the main we have been concerned with the tenets of positivist sociology as they have entered such study. In the next chapter we will discuss and subject to criticism the normative orientation of such tenets and suggest and develop a different and more fruitful perspective on normative phenomena in general and law in particular. It is necessary, however, first to portray the major characteristics of the sociological perspective which we see as capable of the task.

That sociological perspective can best be seen as an extension of the concerns prompting Weber to formulate his study of society in terms of the base category of social action, that is, behaviour meaningful to the actor. Such provided a subject and a suitable matter for sociological study; informed the creation of a methodology in the form of Verstehen (the postulate of subjective interpretation); and indicated the levels and structures of explanation proper for sociology. Since Weber wrote, successive generations of scholars have sought to reformulate the basic idea of 'action as meaningful' and to attend to social action in a way which carries an intent to fix subjectivity as the sine qua non of the discipline. The perspective we are identifying is interpretive sociology.

It is our purpose to point to certain common tendencies in the writings of authors representing the separably identifiable sociological positions of symbolic interactionism, phenomenology and ethnomethodology, but we begin by setting the terms of debate a little wider. To do this we can briefly look at two orientations of thought concerning the nature of man,[1] orientations which find expression in philosophy, psychology, literature as well as sociology. The Lockean tradition, paramount in England and America, asserts that 'there can be nothing in the intellect of man that was not first in the senses', to which the Liebnizian tradition counters 'nothing—save the intellect itself'.[2]

The Liebnizian tradition maintains that 'the person is not a collection of acts, nor simply the locus of acts, the person is the source of acts'.[3] Internal and external stimulation gives way to a view of action as purposive and intentional, and lays the foundation for a sociology cognisant of the properties of social action, properties which presuppose an active thinker and a process of relating this thinker to his phenomenal world, a world of 'objects' with which the thinker has a conscious relationship. Through this relationship these objects acquire their meaning.

The normative structure of much sociology is Lockean in orientation as seen in the formulations of cultural prescriptions, role expectations, role performances—the individual being merely the 'subjective side of culture'. When we look at the 'active thinker' of Liebniz, however, we can be struck by his uniqueness. As Gordon Allport has said, 'each person is an idiom unto himself, an apparent violation of the syntax of the species. An idiom develops in its own peculiar context, and this context must be understood in order to comprehend the idiom.'[4] This context is the 'phenomenal world' of the individual. The phenomenal world is the world in which the individual lives, not the world of sociological theory. It is the pre-selected and pre-interpreted world of which we are all capable of theorizing about, reflecting upon and bestowing with meaning.

We can now indicate how sociology has tried to develop a perspective capable of entering such a world. By keeping statements concerning social actors grounded in the social actors own phenomenology rather than in the conceptual apparatus of theory, sociology has sought to understand the constitutive features of interpretation and meaning in the formation of action in given contextual situations.

SYMBOLIC INTERACTIONISM

Symbolic interactionism, as developed from the teachings of G. Herbert Mead[5] by a succession of Chicago sociologists, rests on three simple premises; first, human beings act towards things on the basis of the meanings that the things have for them; secondly, the meanings of such things arise out of social interaction; and thirdly, these meanings are constructed in, and modified through, interpretive processes used by social actors in dealing with other persons, objects and events encountered.[6]

The first premise is relatively uncontentious but is often ignored in its acceptance: meaning is either taken for granted and therefore regarded as unimportant, or it is regarded as a neutral link between the factors responsible for human behaviour and the resultant behaviour itself. Sociologists who rely on such factors as status, role demands, cultural prescriptions, norms and values to explain behaviour are ignoring meaning whatever lip service be paid to its importance. For symbolic interactionism, to 'ignore the meaning of the things towards which people act is seen as falsifying the behaviour under study. To by pass the meaning in favour of factors alleged to produce the behaviour is seen as a grievous neglect of the role of meaning in the formation of behaviour.'[7]

The second premise of symbolic interactionism stands in opposition to those theories which treat meaning as intrinsic to the thing that has it, or as being a psychic accretion brought to it by the person for whom the thing has meaning. Such a view of meaning is heralded by the oft used, more often misused, questionnaire, which, if relating to meaning at all, relates to it as a distinct entity ready to pop out and be counted on a given signal. Symbolic interactionism views meaning as arising in the process of interaction between people. Reliance on symbolic aspects alone, as in the questionnaire, hides and glosses over the situational context of meaning in interaction. 'The meaning of a thing for a person grows out of the ways in which other people act towards the person with regard to the thing.'[8]

By the third premise we see that the use of meaning occurs through a process of interpretation. This interpretive process involves more than the application of already existing meanings to the situation at hand and must be seen as a process in which meanings are used and revised during the construction of lines of action.

Following from these premises, action is seen as belonging to individuals and, from people engaging in action, concepts of culture and structure can be derived analytically. But sociologists who see action as determined by this culture and structure fail to see that interaction forms human conduct and is not just a forum through which sociological determinants bring about human behaviour. Social interaction is not a coming together of two or more persons to play out a scene dictated by antecedent factors (role demands; status; cultural prescriptions; and so on), nor is it an interaction between factors imputed to those persons. It is a formative process during which action is constructed. Action is constructed on the basis of how people define situations and the behaviour of others in those situations, such definitions being predicted in a process of indication and interpretation. 'Instead of the individual being surrounded by an environment of pre-existing objects which play upon him and call forth his behaviour the proper picture is that he constructs his objects on the basis of his on-going activity.'[9]

Symbolic interactionism at this stage is making strong claims with regard to the nature of man, of action and of society. Perhaps most to be noted, however, are two concerns which go beyond an image of action and move into the realm of methodological imperatives.

First, the situational context of action is stressed but the nature of the actor's situation is given in a phenomenonological cast. That is, the world in which the actor lives is the world of objects with which he has an intentional relation, in other words objects which he notes and which have a meaning for him. Further the process of the generation of meaning is located in interaction. Situational interaction can then be expected to be an important feature to which any methodological stance to the social world must pay attention. Secondly, the interpretive view of interaction does not pre-suppose a world of settled meaning by the application of pre-existing culturally established definitions. Meaning is established in interpretations formulated on particular occasions and is open to reformulation in like manner. For symbolic interactionism, self-indication and interpretation by and through which behaviour is formed do not replace purposes, motives, prescriptions, values, etc. To the extent that the latter factors can be regarded as pre-dating behaviour they are part of the phenomenal world of the actor. His behaviour is not the result of these things but arises instead from how he interprets and handles these things in the action he is constructing. Elucidation of this process is seen as necessary to ground explanations of observed regularities at the level of social action.

It would be tempting to develop symbolic interactionism further, especially with regard to particular studies and the way stability in social definitions is conceptualized. These issues will, however, be brought out in Chapter VI. For now, we will be content to trace interactionism on two fronts. First, the types of concepts it utilizes, and secondly, the methodological position it adopts. On concepts a few words here will have to suffice. First, concepts are seen as the 'method of making contact with the empirical world', and as such they must be true to the character of that world. The empirical world is pre-constituted by the people populating it and sociological concepts must reflect this characteristic, not the presumed characteristics of 'science' in terms of measurable dimensions and neat, mutually exclusive classifications. The construction and use of a concept reflects, obviously, the methodological stance adopted. For symbolic interactionism, methodology 'embraces *all* the important parts of the act of scientific inquiry'.[10] Continuing the quote from Blumer '. . . Every part of the act of scientific inquiry is subject to the test of the empirical world and has to be validated through such a test. Reality exists in the empirical world and not in the methods used to study that world . . . [and] the procedures employed in each part of the act of scientific inquiry should and must . . . respect the nature of the empirical world under study.'

Such respect is not assured by a simple adherence to the protocols of 'good research practice', because within the scientific protocol one can 'operate with false premises, erroneous problems, distorted data, spurious relations, inaccurate concepts, and unverified interpretations'.[11] The approach advocated constructs concepts, problems and propositions in the direct examination of the empirical world—their value and their validity are 'to be determined in that examination and not in seeing how they fare when subjected to the alien criteria of an irrelevant methodology'.[12]

We find with symbolic interactionism a stress on sociology as an empirical science and a determination to respect the empirical world. This is not only meritorious in itself but leads to an appreciation that the only 'given' of sociology is social action, that this is constitutive of social life and that any explanation of social life which disregards this fact is fundamentally and inescapably faulted.

Symbolic interactionism is now vintage sociology: it is strange that its tenets are still regarded as 'recent', misguided and aberrant. The tenets led to explanations in terms of meanings—meanings as part of a reason for action. As such, explanation has the flavour of motive. Symbolic interactionism developed motive explanations, but ones of a particular kind. Motives were not causes of behaviour but entered into the phenomenal world of the actor in terms of which action is constructed. It was left to the phenomenology of the followers of Alfred Schutz to refine this position.

PHENOMENOLOGY

Phenomenological writings have entered into sociology at two distinct levels. First, there are the essays of Alfred Schutz and secondly there are those writers who have endeavoured to take Schutzian ideas and to forge them into a methodological strategy that can be sustained in actual research settings.

Schutz was particularly concerned to analyse those key elements of social life which explain how social life is possible. We can give no account of this phenomenological base-line, suffice it to say that he took Weber's notion of meaning and turned it into a topic of philosophical reflection. Schutz himself was satisfied that until a phenomenology was developed, sociology remained necessarily problematic. But he realized that sociologists could not wait upon such a phenomenology, and allowed sociology to continue so long as it carried with it certain tenets. First, sociology's aspiration to be an empirical discipline concerned to understand and explain real and existent social phenomena is not served by largely ignoring the fact that such phenomena are meaningful for both the actors and the sociologist, and, secondly, sociology must attend to how meanings are constituted and negotiated by and between actors. These tenets serve to disestablish positivism and functionalism from the sociological endeavour.

Phenomenological sociologists have translated these tenets into two methodological imperatives—first, 'get back to the phenomena' and second, 'show how the phenomena are built up'.[13] The first, a descriptive imperative, acknowledges that to be an empirical science, sociology has to be able to describe social phenomena in a manner which retains the integrity of the phenomena. Sociology has to represent phenomena with whatever degree of diversity, uniqueness, similarity, facticity or ambiguity inheres in the phenomena, without shutting off these features because of, say, any fixed conceptual scheme adopted for use.[14] This particular imperative could not by itself enable sociology to move beyond naturalistic description and sociology could never generate any general properties of social action. The second, constitutive imperative, requires sociology to be able to identify the procedures, knowledge and assumptions utilized by social actors in creating the phenomena under study. Since this constitutive imperative by definition questions the presumptions and taken for granted beliefs of lay actors it is necessary for sociologists to remove themselves from the 'attitude of everyday life'. In the 'scientific attitude' the sociologist dispels his belief in the facticity and taken for grantedness of social phenomena in order to show how these phenomena exist for those whose conduct takes place within a world constituted by everyday beliefs and taken for granted assumptions. The actor as subject is conceived of living within a world of objects. These objects stand in a relation to the actor and this relation is called an 'intentional' relation which gives meaning to the objectivities in the phenomenal world of the subject. The subject is conscious, but consciousness is always consciousness of something. These 'somethings' are the intentional objectivities and meanings experienced by the subject and it is the task of sociology in its constitutive mood to reveal how such objectivities and meanings are constructed. In so doing, sociology is specifically addressing the pre-interpreted and structured 'life-world' of the subject to which Schutz gave attention in his essays on concept formation.

In this way, phenomenological sociologists have sought to implement the tenets of Schutz. They have acknowledged that sociology can only continue to study the everyday world of its subjects so long as it gives primacy to revealing the *shared meanings* that people attach to situations and the *'rules'* by which they *interpret* their situations.[15] It can be noted that such a sociology would not use rules (structural functionalism) or meaning (symbolic interactionism) to 'explain' observed regulations, but would address how its subjects recognized and interpreted rules and meanings as operating, and used them in the formation of those patterns of behaviour observable to the sociology is specifically addressing the pre-interpreted and structured 'life-world' of the subject to which Schutz gave attention in his and meaning construction. This characteristic of the interpretive approach to sociology has peculiar relevance for the study of law which has yet to be developed.

Phenomenologically informed sociology can respect the meaningfulness of social action by documenting *actual commonsense meanings* embodied in the construction of typical courses of action. Sociologists can establish validity by demonstrating the continuity between their constructs and the constructs of their subjects. If this be accepted, then most theories of law currently available and most empirical studies are immediately faulted. To the extent that criteria of validity in the studies of law are made explicit they emphasize only the adherence to strict rules of procedure and the evidence of supporting data. But such criteria are internal to the sociological enterprise and do not touch upon the relationship between a sociological interpretation and the everyday world to which it purports to relate.

Ethnomethodology

The term 'ethnomethodology' refers to folk or lay methods, and just as scientists utilize scientific methods to achieve the scientific, so laymen utilize everyday methods for achieving the everyday. Ethnomethodology, then, refers us to the methodic character in which ordinary people (the subjects) conduct their affairs. Common sense is the central object of study and common sense refers to that knowledge taken for granted by the subject and in terms of which he organizes and interprets his life. If it should be asked why attention needs to be given to such lay methods, then the ethnomethodologist may start by reminding us of the dictum of Thomas that 'a situation defined as real will be real in its consequences'.[16]

Having suggested that the ontology of 'reality' is at issue the ethnomethodologist states that we routinely organize everyday activities in such a way as to confirm the real existence of social phenomena. Focusing on lay methods, then, is said to reflect the manner of existence of social phenomena and holds out the 'fascination and promise' of producing more vigorous and empirical analyses of social order than those available in conventional sociology. Within conventional sociology, social order has been explained by reference to the normative paradigm. Interaction is stable because of, and can be explained by reference to, actors' dispositions for acting learned from the culture and communicated by common, shared symbols and the role expectations that are part of the actors' position in society. This, as we have seen, is essentially the picture offerred by consensus and conflict theory.

Within the interpretive paradigm, stability is founded on the interpretive procedures of interacting members of society. Since social order is 'something which members recognise and make recognisable for each other via the use of procedures of practical reasoning . . . then it is to the explications of these procedures that sociology should look for its topics'.[17] But there is more involved than a simple change in topics. There is the theoretical debate within sociology as to whether social structure is reducible to actors' ways of recognising, creating and displaying objectivity, or whether analysis of these procedures is separate from, though perhaps prior to, the analyses of behaviour by reference to objective structural features of society recognized and displayed by sociologists.

This debate, which underlies any attempt to compare and contrast normative and interpretive paradigms, is best entered by reference to a concrete conception within sociology and we take up the issue for the sociology of law by reference to the concept norm in Chapter VI. Interpretive sociology, in its ethnomethodological stance, has refrained from the debate, conceiving the problem not to be whether social order is objective or subjective, but of '*how* social order is accomplished by members for all practical purposes'.[18] It is an approach which, like phenomenological sociology, makes the commonsense world a topic of investigation and focuses in particular on how lay actors accomplish a sense of objective reality.

Since ethnomethodology states that the ontology of social phenomena is a product of the routine organization of everyday activities, then to study such phenomena we must focus on the shared world of social meanings through which social action is constructed and interpreted. Having grasped the construction of courses of social action in terms of a focus on shared meanings we have in an important sense explained the action. To this end the sociologist has to determine which facts and events are interpretationally relevant to the social actors within the chosen area of study. If, in the words of Walsh, '(the) social world is a world constituted by the taken for granted meanings which its members use as a common scheme of reference by which appearances are interpreted and explained',[19] then social 'facts' (events and objects) are to be addressed as 'the practical accomplishment of members' routine practices for apprehending the social world'.[20] This has certain implications for methodology.

First, if 'social reality is produced and sustained by the practical accomplishment of members using commonsense schemes of interpretation', then it is illegitimate to use means of research which avoid the everyday world. The everyday world is avoided if categories of analysis are taken from theories which, however logically tight, remain as closed explanatory systems. The social facts of the everyday world can only be approached by sociology when it seeks to understand how social facts are established by ordinary people going about their day-to-day affairs.

Secondly, these ordinary people will be displaying the natural attitude but, though the sociologist must lay bare the constituents of the natural attitude, he can only do so by dispelling his own belief in the assumptions and taken-for-grantedness of that attitude. Though social life may be unproblematic at times for social actors (it may be routine, obvious, everyday) it remains as *the* problematic for interpretive sociology. The everyday world is avoided if sociologists maintain the 'attitude of everyday life'. We are then being asked to suspend our belief in the facticity of social phenomena in order to investigate how they are achieved, affirmed and sustained in actual interactional settings on the basis of members' commonsense schemes of interpretation and shared meanings. The suspension of the belief in facticity is required to open the everyday world to sociological analysis. If the everyday world exhibits regularity and order, these features can only be analysed through a 'suspension of the belief in the facticity of that order so as to concentrate on the routine practices and procedures of interpretation by which members accomplish it in interactional settings'.[21]

INTERPRETIVE SOCIOLOGY: CONCLUSION

Through the impetus of situational ethnomethodology, sociology has been brought closer to the world of everyday life. In its interpretive cast, sociology has reformulated the topics it is to address and the level of conceptualization to be achieved in a way which is designed to allow the research act to reveal the manner of existence of social phenomena and the general properties of social action.

If interpretive sociology, especially ethnomethodology, appears as esoteric and impenetrable, this is only in comparison with those forms of sociology which fail to question the fundamental basis of their own knowledge. Interpretive sociology is no more esoteric nor difficult than any other branch of science but it does offer a particular challenge and potential to anyone concerned with the renaissance of the sociology of law. In order to realize this potential it is necessary to spell out with reference to concrete research just where interpretive sociology departs from conventional forms of analysis prevelant within the sociology of law. Given the absence of interpretive studies within the sub-discipline we will spell out the features of two empirical pieces of research which can stand as examples of what interpretive analysis looks like in practice. The chosen works are provided by David Sudnow and Don Zimmerman.

David Sudnow[22] has provided an eloquent and unassuming study of the social organization of dying. The methodology (in a narrow sense) was as non-participant observer, and the analysis consisted of organizing extensive field notes and conversational notes. The study, both at the methodological and analytic levels, was backed by a perspective which says that 'the categories of hospital life are to be seen as *constituted by the practices of hospital personnel* as they engage in their daily routinized interactions within an organizational milieu'.[23] In other words death may be a natural state of an organism but it is equally the product of 'organizationally prescribed, practical decision-making'.[24] Recognition of this allows the study of such decision making to highlight the 'social character of these natural states'.[25] The aim of the study is to 'see death' as hospital personnel 'see' it—how the death is 'recognised, named and treated in the organization of the medical staff'.[26] Emphasis is on the procedures utilized to recognise death and to construct institutionalized courses of action on its recognition. Sudnow is adamant that concern is not to be had with, *inter alia*, the effect of death (or even the procedures of recognizing death) on group structure or some other sociological peg, but with the study of death from the perspective of the medical personnel involved, the perspective which gives to death states their socially organized character—'death', Sudnow suggests, can be analysed as a 'procedurally conceived matter'.[27]

Throughout the study, both in methodology and analysis, Sudnow is concerned with the methodic character of routine activities. He is not, qua sociologist, interested in death as such nor with death as a feature of someone's biography with, say, economic and psychological effects on others. He is not interested in death, qua sociologist as a 'problem', something calamitous and something for which social resources have to be set aside. He is concerned with the social character of the medical state as a sociological problem. It is a problem of understanding how social actors construct social action in terms of their own common and specialized knowledge which they take for granted for the purpose of conducting their routine action. The level of analysis is provided by an understanding of the properties of social action provided by interpretive sociology and the level of methodology ensured that the research had such close contact with reality that it would not be co-opted *a priori* by that understanding.

By changing a few key words in the introduction to Sudnow's text we might presume that if attention were turned to law the argument would be as follows: the law has been a topic of academic consideration among anthropologists, sociologists, jurisprudes and men-of-the-law, yet its study as a social phenomenon has been neglected. The taxonomies of jurisprudence, the casework principles of men-of-the-law, anthropological accounts of dispute settlement and the impact of legislation, and of legal needs, all leave the social character of legal states and activities unexamined. The notion of law is treated perfunctorily in terms of its social character and social availability for guiding and grounding action. There has been little work on law as a social phenomenon and nowhere is the social production of legal activity treated. Interpretive sociology would treat legal states and legal activity as constituted by socially organized actions and procedures. The sociological structure of such procedures and the practices of members in making their conduct discernible as legal, rational and coherent can delineate the social components of the phenomena in question.

Zimmerman's[28] study of social-welfare agencies can serve as a further indication of how interpretive sociology draws inferences regarding social action. Differentiating his study from the usual topics within the sociology of organizations concerning such things as, for instance, 'how adequately the formal programme of the organization and the structural arrangements whereby it is implemented provide for "rational" goal accomplishment',[29] Zimmerman sets out his own concern to investigate 'the variety of practices and mundane considerations involved in determinations of the operational meaning and situational relevance of policies and procedures for ongoing, everyday organizational activities'.[30] Further, concern is not had with the distinctions often alluded to in studies of organizations between formal and informal rules; functional and dysfunctional departures from the formal plan; and the like. Rather, the purpose is to see 'how the formal plan of an organization is used by the organization's members to deal with everyday work activities'.[31]

Thus conceived, the problem becomes one of studying how organizational members such as social workers handle routine inquiries and problems in a manner which allow them to reconcile such action with the operational intent of the plan. The implication is that the operational intent of policies and procedures can only be studied whilst studying the everyday commonsense judgements of organizational members concerning the relation of possible courses of action to such policies or procedures. The practical circumstances routinely met by organizational members 'may in fact be consulted by members in order to decide . . . what the formal plan might reasonably be taken to mean and "what it would take" to implement it in the first place . . .'[32] Rather than take rules or the meaning of rules for granted, sociology must be able to specify how rules are given meaning during routine activity (for example, to guide, to account for, or to justify action). As Zimmerman says, the relationship of rules (that is formal rules or 'idealizations') to conduct is to be found by 'investigating the features of the circumstances in which they are deemed relevant and used by members'.[33]

Zimmerman is then concerned with rules, but rather than using the notion of rules to explain social action (that is, 'they did X because of the rule Y') he is concerned with *rule use*. He examines how members of the department used rule Y in constructing line of action X. Further, the reference to rules is the *subjects'* reference, their method of accounting for action, thereby making out their activities as orderly in some fashion. The ability to satisfy others that action X is sanctioned by rule Y is seen to be a necessary step in the formation of that line of action.

We can use an incident taken from Zimmerman's work to display these concerns. The incident referred to the observation that documentary evidence was necessary before certain organizational actions were initiated. For instance, counter clerks required birth certificates, neither the spoken word nor a piece of paper on which was written the date of birth being sufficient for determining say, elegibility for welfare benefits. In other words, 'not just any piece of paper will do for establishing the objective and factual grounds for administrative action'.[34] Zimmerman's purpose became to investigate, *inter alia, how* such records achieve their authority; the procedures utilized to display such an idea of authority; and *how* a 'fact' is established for the purposes of such procedures. In other words he protrayed the processes involved in the use of documentary evidence; the social action behind the production of a 'fact'.

According to Zimmerman, the setting in which the counter clerks operated was characterized by 'the routine collection, production and use of records, and . . . by the way in which the factuality, objectivity and impersonality of the information contained in those records is an everyday practical concern, and an everyday practical accomplishment'.[35] In this setting 'bureaucratic records come to arbitrate and finally establish matters of fact'. Departmental personnel 'simply treat a variety of documents as records of "plain fact" for all organizational purposes'.[36] Further, on occasion, such personnel engage in the 'construction of accounts of *how* a document is to be honoured as reporting "plain fact" '.[37] Since such grounds are constructed and have to be made observable by counter clerks, they are necessary data for an understanding of the accomplishment of 'plain fact' for organizational purposes. As Zimmerman points out, an observer would not necessarily be able to *see* the pertinence of documentary evidence simply by observing counter clerks at work. As a typical work feature, the gaining of documentary evidence could serve several hypothetical purposes, for instance the relief of boredom or getting away from the counter.

Zimmerman's methodological stance, therefore, had to be able to locate the sociological structure of documentation in the process of welfare distribution by recording counter clerks' discussions in 'natural talk settings' (e.g. discussing of cases over morning coffee) and by noting those features of documentary evidence attended to in the accounts generated by the clerks for organizational purposes. With regard to these areas of data acquisition Zimmerman concluded that 'the authority of various documents is made accountable in terms of the routine, organized ways in which these unremarkable projects are geared to one another under the asupices of typified, generally known interests or motives'.[38] But just because a document has these features is not itself sufficient data from which an observer could decide the status of the document. The status of documents is not to be decided 'independently of their occurrence as features of an account delivered on some occasion of work in the setting'.[39] Here then we have a clear account of the close nexus between the analytic level being adopted and the methodological stance necessary to carry it into operation.

Significantly, Zimmerman was dealing with personnel involved in the implementation of statute law, and yet the work bears no real resemblance to the majority of legislative studies discussed or mentioned in Chapter IV. There appear, however, to be two distinct reasons why this is the case. First, Zimmerman's study investigates rather than hides from view the complex features of social action included in the implementation of law. It is then less problematic as a piece of empirical work than these studies which seek to relate 'intent' to 'effect' or to highlight the impact of law on organizational structure without investigating the features of actions which produce 'effects' or 'accomplish structure'. Secondly, Zimmerman works within the topic range supplied by situational ethnomethodology and although that was the reason we chose to give an exposition of his work, it is not the case that all and every study in the sociology of legislation undertaken from an interpretive stance will necessarily follow such topic choice. The sociology of legislation undertaken by Carson[40] displayed a marked awareness of the strictures of interpretive sociology and yet succeeded in developing work with no obvious resemblance to that of Zimmerman. We would argue, however, that Carson's work has a strong affinity to the study of counter clerks just offered and we can display this affinity quite briefly.

When Carson analysed the implementation of the 1961 Factories Act, he had various alternative structures of analysis open for use. For example, there were the structures of the criminological literature on 'white-collar crime' or of the legal work on strict liability. But Carson chose to rely on the 'logic in use' of the Inspectorate to organize and guide the research. As a direct result of choosing as his analytic level that of the Inspectorate's social action, Carson was able to proceed with the analysis of implementation by looking to how the Inspectorate 'made sense of their own decisions at the time'. We can say that whereas Zimmerman would have as his subject-matter (the

level reached by the methodology) 'social action' and as his topic
'features of social action', Carson had 'social action' as subject-matter
but a topic selection more reminiscent of conventional sociology of
law, i.e. 'implementation'. Whereas Zimmerman would have
analysed in detail how it was that the Factory Inspectorate accomplished certain decisions and the status of the assumptions and commonsense knowledge which constituted the procedures to be utililized
in making decisions, Carson utilized the Inspectorate's perspective to
inform him as to the process of implementation. The difference is
clear but so also is the similarity. The latter comes out most clearly if
we look to Carson's method.

As Carson was committed to a resolute empirical approach, his
analysis was only capable of being carried out by close contact with
the everyday work performance of the Inspectorate. And as we have
seen from Zimmerman's work, simple observation is not sufficient to
lay bare the operative structure of work performance. Having
rejected participant observation because of the exigencies of the
research situation, Carson utilized as the prime source of data the
documentary evidence provided by the Inspectorate as an integral
part of their work performance. Parallelling work activity, the
Inspectorate routinely produced a documentation of that activity
which provided direct evidence of the significance of features of situations to the Inspectorate. It is important to note that the documentary evidence is used only for this purpose by Carson. It is not a case
of the Inspectorate doing the research themselves; the documents are
not accepted as a faithful rendition of work performance nor for an
observers' assessment of the success or rationality of the work performance. They simply allow one to understand the action of Inspectors
with regard to those features they saw to be significant, so that the
researcher gains access to the assumptions and types of knowledges
utilized in the work performance. It was a procedure more successful
than the reliance on questionnaires employed in Smith and Pearson's
study of strict liability.[41]

The latter study had used questionnaires and had concluded, *inter
alia*, that an emphasis on previous warnings was a means of overcoming problems of proof in court. Carson was able to show by his
method that the emphasis was in no way so limited. Previous warnings were, first, a separate and identifiable method of enforcement
built upon the Inspectorate's own understandings of the job at hand
and the exigencies surrounding compliance, and, secondly, far from
being concerned with proving the *actus reus* in court settings, served to

limit the cases taken to court to those in which a strong and demonstrable element of *mens rea* was present. The questionnaire of Smith
and Pearson was shown to be a faulty vehicle for investigating social
action; the properties of social action had to be studied in order to
build a sociological analysis and a particular methodology was
required to put this analysis into operation.

Even when looking at historical material on the nineteenth-century
factory legislation, Carson still maintained contact with the subject-
matter of social action. Documentary evidence again was used but
again with a specific purpose which forwarded the chosen level of
analysis. The documentary evidence was not used as an 'objective'
picture of history with which to interpret the significance of past acts
and events nor from which to infer a determinate historical or functional process, but as data from which to analyse how certain people's
concepts of social developments and self-motivations were implicated
in their own construction of history.

By reference to the types of work indicated above we can, while
appreciating the evident differences between them, illustrate the
points at which analyses informed by an interpretive perspective differ from those offered by the majority of work currently available in
the sociology of law. The points can be arranged under certain headings: subject-matter and topics of inquiry; methodology; analysis and
conceptualization; and theory and explanation.

Subject-matter and Topics of Inquiry

The main distinction drawn by differentiating between subject-
matter and topic of inquiry is between that with which our methods
make contact (and which may hold methodological imperatives) and
a convenient depiction of the particular section of the social universe
to which research aims to pay attention. The continued emphasis we
give to subject-matter parallels the discussion in Chapter I concerning
the unification of sociology as a social science of social action. We
have to distinguish, however, between social action as the subject of
interpretive sociology, and particular topics researched by interp-
pretive sociology such as 'death'; 'counter clerks'; and 'legislation'.
Further we have indicated above that even within 'interpretive'
analyses, topics can be handled very differently. Zimmerman studied
counter clerks not only in a way which recognized social action as the
base unit but in a way which really kept social action as the actual
topic of analysis itself. With Carson this was not the case; social action
was subject but took a back seat to the topic of implementation of

legislation. Despite this difference the distinction still holds for the purposes of exposition. Let us reiterate the importance of subject-matter and its identity.

First, we have accepted that within general sociology there is an acceptance that the science studies a unified subject-matter—the study of social action not only defines sociology but defines it as an empirical science.

Secondly, assertion that social action is studied is not enough. We have to demonstrate that our methods do in fact reach this level.

Thirdly, given the nature of science, knowledge of a subject-matter is never complete and each piece of research should not only be guided by prior knowledge but must be aware of the danger of accepting *a priori* assumptions about the subject and be able to defeat such assumptions thereby advancing the science. This we have called the dialectic.

Fourthly, the above points are predicated on an awareness that the actual subject-matter approached will relate to the methods chosen and we must not let our methods be the master and dictate what our subject is to be.

Fifthly, interpretive sociology has criticized conventional analyses for accepting too complacently normative conceptions of social action; that these conceptions are the result of closed theoretical edifices; and that these edifices are contradicted by empirical work alive to the features displayed through interpretive analyses of actual research settings.

Within the sociology of law one finds a reluctance to face the importance of the subject-matter being studied but we have endeavoured to depict the levels at which the various methods used have been directed. In other words we have tried to depict the subject-matter even if that has been attained by default rather than by persistent effort. Within the area of 'law and society' studies we have discussed the subject-matter as being either 'law' or a sociological concept of 'law as norm'. Durkheim also based his sociology on a base unit of norm, similarly taken to be unproblematic. Weber claimed to have social action as his subject-matter and such was the definitive referent of his science of sociology. He did, however, use normative conceptions in his ideas of social action from which he drew his definition of law. But none the less, Weber's normative conception of action was the *ideal actor's* own ideal conception rather than an observers' construct; social action remained the level at which methods were directed, and the concept of law was built up directly from his idea of action. These aspects of Weber's work are reflected in the structure of Carson's research on legislation. Both Weber and Carson addressed social action but both did so only to the extent necessary to further investigation of a major topic concern.

Apart from Carson's work, and certain 'legal actors'' studies which treat the 'social' as complex, analyses in the area of 'law and society' do not usually address subject-matter as a problem at all. It remains an uncontrolled consequence of a method research, such as attitude scales; questionnaires; etc.

The significant feature of general interpretive sociology is its denunciation of research which in its approach to particular topics fails to implement the Weberian concern with social action as a unifying theme. For interpretive sociology, the topic is either features of social action itself—the setting of research being largely gratuitous (Zimmerman)—or is chosen for interest but treated with due regard to the nature of social action (Carson). The methodological problems of investigating the topic of law flow from an appreciation of the centrality of social action.

Conventionally within the sub-discipline topic selection is either based on a problem in an existing theory (Bredemeier) or is chosen for interest ('relevance' topics). Whereas for interpretive sociology, social action is always an operative consideration, topic selection within contemporary sociology of law is usually treated as being the prime problem in itself and as posing the prime methodological barriers. The barriers are a series of pragmatic decisions: how do I gain access to the setting; should I use a long or short questionnaire; how can I make my research theoretically significant? Once a method has been chosen and refined, it is treated as a neutral vehicle for collecting data on the topic. The extent to which the topic is conceptualised independently of the properties of social action is the extent to which research within the sub-discipline is divorced from sociology. Carson did not conceptualise the topic of his research in this independent manner (the study of implementation was the study of how the Inspectorate made sense of their own decisions at the time) but that has been the fate of most studies. Finally we might say that interpretive sociology is not unaware of the pragmatic problems of research; it is not an approach immune from such difficulties. It is just that their solution is not sufficient for the pursuit of empirically grounded sociology.

Methodology

It is undoubtedly the case that within the sociology of law various research programmes have succeeded to differing extents in resolving the traditional methodological pitfalls of bias, error and so forth. But we have also indicated that there is more to a method than the employment of techniques to reduce or hold constant external defects. Similarly, research varies with regard to its internal consistency, but again discussions earlier in this chapter showed that such do not constitute an adequate resolution of the problem of methods. Our concern is that methodologies, albeit well used, determine the subject-matter of study.

Phillipson has provided a documentation of the way various research methods (e.g. panel studies; opinion polling; statistical collation) imply a conception of a social actor as an 'object controlled by external forces' and as 'a passive carrier of attributes'.[43] In the face of such methods, social action becomes the result of forces or attributes rather than a meaningful accomplishment. But this idea of action (that it is so controlled) is not a 'finding' but is implied in and is a result of the methodological stance. The methods imply this conception and they never reach the level of social action sufficiently to find out whether they are correct. Within the sociology of law one can find such stances taken as indicative of 'good research practice'. We can use the example of the questionnaire as used in knowledge and opinion of law studies. The subject-matter of the chosen methodology becomes by default 'responses to questions'. No indication is given at all of the utility of 'opinions' as a building block for sociology nor of the assumptions made concerning the relationship between a static, objective concept of an 'opinion' and the construction of patterns of regular action represented by the legal system. Blumer has made the point with regard to opinion polling generally. As he says, 'the findings resulting from an operation or use of an instrument are regarded as contributing the object of study. The operation ceases to be a guided procedure on behalf of an object of inquiry; instead the operation determines intrinsically its own objective.'[44]

Interpretive sociology rejects such methods because of their determining effect on subject-matter and inherent assumptions concerning social action. It has to adopt methodological stances which enable it to use research situations to obtain knowledge of the features of social action and the operating processes of social action which produce the phenomena identified as a topic of inquiry. To an extent an emphasis on the features of social action (invariant properties) marks an ethnomethodological orientation and an emphasis on processes of social action marks a symbolic interactionist orientation. It is, however, with their common emphases on social action that we have been most concerned.

ANALYSIS AND CONCEPTUALIZATION

We have spent considerable time delineating aspects of analysis and conceptualization in earlier chapters and it should now be clear how inextricably linked each is with the question of subject-matter and methodology. At this juncture we wish only to make some simple distinctions between the major perspectives of sociology and to stress that great circumspection is required when deciding exactly what 'analysis' means and, having decided that, when using concepts during analysis.

If we cloak together behaviourist, positivist and functionalist sociology, we can say that they use analysis to disprove or support substantive assertions thrown up by theory or meta-theory, or to generate assertions through the use of meta-theory. Distinctions in the form taken by analysis become apparent if we utilize the dichotomy drawn in the last chapter between substantive theory and meta-theory. As an example of the former we have Parsonian functionalism and when using the substantive theory of Parsons, analysis becomes the focusing of general propositions onto patterns of social life. Data are identified through the theory as in the analysis by Bredemeier of 'law as an integrative mechanism'. This 'analysis' brought an area of social life more fully within the Parsonian theoretical edifice. Compare to this the situation when a meta-theory such as behaviourism is brought to bear directly onto research. Here, 'analysis' has a different character. The way in which behaviourism construes the world requires the identification of 'entities' which are discrete and measurable. These entities are discovered as data by a chosen method such as the questionnaire, and then the data are analysed by statistical techniques designed to allow cross-tabulation and the identification of correlations. 'Analysis', then, highlights relationships (statistically based) between entities aping the form of scientific 'laws'. In distinguishing between substantive functionalism and meta-theory behaviourism, we can say that in the former 'analysis' is the interpretation of social life through the theory, whereas for the latter 'analysis' is the subjection of collected data to statistical techniques.

The break with interpretive sociology is established if we recognise that analysis here is analysis of social life seen as comprising social action. Interpretive sociology, by definition, accepts that the subject-matter of sociology is social action and, further, that the task of sociology is to analyse social action as such and not to translate social action into the language of a social theory, nor to encapsulate such action in the discrete entities required by numerically based categories. 'Analysis' ceases to be an arcane sociological step in the sociologist's attempt to understand how social action is conducted; what social actors are doing; and what types of activity, forms of reasoning and so on constitute a particular area of the social world. We have drawn the boundaries of interpretive sociology sufficiently wide to contain both Carson and Zimmerman. In each author's work we can see a concern to analyse precisely what it is that, say, factory inspectors and counter clerks do rather than to look at their activity through functionalist spectacles or via statistical techniques.

The break between conventional and interpretive sociology is visible also within the process of conceptualization. In conventional work, conceptualization serves the purpose of solving certain logistic problems inhering within particular varieties of research, for instance problems of operationalization or problems of gearing a social theory into the social world it claims to encapsulate. For behaviourism, for example, concepts are dominated by topic selection. Ask the question 'Can disparities in lawyers' victories be traced to lawyers' characteristics?' and the necessary concepts are contained within the question. A concept of 'victory' is required and must be operationalized to permit quantification—for that is the basis of the behaviourist method. So too must the characteristics be identified and made fit for the behaviourist research act. We saw in the last chapter that this mode of research was capable of missing or misconstructing anything significant about, or particular to, the judicial process. Concepts within functionalism are similarly removed from social action. The pincer movement in the development of functionalism closed off social action from scrutiny and concepts remain the only means of identifying those segments of social life that are to be held within particular parts of the social theory. These characteristics of concepts are important, because in any form of sociology, analysis is dependent upon conceptualization. But it is the fate of conventional sociology that its concepts are parasitic on assumptions located in theories or methods of research that are removed from and have no contact with social action.

For interpretive sociology, in contrast, concepts either derive from the categories of action performed by social actors (Carsons's 'moral fault') or reflect features of that action so performed (Zimmermans' 'fact as practical accomplishment'). In both cases concepts derive from and are inextricably linked with social action. From this follows two points. First concepts are generated directly from subjective, meaningful behaviour, and so can, and should, make no claims to contribute to objective, scientific laws of behaviour. Secondly, being derivative of action they neither can nor should be regarded as potential explanations of that action. The inevitable tautology is as clear in this case as is the source of concepts. It is when the source is cloaked that the tautology may escape notice.

Theory and Explanation

In Chapter One we detailed the variable treatment offered of theory within sociology and pursued certain arguments concerning the relationship between theory and explanation. More focused comments were made with regard to substantive research in Chapter Four. We can now see that the major perspectives within sociology have themselves a variable relationship to these issues. We will here only indicate the major configurations and will utilize the distinction between meta-theory and substantive theory given in Chapter Four.

Behaviourism, functionalism and interpretive sociology all contain more or less explicitly formulated meta-theory. The meta-theory of behaviourism is one of stimulus-response; it explains by formulating 'laws' and gives primacy to analysis by 'cause'. The meta-theory of functionalism explains teleologically, primacy being given to analysis by 'functions'. In these two instances we can say that the meta-theories work *directly* on research. By this we mean that the assumptions built into the meta-theories regarding social action are personified and acted out on the stage of the real world. For instance, behaviourism has to use methods which allow for the language of stimulus-response and the generation of 'laws'; these methods, the tools of inquiry into the real world, are but the reflection of social actors seen as mechanical responses to internal and external determining conditions. With functionalism, in the meta-theoretic guise of 'voluntarism', we saw in Chapter Three that social action is equally castrated, voluntarism merely attributing to social actors an ability subjectively to recognise which response is appropriate to which determining conditions.

This aspect of the meta-theory of functionalism we saw as significant in the development of functionalism's substantive social theory; it made easier the pincer movement which defeated claims to subjectivity. It is the substantive theory of Parsonian functionalism which provides the example of meta-theory working 'indirectly' on research. The meta-theory works indirectly because it becomes subsumed within the pattern variables which imprison the social actor and his unit acts—the meta-theory operates but is closed to scrutiny.

Interpretive sociology, like behaviourism, always works directly from a meta-theory into research. We have, then, in particular to distinguish it from behaviourism if we are wanting to pursue interpretive research to the exclusion of positivism. Two distinct points need to be borne in mind.

First, working directly with a meta-theory allows us to test the postulates of the meta-theory against the subjective world. 'Allows', note, does not mean 'automatically allows', and the extent to which it is achieved is the extent to which the meta-theory is capable of generating research with the dialectical relationship to sociology indicated in Chapter One. Interpretive sociology lays claim to, or we have made claims on its behalf to, such a facility. The claim is based on the character of its meta-theory; the meta-theory necessitates that research address the nature and features of social action—indeed the meta-theory is no more than stipulations concerning how this can be achieved. A further characteristic of the meta-theory is that it allows any research undertaking to deny the assumptions concerning social action that inhere within the meta-theory. How is this done? As an idea, the answer is quite simple. Interpretive sociology neither works indirectly via a substantive theory which involves a substantive classification of the social world, nor by a meta-theory which involves the scientific classification of that world; it needs neither substantive boxes nor discrete categories in which to put the world. Its aim is not to create a sociological world but to understand the social world as it is.

The demarcation from behaviourism is clear. Behaviourism explains by 'laws' which require discrete categories; interpretive sociology explains by showing the interconnectedness of social phenomena and the forms of social processes, reasonings and knowledges used by people to establish social phenomena and act in regard to them. The method of explanation operates on exactly the same level as the meta-theory; the intelligibility of the meta-theory is always on trial in a manner which behaviourist research could never emulate. For completeness sake we can also say that the demarcation from functionalist substantive theory is equally clear. The inability of the latter to engage in dialectical research, we have already documented.

As an idea, the above differences are, we think, intelligible. Interpretive sociology does not theorize about and explain objective phenomena but seeks to show how the people it studied create phenomena —phenomena which may themselves be perceived *as* objective.

Secondly, we have to bear in mind that although all perspectives presently available within sociology have more or less explicitly formulated meta-theories, this allows important divergencies in the extent to which such meta-theories *are* explicit and formulated. Here we can usefully compare interpretive sociology and behaviourism. Behaviourism's meta-theory is less explicit and less formulated than most. We have seen Nagel's embarrassing attempt to specify behaviourism in operation and saw clearly that despite all scientific pretensions the main feed for research remained the researcher's own common sense. The meta-theory does not provide for research. Interpretive sociology operates a clearly formulated and explicit meta-theory encompassed by its specifications and stipulations concerning how to research the properties of courses of social action.

In conclusion it is possible to use the appreciation of the differential development of explicit meta-theory between behaviourism and interpretive sociology to underpin our previous assertion that the two perspectives, though both operating from meta-theories, diverged in the character and place of 'analysis'. Behaviourism not only demands a translation of observations into categories and laws, an analytic step, but it further requires an augmentation to its meta-theory because the meta-theory is largely an illusion. Analysis becomes the injection of inexplicated common sense as a resource in the research act. Interpretive sociology seeks, not always successfully, to implement its meta-theory, which in itself holds directions for excluding common-sense theorizing. The researcher is specifically required to bracket away his sense of the common properties of situations and actions in order to engage in analysis, analysis here being the methodic approach to common sense as topic, not resource. The bridge between behaviourism and interpretive research is broken, then, at the most significant level, that of meta-theory itself.

CHAPTER VI

Law in the
Presence of Sociology

It was our concern in the previous chapter to display the reasons why contemporary sociology of law treats the social nature of law as inherently unproblematic. The reason lay primarily in that the conventional approaches to sociology adopted by the sub-discipline, sociology in the presence of legal phenomena, treated such phenomena as factual and as 'obvious'. The concrete entity of law was established as a point of departure for, rather than as an aspect of, sociological inquiry. The alternative sociology, interpretive sociology, was seen as capable of treating the sociology of law as the study of social action with a legal referent and of raising as a sociological problem the relationship of social action to the 'obvious' facticity of law. The strength of this approach lies in the commitment to the study of social action as a force capable of focusing the fragmented state of the present literature. The requirement for advancement was seen as the need to achieve a working conception of legal phenomena suited to the study of social action.

That the sub-discipline has for so long taken its nomenclature for granted is evidenced by the prevalence of normative conceptions available in the literature and justified by reference to normative sociology. Such conceptions have had a dual role which we need to look at briefly in order to build up an alternative. First, they imply that social action is methodologically subservient to normative phenomena; in other words social action is normatively regulated—norms explain action rather than vice versa. Secondly, such normative phenomena are themselves unproblematic, existing as factual entities to be used as a tool of analysis. Of all such factual entities, law is given as a prime example and normative conceptions enter into existing forms of work in a manner which excludes analysis from investigating the facticity of law. Not surprisingly the manner in which normative conceptions are implicated in making law unproblematic will differ from writer to writer and so we deal separately with the most significant examples.

(a) *Weber:*[1] Weber defined sociology as the interpretive understanding of subjectively meaningful behaviour or social action. To engage in this form of analysis Weber utilized the method of 'ideal types'. Ideal types allowed an understanding of the meaningful relationship between phenomena (required by the character of the social world) to be subsumed under general rules (required for a causally adequate explanation). We need to ascertain whether or not Weber achieved this level of sophistication at the cost of hiding problems of normative regulation inside his definition of the base unit of social action.

Talcott Parsons discerned a normative thrust in Weber's work. As he argues, 'it is inherent in the frame of reference of "action" which is basic to Weber's whole methodology, that it is normatively oriented'.[2] Here Parsons refers to Weber's concept of action in which a social actor constructs behaviour in terms of expectations held of how others will act either towards himself or to some social artifact. It is clear that Weber is not intending to explain action by reference to a norm, but the level of explanation which he does achieve is dependent on a base unit which is 'normatively oriented'. In Weber, this normative orientation is always an ideal actor's own ideal orientation rather than being inferred from the properties of a social system of behaviour, but being shielded from study as an implicit factor in the definition of social action, the status of norms as a sociological concept is not opened to scrutiny. It is here that we located the reason why Weber did not act as a catalyst for interpretive analyses in the sociology of law. Weber had identified law in terms of a particular orientation of social action and normative conceptions are, therefore, implicated in the concept of law.

(b) *Durkheim:*[3] The operation of a normative structure is strongly evinced in the work of Durkheim. The normative structure supports and sustains social life. Norms are external to and constraining on social actors and stand in relation to social action as cause to effect. Law is the most significant normative structure for the purposes of sociological analysis. It stands as an unproblematic body of rules external to the individuals and corresponding to the form of solidarity displayed by society. Law is a social fact; and its factual character is for Durkheim sociologically unproblematic.

(c) *Renner:* [4] If we turn to Renner it is clear that a break is made with conventional depictions of normative regulation and it is equally clear that the dominant conception of law is not an adaptation of the normative ideas of sociology. Renner, however, does give law to us as a 'crystallized form' of objective content and therefore perpetuates a style of legal conceptualization remarkably similar to those displayed by Durkheim. Although Renner locates the engine-room of societal change in a Marxist analysis, his insistence that sociology refrain from defining law leads him to the unacceptable position that law is external to the action of individuals . . . 'the notions of the individual are removed from the control of his floating psychology and are made permanent'.[5] Our concern is that such a view legislates away the right of sociology to treat the social nature of law in terms of an intersubjective construction and affirmation of meaning. Rendered impotent sociology may use notions of norms as representing stable and fixed social entities without in fact inquiring into the legitimacy of conceiving norms (including law) as being such stable and fixed entities.

(d) *Parsons and Bredemeier:* [6] In the work on law of Parsons and Bredemeier we see the operation of a picture of the social world as an homeostatic system, the component parts of which are explicable in terms of their functional relationship to the whole. The constituent parts of the resulting order involve conceptions of norms, roles, role-sets, role-expectations, role-performance and the like. The individual social actor, as the intermediary necessary to the functioning of law as an integrative mechanism, is involved in action which is normatively regulated. The individual himself is expendable; indeed the expendability of the individual becomes a system need. Once expendable, the individual is denied potency to talk back to the theory; we are left only with the theory's own component parts, and, such being derived from the theory, they are unlikely to deny it. Having established norms as immune from study, as concrete building blocks of society, norms are further used to underline the operative conception of law. Two features of functionalism, therefore, give cause for concern. First, it offers a model of normative regulation in which norms explain social patterns without themselves being established as a topic of inquiry and secondly, it makes use of normative conceptions in depicting the character of law.

(e) *Chambliss and Seidman:* [7] Although standing at the opposite end of one sociological continuum from the functionalists, Chambliss and

Seidman define their object of study (law) via the use of base sociological concepts of role; role-expectation; norm; and sanction. Again the character of law is set *a priori* in terms of normative conceptions, regarded as mere tools of analysis and therefore immune from question.

The above writers display an attitude towards law which seems in part at least related to prevailing normative conceptions. We can, however, add that the introduction of such conceptions is done with a conscious determination that norms are a fitting component of sociological analysis. While we may disagree that the conept of norm has such an aptitude, at least the above writers make it relatively easy to identify the points at which norms and normative conceptions are being used and to subject such use to scrutiny.

If we are not to be complacent with regard to the adequacy of sociology's understanding of norms and normative conceptions, then such scrutiny is necessary. Unfortunately there is a pernicious development in contemporary sociology of law which not only takes law for granted but which makes it difficult to identify the point at which law is rendered unproblematic. We can hazard that in those works which flirt with functionalism, the facticity of law is related to the functionalist's normative apparatus. In the studies of the profession which remain unobscured by functionalism, in the studies of legislation which endeavour to follow an intent-distortion or an impact model, and in studies of legal services, treating law as unproblematic seems tied to the types of statements such studies seek to make. The sociology of the legal profession may need to pay as little attention to law as the sociology of doctors pays to medicine; legislative studies are predicated on a logic which excludes the pertinency of any investigation of the nature of law; legal services research is so encumbered by the gargantuan ideal of justice that to quibble about law may seem inopportune at least. With behaviourism, enough has already been said to show how the chosen methodology necessitates the compartmentalization of social life such as to render norms, justice, etc., non-problematic entities by way of operationalization.

Finally it must be added that many works which pass as sociology of law simply develop no operating conception of law and appear to disregard the possibility that such an eclectic approach to law may damage the value of their studies. Survey researchers administer instruments which are based on a certain view of social action, for example the unproblematic interpretation of stimuli (question) and interpretation of response (answer) and a normatively conceived notion of social life (for instance, the relation between behaviour in situations and the recognition of situations as being situations for which a particular behavioural response is called). No attempt, however, is made to see whether such assumptions are consistent with an operating conception of law, and survey researchers seem so negligent that the assumptions implicated in the structuring of their instruments act, by default, to generate a conception of law. By default the conception is one of law as objective, as factual, as able to be expressed and subsumed within the survey instrument. In other words law is taken for granted without any theoretic or methodological justification. This is particularly the case in knowledge and opinion studies. Not only do they take law and particular legal prescriptions for granted but they do so not with any conscious determination but with an unreflexive attitude to the difficulties of embodying law in questionnaire instruments. If anything can be said about such studies then it must be that they achieve consistency; sociology is taken for granted; social action is taken for granted; meaning is taken for granted. Why should we complain if law is equally taken for granted?

But we do complain simply because work which does take law for granted can gain a spurious justification for its position via an overriding consensus operating within sociology that norms and normative conceptions *are* unproblematic and *can* be taken for granted. This we cannot accept as anything but sociological blindness. No one denies law's normative character—its character as a body of rules established with the intent and in the expectation that people will orient their conduct in accordance with its provisions. This, however, is no more than our *commonsense* understanding of law and leaves open the question of how *sociology* may legitimately set questions with regard to the manner of existence of legal phenomena.

LAW AND NORMS

Law has itself been used as justification for normative conceptions of social order. The obvious facticity of 'legal regulation', with the elements of control and coercion, has been used to support a view of 'normative regulation'. From people orienting conduct to, and acting in terms of, a particular type of normative order (the law) a view of social life has been justified in terms of dispositions, expectations and sanctions prevailing within a society which itself is given the character of a normative order (the social system). In this view of social life, norms become part of the explanation of order or observed regularities, and the manner of existence of normative phenomena becomes excluded from sociological inquiry. To criticize this position we need, therefore, to (a) look to the meaning of 'norms' in conventional sociology; (b) indicate the use of norms by major perspectives; (c) consider the way norms are identified; and (d) outline the most sophisticated attempt to show that norms can be used in sociological explanation in such a way as to circumvent the problem of meaning.

Norms

Most obvious, before distinctions as to type are made, is the factual character of norms. Norms are external to individuals and constrain their action. As sanctioned ways of behaving in particular situations they explain the resultant action.

This facticity of norms is further evidenced by sociology's ability to refine the concept. We are seduced into believing in norms by the very concrete taxonomies developed in major introductory text books between 'set and received' norms; 'obligatory and permissive' norms; 'behavioural and attitudinal' norms; as well as by the efforts to identify the source of norms; to explain the existence of particular norms; and to trace the identification of norms through a further taxonomy of types of sanctions—restitutive; repressive—and of sanctioning agencies—self; primary group; reference group; society. Further, writers have found in 'norms' a conception amenable to the major perspectives on social order of behaviourism, conflict, theory and functionalism and, via reference group theory, interactionism.

Perspectives on Norms

Behaviourism: Being required to package social life into unproblematic constituents for the purpose of stimulus-response analysis, behaviourism is particularly susceptible to conceptions of normative phenomena. In behaviourism, as the term suggests, norms are evidenced in simple observation of regularities in social life. Placing such regularities into a concept of norm to be reintroduced in the explanation rarely succeeds in camouflaging the obvious circularity.

Functionalism: In functionalism, standards of proscribed and prescribed behaviour exist in terms of expectations and dispositions to act gained through childhood and adult socialization. Social order is explained in terms of cognitive consensus and social variance in terms of differential socialization. Norms themselves are explained in terms of system needs, and explanations of behaviour are therefore teleological in character, depending on norms whose existence serve overt or latent functions.

Conflict Theorists: The sociology of Chambliss and Seidman demonstrates the manner in which conflict theory is predicated on normative conceptions of social order. This is evidenced in the use Chambliss and Seidman make of role theory in determining the characteristics of law. Roles, in sociology, are identified in terms of the normative expectations to which a role player is subject. For Chambliss and Seidman, however, it is not system needs which explain particular norms, but the power dimensions in society which construct, legitimate and enforce a particular normative order.

Interactionism: The extent to which interactionism is open to simplification in terms of 'ego's perception of alter' and 'alter's perception of ego' is the extent to which it can embrace normative conceptions of order. In an introductory sociological text by Aubert we find a determined attempt to infuse interactionism with a view of normative regulation by analysing patterns of conduct in terms of ego's expectations of alter and vice versa. The construction of action is, therefore, normative. Here norms are explained in terms of their source either in family socialization or reference groups, but not at the higher levels achieved by conflict or functionalist grand theory.

It is worth remembering that role theory and reference-group theory have two major variants, one of which is open to such normative interpretation, the other one of which is openly critical of such interpretation.[8] To the extent to which the former is used to justify the use of normative conceptions in interactionism the result is to achieve more of the imagery of interaction than a hard reflection of its basic premises.

The Identification of Norms

We saw above how law is used to justify a reliance on norms in explaining behaviour and this is closely related to an ability to identify operating legal rules, either by reference to written codes or to the expertise of a recognisable professional body of lawyers. Identification of other variants of norms, however, is also required and in a manner which circumvents the problem of meaning. How then does sociology identify norms for the purpose of explanation? Let us have recourse to an oft-cited example: norms are identified by the operation of sanctions. When sanctions operate a norm has been broken. This then should allow us to relate particular norms to particular situations and further to inquire into the purpose of that norm—is the norm supportive of, and in turn supported by, a powerful interest in the situation, or rather is the norm required for the orderly character of the situation? Imagine a defendant in the dock swearing at the judge and, further, the judge rebuking the defendant and threatening his expulsion from the proceedings. A clear sanction. Now attempt to identify the operating norm without utilizing your own knowledge of the trial proceedings. In other words could a cultural alien identify the norm, for this is required for the identification to circumvent the problem of meaning.

Take a different example:[9] a student enters a seminar carrying a crocodile; the seminar leader (a) sends him out, or (b) laughs. Are sanctions operating in each case? And if sanctions operate in either case what norm has been breached? Our cultural alien will be in difficulties again. Is the crocodile relevant? Is the identification of the particular student relevant? Or the time or place? We, of course, would have no such difficulties because we can rely on our own understanding of the meaning of a seminar, but our common sense tells us more than this. It tells us that strict identification of something called a norm is impossible, spurious and indeed unnecessary for the purpose of regularity and order in social discourse. It tells us that seminar leader A could rebuke the student having addressed his behaviour as carrying the meaning to disrupt the seminar while seminar leader B could just laugh, addressing the incident as meaning a rag stunt and without the whole edifice of social networks crumbling in ruins. Any attempt to resurrect norms by limiting them to particular situational experiences (that is identifying the norm as 'students must not bring crocodiles into the situation of a seminar unless in furtherance of rag-week festivities') not only produces a norm which it is hard to endow with any concrete existence prior to the particular occasion, but also demonstrates the extent to which the identification of a norm is dependent on the observer's understanding of the meaning of the situation.

The factual character of norms becomes somewhat mythical when we examine the manner of their identification. Not only is such a 'norm' shown to be *situationally* dependent (rather than concrete and external) but its manner of existence is further shown to be one of construction in, rather than determinant of, social action.

Further, any attempt to support a general norm of 'non-disruption of seminars', say, by referring back to a sub-system of values, is equally problematic. If norms are identified in terms of values around which a consensus exists, 'values' produce as many problems with regard to their own identification as do their normative auxilliaries. And, returning to the trial example, we would argue that it is no more possible to posit an external and constraining normative framework of law, legal procedures or the ability of the judge to invoke sanctions.

NORMATIVE SOCIOLOGY AND THE CIRCUMVENTION OF MEANING

We have already seen that interpretive sociology asserts that 'meanings' are not fixed and pre-given but are somehow accomplished and situational. How does such an idea tie in with social regularity and order? It could be argued that if meaning is always problematic, society would not possess features of stability and would only have a precarious existence. In fact, it would have no existence separate from its construction and affirmation during causes of social action. Does it follow that the existence of social regularity refutes interpretive sociology's emphasis on meaning? We can best illustrate how interpretive sociology handles social regularity by reference to two examples.

(i) It is clear that in certain situations 'meaning' is unproblematic for the participants; they know what is going on. Interpretive sociology might analyse such situations in terms of what the parties take for granted about the occasion. The orderly character of the occasion is related to the existence of trans-situational features which parties take for granted as operating. These are not necessarily made explicit, in other words no reference is made to them. To the cultural alien the situation may be meaningless just as we might be unable to interpret a line of discourse if we did not know the frame of reference on which it was predicated. To understand such situations, or such discourse, it is necessary to see the meaning of that action or discourse in terms of the background features taken for granted by the parties. 'Indexicality' has been used to refer to this dependence of meaning on trans-situational features which are implicit and reaffirmed in courses of action.

(ii) In some situations it may be that participants have no clear idea of what they are allowed to rely upon as indexing the meaning of the evolving course of action. Such may be the case for instance at the time immediately prior to the arrest of an innocent party. In such a situation the party is likely to use such things as police attitudes or the tenor of remarks made, to try and make sense of what is going on. Such a use of what are called 'indexical features' has been referred to as 'documentary interpretation'. Wilson says that such interpretation 'consists in identifying an underlying pattern behind a series of appearances such that each appearance is seen as an expression of the underlying pattern. The underlying pattern is itself identified through the individual concrete appearances. The mutual determination of appearances and underlying pattern is referred to as indexicality.'[10]

Indexicality, though a complex notion, is in essence based on simple observations which we can usually recognize on internal reflection. Ethnomethodology in particular has been concerned to analyse how participants use indexical particulars or background expectations to sustain routine action, in other words, how shared meanings are possible. This is the relation between meaning and order in interpretive sociology. For conventional sociology to attack the ability of interpretive sociology to handle social order, it has to attack the concept of indexicality. Goldthorpe,[11] for instance, while not ignoring meaning (he is not saying 'meaning is irrelevant, look to the norms') tries to show that for some situations, meaning exists in a manner not dependent on indexicality. The key to the argument lies in a Popperian approach to trans-situational meanings. Goldthorpe argues that some areas of trans-situational meanings do depend for their analysis on indexicality but that in other areas trans-situational meanings exist as autonomous domains, independent of indexicality and individual states of consciousness, and lie within the area of 'objective content of thought'. Such meanings are independent of inter-subjective states. This is what 'objective' means in this context; it relates to the manner of existence of certain meanings. If law is shown to be of objective content, then its normative character would be established in a very factual manner and could be used as indicative of the equally factual character of other norm-systems within the hierarchy of habits, rules, norms, law.

If meaning can be circumvented in some situations such that we can speak of and identify the operative 'norms' then conventional sociology is particularly well suited to the study of such situations. The issue of the legitimacy of both normative and interpretive sociology, then, is an empirical issue to be decided in terms of the extent to which actors depend on indexical features to sustain social action and the extent to which they are 'programmed' by their culture.

248 *Sociological Inquiry and Legal Phenomena*

If that is the point then we can accept it. It only remains to investigate the manner of existence of norms. Are they constraining and objective or are they produced in interaction? This is the type of question interpretive sociology has demanded to be asked. If an action situation is being upheld by reference to indexical particulars this has a lot to say about whether we can conceptualize the situation as one dependent on a pre-existing normative structure independent of its affirmation in routine social settings. Goldthorpe, however, is saying that some situations can be so conceptualized. He suggests that there exist trans-situational meanings independent of inter-subjective states. In some areas, then, meaning is unproblematic.

We have to do two things to defeat this argument: (a) show that meanings only enter into the construction of lines of action to the extent that they exist in inter-subjective states; (b) show that they exist in inter-subjective states in a manner not well conceptualized by the idea of objective content—in other words, we have to show that such objectivity is only of achieved status constantly being reaffirmed in social action. Since Goldthorpe takes law as his prime example, we can use this to base discussion. With regard to law, Goldthorpe says:

(a) A law exists without anyone knowing it; it exists independent of anyone's mental state.

(b) A law exists 'as an intelligible even when it is in no one's mind. It is there to be . . . invoked and appealed to . . .'[12]

So a law may be a negotiated version of reality, but it is capable of existing independently of the actors who created it—a constructed social order it may be but such is not like a dream, it does not necessarily vanish 'once no longer represented in individuals' mental states'.[13]

We can begin by accepting in large measure these statements from Goldthorpe. Sociology certainly cannot deny the existence of a statute that has been long forgotten, nor could sociology deny to that statute legal validity so long as it meets the requirements of validity as accepted by the legal system. We can, however, ask the relevance of all this. What of the statute's *social* character? To the extent that sociology is concerned with people doing things, a law which no one knows about is unlikely to have a great effect in the social world. Once it is recognized (appealed to or invoked) then we can be concerned with who can invoke it and how they interpret and use it; but all these questions depend on at least some people being cognizant of the law and somehow establishing the meaning embodied in the law to construct a line of action or to foster some legal process.

Further, though we can accept the commonsense approach by which laymen are seen as facing laws whose content they do not determine, to adopt the layman's attitude is not particularly sociological. The legal profession sustains an interest in legal rules and manifests them in particular action settings. What the layman faces is not an independent realm of objective thought but the product of the social interaction and subjective processes of those competent personnel who play a major role in sustaining the social import and meaning of law.

Finally, it seems as if Goldthorpe is using a sleight of hand to make us believe that his comments on law as objective content somehow undermine interpretive sociology. Interpretive sociology is only saying that the manner of existence of such things as law and how they enter into courses of social action must become a topic of inquiry rather than being legislated out of existence. Rather than saying that social phenomena do not exist apart from how members perceive and account it, interpretive sociology says that social phenomena only attain a social character and only exist as a resource for social action in terms of such perceptions and accounts. The social world may not be only inter-subjective, but as a resource for action it is inter-subjectivity which has to be addressed.

Let us go back and reaffirm the importance of Goldthorpe's argument. He is trying to circumvent the problem of meaning in order to shore up a normative conception of social life and, since law can be taken as a normative order par excellence, a demonstration that the meaning of law is not of inter-subjective character could then base an argument that other such orders (habit, custom, rule, etc.) have an equivalent status in social life. Our argument so far is that the status of law in social life *is* inter-subjective and that meaning cannot be circumvented simply by adopting a layman's approach and showing a law to have an existence independent of his (your or mine) subjective state. We now have to show that the 'objectivity' of law is only of achieved status and has no existence independent of individual states of consciousness.

In a sense law is obviously objective; the layman cannot deny it and should he try an army of lawyers will (or may) prove him wrong, and in some countries an army of soldiers may do so even more effectively. Sociology need not take the layman's approach nor take the layman as its point of reference. If it does so it will achieve only a lay sociology and of that there is an abundance. But what does it look like to take an alternative approach? Let us try and create a concrete example.

We can begin with stability in case law. Case law has all the rudiments of objectivity, right down to recorded and legitimated pronouncements on 'the law'. Now it is clear that Goldthorpe is arguing more than that the law is objective because it is written down. He is saying that the meaning of that writing is of 'objective content'. If we stay at this level, however, we can easily see that there is nothing 'objective' about it. There is nothing objective about stability in case law. Such stability is achieved by competent personnel whose competence is assessed in terms of their conscious readiness to resist reinterpretation of 'fixed' case law. But case law is not fixed independent of such determination. A settled decision on the meaning of a word may be continually reaffirmed and thereby non-problematic for these competent personnel, but the nature of that reaffirmation remains a problematic for sociology. To make the example more concrete, take the specific example of the House of Lords declaring itself not bound by its own previous decisions. One day it is bound, the next it is not—by self-ordination. This conscious application of special competence demonstrates the contingent nature of the previous normative idealization. The previous rule had nothing objective about it except what was sustained in it by social action and could base only a legislative and not a sociological analysis of stability in case law.

It should be clear that we are not denying norms a factual, objective character simply because they can change.[14] Conventional depictions of norms could certainly accommodate to changes in the content of norm. What we are addressing is the question of how norms exist, be they stable or changing. We do not have to treat the notion of a norm as unintelligible to be able to question conventional depictions of how they can be said to exist and their relation to social action. The problem of conventional depictions is that the method of treating norms *decides* the question, rather than the question being left open for empirical analysis of norms as they do, or do not, operate in social life itself. Goldthorpe may well argue that changes in the content of norms says nothing of their factual existence. What we have tried to show, however, is the character of that factual existence (objectivity) as being established and sustained in social action. To use an 'objective' rule to explain earlier decisions might be to engage in legal analysis but that is the province of lawyers. For sociology, it illegitimately reifies the manner of existence of such rules and meaning. The lawyer is relying on his own common and professional sense, and such a reliance should be studied by sociology and not taken for granted and fed back into an 'objective' explanation. At the level of sociology, social action explains objectivity not vice versa.

Conventional treatments of norms and critics of interpretive sociology's emphasis on intersubjective states, have failed to shore up normative conceptions of social order. Law can no longer be used to underpin the normative character of social life and without such a base the weaknesses in the factual character of norms become all the more evident. Norms can no longer be used to underpin the orderly character of social life.

It appears that whether attention be given to norms per se or to the more sophisticated treatment of law in terms of 'objective content', we are brought back to a particular level of question—how do participants provide for shared meanings in the construction of routine lines of action?

To put the issue in context, we will first look at the situation of the trial, secondly discuss briefly depictions of the judge suggested by interpretive sociology and thirdly discuss the conception of normative phenomena lying behind such depictions. This will allow us to answer the final attempt of conventional sociology to resurrect normative analysis before proceeding with a discussion of our own work within the sociology of law.

As men in the world we are frequently confronted with situations in which one person can, by his control over objective resources, determine the life of others. One such situation is the trial. A judge is, to our common sense, in control of sufficient resources to constrain the defendant. The defendant can give meaning to the sentencing (for instance, reject the legitimacy of the court) but cannot escape the situation constructed by others. How, then, are we to analyse such a situation?

A conventional account may be given in terms of social control or power, and such terms may seem particularly relevant given that the trial process appears to our common sense as having an objectifying character. The defendant is in a sense objectified, at least to the extent that he is unable to act in the situation in a way which affects his own biography. If the defendant can be physically incarcerated, then this fact assumes enormous significance because it is such a dehumanizing act. If we can, however, relinquish our sympathies or prejudices, what does the trial process offer by way of promoting a sociological discussion? We can begin with the fact that the word 'trial' refers to particular action scenes in which certain personnel promote a legal process.

In the trial the judge says: 'I sentence you to . . .' but it would be an incompetent account if, when asked to relate what happened, you remarked that the judge uttered the words 'I sentence you . . .' The judge doesn't just say something, you do not just observe him saying something, he *sentences* and you observe him *sentencing*.[15] Now, what is it that gives the judge's words such a character with their specific implication for social action? To answer this you have to see the judge in relation to the meaning structure of 'a trial'. The statement of the judge contains an implicit prediction, backed by the objective deployment of resources. If the judge could not say 'I sentence you . . .' and expect his statement to contain an implicit prediction, then we would not call the situation in which the words were uttered 'a trial'. If the words were uttered in a mock trial or during a play rehearsal, they would not have the same relevance. The significance attached to the sentence would be completely different and could only be explained in terms of the total meaning situation in which it was performed. If the conventional sociologist counters that this shows nothing about meaning and that the determining factor is 'the deployment of objective resources' we can counter by giving the example of a court in this country sentencing a member of the Rhodesian post-U.D.I. government. This sentencing would not be backed by such a deployment but the sentencing would not be in the nature of a mock trial—its significance would be dependent on the meaning situation in which it was performed, although in this particular situation the judge would recognize that any sentence would not be implemented by the executive power in Rhodesia. A sociological understanding of the trial, therefore, depends on a recognition of the relationship of the judge to the meaning structure of the interactional setting. It is at this level that alternative approaches could enable sociology to gain an understanding of the trial and sentencing process.

Cicourel's views are suggestive in this context because his conception of normative phenomena is the basis of an attempt by certain sociologists to regain a place for conventional normative explanation. Cicourel[16] suggests that the judge may be viewed as interpreting 'a highly formal system of rules' in order to justify a claim that, say, a particular legal determination falls under a rule, practice or policy. It is clear that Cicourel himself is concerned with the properties of everyday language and how such language is used to provide for 'objective' accounts of situations, for instance with regard to how things such as police or probation reports ('empirical displays') become idealized accounts independent of the contingencies of their production and the language of their expression.[17]

We can suggest, therefore that interpretive sociology might extend the analysis of the trial situation in two primary directions. First, rules would be addressed not as part of an objective explanation, but as to their manner of use in the construction of courses of action leading to, say, particular legal determinations.

Secondly, analysis would address how judges, say, provide for the objectivity of particular laws, or the objectivity of particular 'empirical displays' by 'assigning normative sense to the structure of sentences and thereby detaching them from their common-sense and situated meaning, thereby transforming them into context-free claims about social reality'.[18]

Lying behind Cicourel's statements regarding the judge is a distinction which he himself draws between 'surface rules' (the norms of conventional sociology) and 'interpretive practices'. The latter are procedures whereby social actors recognize a surface rule as operating and determine its operational meaning. For Cicourel the 'interpretive procedures provide a sense of social order that is fundamental for normative order to exist or be negotiated or constructed'.[19] Although it is clear that Cicourel is attempting to say something profound with regard to the ontological status of normative orders (including law), Dreitzel amongst others has argued that the distinction between surface rules and interpretive practices demonstrates a place for the conventional analysis of norms. Interpretive sociology, it is said, is dependent on normative sociology to the extent that conventional sociology takes as its task the study of normative orders. Can such an argument be supported? We think not, and for two reasons.

First, if Dreitzel is attempting to resurrect normative analysis when he says that we cannot analyse the interpretive practices without regard to the normative rules,[20] it is based on a non-sequitur. Cicourel's position does not suggest that you can. As Cicourel states the position: 'The interpretive procedures provide a sense of social order that is fundamental for normative order to exist ... the two orders are always in interaction *and it would be absurd to speak of the one without the other.*'[21]—which, rather than leading to the position Dreitzel sees as untenable, leads only to its converse.

Secondly, it has to be recognized that the issue of central concern *is* the ontological status of normative orders. Cicourel's position has much to say about how we can conceptualize and understand normative orders. The study of normative orders has to be based in the manner of their existence in the everyday world. If it is a normative order constructed, continually sustained and reaffirmed, the analysis has to be at this level rather than subsuming the order into an objective explanation disjunctive with its very manner of existence. Analysis has to be at the level of how actors come to sustain a sense of meaning in interactional settings by recognizing the particular form of normative orders, seeing such orders as relevant, affirming and sustaining the operational meaning, objectifying its substantive content, and finally, accounting their behaviour in its terms so constructed. These social practices sustain the normative order. To have the order sustain the practices, and this is what is claimed by conventional conceptions of normative regulation, is to turn a topic of investigation into a resource for explanation. It is to ignore the words of Blumer, given to sociology over two decades ago, when he said that '(it) is the social process in group life that creates and upholds the rules, not the rules that create and uphold group life'.[22]

A RECONCEPTUALIZATION OF LAW

It appears that if we can for one moment put aside all things we have 'learnt' about law, then the most immediately obvious character of law is its expression in language. This recognition serves to base two ideas.

First, law, like language, establishes meaning by abstracting certain features of the phenomena to which it relates and, by embodying those features in certain syntactical propositions, constitutes a way of looking at that phenomena. We give a short example of this in relation to child care legislation below.

Secondly, we can conceptualize law as a 'categorisation of experience', by which we mean that the law provides in some sense for certain acts, events and objects, and for relationships between them (for instance, 'making a will', 'an intestate death', 'an heir' or, from another branch of law, 'drawing up a lease'; 'a sale of property'; a 'tenant of an unfurnished flat'). The second idea gives the impression that the law allows certain possible experiences (such as being 'the tenant of an unfurnished flat') while the first idea suggests that law abstracts certain features of, say, a relationship between two people and provides a way of looking at that relationship, for instance the relationship as embodied in statutes concerning 'landlord' and 'tenant'.

At first it might appear that a tension exists between these ideas and the view expressed by interpretive sociology that meaning is constructed in courses of social action—the latter would suggest that the meaning of 'an unfurnished flat' is given by the routine procedures utilized in the depiction of property as belonging or as not belonging to that category by those competent to make such designations. It is, therefore, necessary to remember that the question of sociological importance is the relationship of social actors to legal propositions, however the latter be conceptualized. If, however, we are not to *assume* a relationship, for instance that social actors do *use* legal propositions or that the meaning of legal propositions is constructed in social action, we have to develop a level of conceptualization which is neutral as far as the substantive content of social action is concerned whilst *sensitizing* analysis to the properties of social action.

We have, then, to try and answer two questions:

(a) Can we justify our conception of law?
(b) How does it sensitize us to questions concerning social action?

The Conception of Law

We claim that the statement 'law is a categorization of experience' adds nothing to what is necessarily entailed in the concept of law. This should serve to distinguish the conceptualization from statements such as 'law is a form of social control'. If 'law' is not a categorization of experience, then it does not exist as a social phenomenon but only as a string of three letters. If, then, the statement can be said to be true *a priori*, then it adds no ordering assumptions in the guise of conceptualization. The term does not imply anything about the substantive content of men's action or their relationship to the objects, acts and events embodied in the syntactical propositions of the law.

We are then able to adopt a form of conceptualization which allows contact to be made with a phenomenon 'law', for instance, by beginning analysis with certain syntactical propositions, and yet allows that the subject matter of this branch of sociology, that is men's action in relation to such propositions, remains within the world of empirical actuality.

For instance, that law is a categorization of experience does not allow us to assume that men do in fact act in terms of the meaning structure established by the law, nor that men in constructing courses of action orient themselves to, or are cognisant of the propositions of law. A crude example can be given from the law itself, in that ignorance of law is no defence. Action undertaken in the context of a universe of meaning unrelated to any legal proposition does not offer immunity to the specified consequences of that action. But for our purposes 'ignorance of law is no defence', is to be treated as one of those propositions of an existent legal system that exists as a categorization of experience. Although an actor may or may not be cognizant, the proposition exists as a categorization of experience in the sense that it constitutes a peculiar construction of the relationship between knowledge of the law and immunity from it.

At this stage, then, it is in terms of its analytic potential that we seek to justify the level of conceptualization.

Conceptualization as sensitizing inquiry

First, by conceptualizing law as a categorization of experience we are immediately faced with the central question of the relationship between this conceptualization and the properties of social action which allow men to ascribe properties to phenomena, to construct or affirm their meaning and the relationship of this meaning to the construction of courses of action. In other words we are unlikely to be able to assume a relationship between legal propositions and social action and the relationship stays as a central topic of inquiry. This central topic of inquiry presents itself almost automatically from the level of conceptualization and does not have to be fought for.

Secondly, we are again almost automatically faced with the question of the relationship between the commonsense 'objectivity' of law and the mundane practices and procedures, organizational determinants, prescribed decision making or whatever relevant features stem from investigation, by which such objectivity is provided for and sustained.

Thirdly, Bruner[23] argues that the actor's capacity to think in the first place is based on his capacity to categorize. '*Categorizing is the means by which the objects of the world about us are identified.*'[24] We can perhaps hazard that our approach to law may find a commonality of interest with those sociologists and linguists which have been responsible for developing the contemporary state of interpretive sociology. And not only from such people as Bruner. If we take Brown's formulation of the Whorfian hypothesis, we learn that 'each language embodies a particular world view. The speakers of a language are parties to an agreement to perceive and think about the world in a certain way—not the only way. The same reality—both physical and social—can be variously structured and different languages operate with a different structure.'[25] This again warns us against giving a constructed reality the status of an objective reality, it again sensitizes sociology to the relationship between social action and legal propositions. The relevance of the Whorfian hypothesis would be lost if we began by a conceptualization of law as, say, 'an integrative mechanism' and would be far from obvious if we began with a view of law as 'one form of social control'.

Fourthly, the sociology of law is intimately tied to the types of questions asked by Cicourel, questions concerning the form of legal language, and the structure (indexical) of everyday discourse. The question most obviously raised is the manner in which the everyday language structure used in legal talk is utilized and handled to provide for and sustain the objective nature of normative idealizations.

We hope then that it is not too much to say that the approach so far adopted does sensitize sociology to questions concerning social action. It is predicated on the need to avoid an imposition of substantive assumptions on to the social world in order to investigate the manner in which the meaning of certain acts, objects and events (social phenomena) are created and sustained, and their relationship to the construction of courses of social action. We can then abstain from any assumption regarding these relationships and allow investigation to be informed by, and in turn inform us as to, the nature of social action in certain specified areas of social life. Whether social action is constructed in terms established by law (and we should add whether the terms of law have a meaning constructed in social action) is an empirical question. That law is a categorization of experience is a statement regarding the status of law in social life—it does not imply a fixing of experience dominating men's action. The categorization holds within it the possibility for originating and transforming the conditions in terms of which social action takes place.

If study is sensitized by the conceptualization, then this in part is due to the crucial and unavoidable question concerning the relationship between how social actors assign meanings and references to an environment of objects, acts and events and the conception of 'law as a categorization of experience' providing a meaning structure for certain objects, acts and events with the social world. An example should clarify the levels of analysis avoided and that which is attained.

The example is from child-care legislation. In looking at this example we can discuss the manner in which legislation has traditionally been studied.[26] Generally, traditional sociology has addressed itself to a very rich and diverse set of questions with regard to legislation, but these questions have a particular relationship to the subject-matter under study. They have not been oriented to the nature of social action, but, rather have elected to deal with issues such as the impact of legislation or the relationship between 'legislative intent' and the ensuing distortion of that intent. With child-care legislation, impact studies would be concerned with the consequences of the legislation for a range of areas of social life. Questions might be addressed to the number of children taken into care, the impact on family structure and on the organizations delegated to apply the legislation. In the case of child care legislation these organizations include Social Services Departments and questions could be addressed concerning the effects of the legislation on social-work training, the increased resources required or the conflicts generated between social work and other agencies. 'Intent-distortion' studies in one sense look quite different. Such studies tend not to take legislation for granted, the object of the studies being to reveal the correspondence or discontinuity between intended and actual interpretation.

The studies, however, either fail to address or completely misconstrue the relationship between legislation and social action. In both types it is assumed that sociology can go to an action scene without inquiring into the properties of the social activity that constitutes that action scene. Secondly, they take for granted a problem to be addressed and see the action scene in terms of that problem as defined by the sociologist or by the legislation itself. These two features make it certain that each social actor is viewed in terms of this prescribed problem rather than in terms of the particular problems which he himself faces in the construction of his own activity. So for instance with regard to child-care legislation, social-worker activity is seen in terms of the social problem of deprived children rather than in terms of the social workers' professional problems of utilizing resources, achieving a competent performance of his work activity and handling a myriad of organizational concerns. His activity is then interpreted in a manner divorced from his own phenomenal relationship to the situation. In so approaching situations, traditional ways of studying legislation close off sociological concerns and do violence to the sociological subject-matter.

In terms of the level of analysis which we feel is sociologically more fruitful, we can only begin to develop it here. We can begin with a brief look at child-care legislation in terms of our view of law. Inquiry would first be addressed to the constituent features of the legislation before seeking to investigate the manner in which such elements enter into the construction of social action. We can give a short account of the first concern here while leaving the latter concern to be documented later in this chapter.

Section 2 of the Children Act, 1948 reveals a number of constituent elements. Under this section a local authority may assume parental rights in respect of a child in its care if it appears:

(a) that his parents are dead and that he has no guardian; or
(b) that a parent or guardian of his has abandoned him, or suffers from some permanent disability rendering the said person incapable of caring for the child; or
(c) is of such habits or mode of life as to be unfit to have the care of the child.

Each of these propositions is an abstraction of certain features of the parent–child relationship and is an invitation to view the relationship in a particular way for the purposes of applying a certain proposition. The approach to law signifies that such propositions are not bounded categories, they do not set the relevant features of the situation for analysis, but they do constitute a taxonomy of possible experiences of the child–parent relationship which can be investigated in terms of their relationship to the social activity of those responsible for the welfare of children. The problem of welfare, however, is not established as the problem of analysis. Rather, analysis concerns the way in which such propositions enter into the professional routine activity of, for instance, social workers. Where these propositions so enter into the symbolic universe of a social actor, to be taken into account in undertaking action, they constitute sets of experiences which are routinely handled and given meaning within the experiences of patterns of social action constituting one aspect of the provision of welfare.

It is clear from Section 2 that the meanings any actor can attribute to a proposition are limited in part by that proposition. It needs little reflection to realize that an actor could hardly construe 'dead' in proposition (a) to mean that the parents lead a fairly quiet existence. Other propositions such as (c) appear to offer more scope for interpretation. There is nothing 'objective' about the limitation identified—that such limitations do obtain reflects our understanding of the socially sanctionable and situated range of uses of a particular linguistic item such as 'dead'. It is the mechanics of how a phenomenal relationship is established with such (and all such) propositions which must be the first line of analysis for sociology. Let it be said, however, that the concern is not to assess the 'correct' interpretation but to understand legal propositions in terms of their relationship to social action, thereby enabling sociology to be informed as to the meaningful and interpretive character of social life.

This level of prior analysis is geared to an understanding of social action without in fact establishing the relationship of law to social action in an *a priori* fashion. The example should have shown in part the relationship which obtains between the nature of legal propositions as establishing sets of experiences and the routine construction of lines of social action by actors whose phenomenal world includes in some manner these propositions.

The world of everyday life is a subjective world, but equally it is an inter-subjective world allowing for the construction of shared meanings. If this were not so, then the very basis of law as a rational activity would vanish. It is only man that can give meaning to the world he experiences but man can also make classifications and embody them in a particular language with a particular structure for viewing the objects and events of the social world. Turning this awareness into a methodology for the sociology of law is our central concern and whıle such a methodology cannot claim to be able to address 'the distinctively legal' or the 'properties of legality' it is sensitized to the question of how, and to what extent, legal classifications are constructed, negotiated and used in constructing lines of action, and how they are given meaning and assigned relevance by social actors. In this manner law can be approached without making substantive assumptions concerning social action. This avoids the reification of the purpose of law with the subsequent danger of distorting the phenomenal world of the social actor being studied. The approach is securely based in the analysis of a specialized language expressing concepts embodies in rules, policies and procedures allowing an understanding to be achieved of how language and meaning enter into, promote, affirm or sustain social life.

Three steps for analysis have been suggested by interpretive sociology:

(1) suspend the assumption that social conduct is norm-governed or mounted from shared meanings which assume a concept of norm;
(2) observe the terms in which lay and professional actors describe

and achieve regular, coherent and connected patterns of action;

(3) treat the appearances of patterned social activity as *appearances produced*, and study the routine procedures of such production in terms of the phenomenal world of the social actors concerned.[27]

THE PENETRATION OF THE NORMATIVE ORDER

We now wish to demonstrate how the tenets of interpretive sociology can underpin particular research endeavours within the sociology of law and how our view of law as a categorization of experience can act as a sensitizing device for attuning attention to the social processes constitutive of group life.

To avoid misunderstanding we must reiterate that no more than orientation is derived from our notion of law, an orientation which above all resists the foreclosure of law from social action seen to occur in normative conceptions. We do not possess a unique sociological sensitizer in this respect. Others may be equally appropriate. We claim only that the notion is practically sufficient for that purpose. The notion cannot indicate particular topics for investigation; it cannot frame hypotheses; it does not possess the status of a high-order proposition in a deductive system; it cannot partake of substantive conclusions; it does not eliminate the need for research itself. The notion does, however, point research attention to features of social action and facilitates the necessary suspension of belief in the objective facticity of law; it does provide a linkage with the touchstone of sociology and a path by which to achieve the sociological penetration of the normative order.

We can accept that there are 'things' such as law, customs, habits, rules, etc., which are thought of and acted towards as 'real things' in social life; we can further accept that the term 'norm' is not applied totally fictitiously to the patterned regularities of expectations and actions seen and understood to exist in social life. Sensitized by our notion of law, however, this level of acceptance can be suspended as preparation for the sociological penetration of the normative order, a penetration to be achieved by an investigation of the processes in group life which uphold normative rules and which enable the rules to be identified in the first instance.

The demonstration to be given of the utility and viability of the adopted approach is built around an account of legal rules in the setting of local authority social work. The account is not given as a formal presentation of completed research since it is the style of analysis which we are concerned to display rather than substantive findings. The account is presented, therefore, as a life history of the analysis. We will indicate both how it displays a serious commitment to the tenets of interpretive sociology and how it departs from alternative styles of analysis available. Such direct comparison should facilitate our attempt to translate the imagery of interpretive sociology into actual research practice.

The issues raised refer to such topics as the predicates on which law is or is not introduced into the social worker/client relation, and how legal categories become or do not become a referent for routine activity both within social services organizations and between social workers and their clients. We take such issues to be self-evidently authentic matters of interest to sociologists of law and we take social-work departments to constitute at least as valid an object of attention as, say, the police. Social-services departments are established under statute; departmental agents are specifically authorized to administer large portions of welfare legislation; social workers are routinely implicated in situations in which legal propositions are of actual or potential importance to the matter in hand; their clients are shrouded in a welter of legal rights and duties. Any of these legal aspects of the social-work nexus could base the interest of the sociology of law.

It may however be thought that, whatever the potential of such issues to constitute an object of research, they are unrelated to those concerns seen already to exist and considered as legitimate for the sociology of law. Ours might then be construed as an idiosyncratic project. We can show this not to be the case by reiterating certain features of contemporary work as discussed in earlier chapters.

The analysis to be given impinges on established issues in the sociology of law in five specific areas.

(a) *Studies of Legislation:* The sociology of law has spawned a variety of approaches available for studying legislation and its implementation. The analysis here stands as a comparison with conventional work on implementation.

(b) *Discretion in Welfare Administration:* Discretion has been an operative category for a great deal of work on the implementation of law and the administration of welfare. Rather than describing or explaining administration in terms of discretion, we can ask the sociology of law to describe 'discretion': that is, what does discretion look like in practice? If discretion is either the absence of formal rules or the category in which cases are decided on merit, this leaves untouched the issue of *how* cases are decided on merit. The analysis offered here could assist in untangling the congeries of practices, beliefs and background assumptions which are collectively depicted as discretionary action.

(c) *Legal Actors (Decision Making):* To the extent that research on legal actors has been concerned with decision making, we had cause to remark in Chapter IV that the style of analysis undertaken misconstrued the actual basis on which decisions in the legal process are made. The inputs and outputs, political affiliations and so on, used to explain decision making distorted rather than illuminated that process. The analysis given here is relevant to the investigation of how decisions are made in social-work settings with regard to law and to the decision-making processes involving other legal actors.

(d) *Legal Actors (Sociology of Professions):* We saw in Chapter IV that some critics of the functionalist approach to professions had emphasised the bodies of knowledge utilized by professionals in their tasks. The analysis to be given here investigates the manner of existence of 'professional knowledge', the grounds of its invocation, variance in its use, and its relation, in one particular setting, to law.

(e) *Legal Services:* The involvement of social workers in the distribution of legal services allows our own analysis to extend previous work on the deployment of such services. Our own work is able to direct attention to the inner workings of what has been referred to as the 'complex social process' by which clients actually come to encounter a legal service.

These five areas can be borne in mind in reading the analysis to be presented. The major question, however, must relate to the ability of the style of analysis portrayed to reach the level of action. The style of analysis can only be successful if it is able to make contact with the sociological subject-matter and, having done so, is able to revise our estimate of the nature of that subject-matter.

In the analysis which follows, no attempt is made to isolate the peculiarly legal element from the context in which such elements appear. We will first consider the processes by which a client of a social services department presents a problem to the department and how, in the ensuing patterns of action the problem is treated and given a status as treatable. Particular attention will be given to the so-called process of 'redefinition' of clients' problems and to a comparison of interpretive and conventional accounts of this process. Secondly, we will direct attention at the processes within the organization which make law available for use in case settings in addressing (re)defined problems. Finally, and working from these two analyses, we will explicate the relationship of law to social workers at an action level. Throughout we rely predominantly on knowledge of social-work agencies which is available to any aware observer and need to stress therefore that the analysis as portrayed does not allow for any substantive documentation. We merely wish to stress a style of analysis that is both different from conventional styles and yet applicable to similar areas of concern. The manner of presentation is predicated on the need to demonstrate the potential of interpretive sociology for the study of law without presuming a great deal of specialized knowledge of the legal content of social work on the part of our audience.

AVAILABILITY OF EXPLANATION

It is almost a byword in conventional studies that social workers redefine clients' problems. The pervasiveness of this prevailing wisdom is such that commentators have felt able to repeat it as an entirely uncontentious observation. Compare Morris, for instance, saying that 'success as a social worker tends to be evaluated through persuading clients to redefine the problem in such a way that the social worker can himself take some necessary action or alternatively can persuade the client to accommodate to the situation'.[28] This conventional depiction of the social worker/client setting as one in which clients' problems are replaced by problems as seen by social workers has both a superficial attraction and a superficial resemblance to what takes place.

Observers have noted, rightly, that 'presenting case' does not necessarily equate with 'case addressed by social worker'. In the department in which one of the authors worked for six months, for instance, a fundamental distinction was made between presenting problem and problem to be addressed, and this distinction was routinely allowed for on initial interview forms. But a determination by a sociologist to accept and treat situations in terms of 'redefinition' constitutes an over-identification with the client, whilst necessitating a view of him as an empty recipient of service. Such is not the case. Clients can and do evaluate service, and since in all but a few cases the client can withdraw from the worker/client setting, client evaluation and satisfaction constitutes a limit upon social-worker action. In that contact is maintained, therefore, the social worker cannot unilaterally do anything. The situation is one of negotiation not redefinition, though this is not to say that one party may not negotiate more than the other. We have to be able to understand such non-symmetrical negotiation.

To the extent that analysis becomes committed at this early stage to emphasise the *negotiated* character of problem diagnosis, certain facets of social worker/client relations are prone to become elevated for consideration. First, negotiation constitutes a process qualitatively different from that of a decision: the latter has the character of a discrete act and need involve only one actor; the former partakes of a processual character involving more than one actor, with actors being in some way oriented to one another during the course of negotiation. We need to note that the reasons for making a decision, for instance the 'decision' to redefine, may be elicitable in a manner not replicable for negotiation settings where actors' reasons, motives, strategies and purposes may vary over time and where an actor's account of what is happening may vary according to the stage reached in the negotiation. An exhaustive report of negotiation is unlikely therefore to be achieved through the use of survey or interview techniques. Secondly, negotiation implies some common ground between parties. The extent and nature of that common ground may vary enormously but at a minimum it is likely to consist of an agreement that one is to be the recipient of service and the other the provider. Thirdly, negotiation may never have a settled outcome, nor may participants appreciate that no outcome has been reached or that the outcome remains in doubt. No imputation of success is required. Fourthly, negotiation is only possible through language and talk, in settings whose character is important to the way in which discourse proceeds—compare for instance settings in which a client and social worker discuss a problem presented, and others in which two friends discuss a problem experienced by one of them.

Such facets of the setting, once identified, help to focus attention sufficiently to gather data capable of enlightening the issue of redefinition. Redefinition, however, does not set the terms of research, it simply stands as a feature of a setting to be enlightened by investigation with a broader compass. To start with 'negotiation' neither presumes the specific outcomes of social worker/client interaction nor does it run the risk of moulding data into a pre-existing conceptual scheme.

We can usefully compare the skeletal framework provided by the elevation of 'negotiation' with a conventional account of redefinition. A conventional account would be framed as a power differential in the social worker/client relationship. Redefinition takes place because the social worker has more power than the client. The impression is conveyed, then, both that we can identify something called power and that power determines the social world. Neither is an unproblematic assumption, but even their acceptance somehow fails to say much about how the trick of redefinition is actually performed. Power, may be, but power in which particular guise and employed quite how? Further, we must contest that the introduction of the concept of power in this way can stand as explanation. Essentially, the notion of power is descriptive—we collate certain events and relationships portraying a certain similarity and assign the concept to comprise this similarity (for instance, situations in which one person A gets another B to do something that B would not otherwise have done). To *explain* a supposed instance of power—redefinition—in terms of the concept is tautologous because the only index of power operating in the situation is the redefinition itself. The aim should be not to ascribe explanatory potential to a descriptive notion referring to the identified phenomena of redefinition, but to ground empirically the notion that one is wanting to use. If we are constrained to be committed to the notion of power we can at least try and illuminate what power looks like in the setting which it is used to explain.

As we tried to indicate earlier, in the discussions of the trial examples, alternative accounts of situations seeming to invite the power treatment can be given from an interpretive standpoint. It should be clear that interpretive sociology treats action as belonging to men, not to power relations. Men act in terms of whatever is at hand, creating behaviour by determining (in the weak sense) the meaning structure of the interactional situation. Alternative approaches need not define power, nor locate power in terms of behavioural effects, but can treat situations in terms of categories grounded by reference to routine social activity. We need to pay attention to those mundane empirical issues which might illuminate how the trick of redefinition is performed. If one begins with questions such as 'do clients always accept redefinition' and 'if so, on what grounds' and 'on what can social workers be seen to be relying' then it is likely that explanatory circularity can be avoided by a firm grounding of the account given. We will return later to a fuller consideration of the use of the concept power; for now we can simply reiterate that the bearers of such notions possess no monopoly of competence to give accounts of certain settings; alternative approaches can have validity, although not by offering reformulations of problematic sociological concepts but by addressing directly the settings in which such concepts are held to have analytic and explanatory potential.

Under such a banner we turn to address directly the negotiated character of problem diagnosis within the social worker/client setting, the proximate context of 'redefinition'. As an entry to further analysis we can note that it has been suggested by Rees[29] that the importance of the client in resisting redefinition will depend upon his realization that he is in a bargaining situation. The key to an understanding of the negotiation process would then reside in the degree of consciousness of the client. But this assumed relationship between consciousness and action does seem to legislate certain possibilities from existence. Even without such an awareness the client need not be duped. An attempt to redefine an application for a bus pass in terms of, for instance, anal/oral conflict, with the subsequent imperatives for therapy, would be rejected by the client and would be a demonstration of incompetence in the field of social service. The example is fanciful, but what makes it fanciful is the 'obvious' limit on the social worker in terms of, inter alia, client satisfaction. Client awareness of self-involvement in a bargaining transaction may strengthen a stand against social-worker redefinition, but the stand need in no way depend on such recognition. There are more reasons for leaving the relationship than that covert negotiation has broken down and become visible to the client. Cultural knowledge is available to locate certain situations as 'non-negotiable' and to deny legitimacy to certain attempts at redefinition.

A recognition that client satisfaction constitutes a limit to social-worker action, over and above any limit implied by client insight into the character of the social worker/client setting, leads us to consider certain correlates of that satisfaction. Client satisfaction can be seen to be related to the nature of the demand made—the presenting problem—along two important dimensions.

(a) *Specificity of Demand:* We have to distinguish presenting problems according to their degree of specificity. If a demand is specific, then the client can be held to recognise with some ease either attempts to redefine his demand or a failure by the social worker to address directly his problem. Client evaluation is a distinct possibility and client dissatisfaction a constant threat to unilateral action. A specific demand might be a request for a bus pass, and in such situations there would seem little scope for redefinition. If the demand is general on the other hand, a recognition by the client that redefinition has taken place, and that the social worker has failed to meet the presenting problem, is less likely. Indeed general demands, to the extent that they involve no more than a presentation of a situation, are almost an invitation to redefine. Deprived of his own measuring stick through the character of the request, client evaluation and dissatisfaction are more remote. A general demand might be a request for alleviation of social isolation. Such demands invite redefinition in terms of an absence of a telephone or a television, client personality, intra-familial relations or even personal hygiene or, perhaps, lack of a bus pass.

(b) *Relationship to Professional Knowledge:* Even specific requests can take a multitude of forms. Consider for example, the two specific requests 'I need a bus pass' and 'I need my daughter to stay at home in the evenings.' Both demands are in their own way quite specific. None the less they vary dramatically in terms of their relationship to professional knowledge, and this indicates a second dimension along which demands vary. The request for a bus pass is likely to be accounted for simply in terms of cultural knowledge, and the background to the request will be comprehensible and actionable. At a very commonsense level there is no difficulty in comprehending the configurations of circumstances leading up to such requests, even though the particular reason for a request may differ from case to case. Further, processing a bus-pass request need not transcend mundane information acquisition, such information being collected in terms of relevances embodied in departmental policy, procedures and forms, and a relatively unproblematic decision. The same is clearly not true of the latter request. A detailed assessment of family circumstances, further interviews with parents and child and a more or less sophisticated diagnosis in terms of professional knowledge would precede treatment itself. It might be incompetent social work to redefine a bus pass with reference to anal/oral conflict but it would be equally incompetent to incarcerate physically the child within the home, and this simply reflects the character of the request as pertaining to issues with a problematic background requiring analysis prior to a departmental response. Such situations cannot be accounted fully by cultural knowledge.

In the light of such observations we can see that the limit of client satisfaction can be successfully differentiated in terms of the nature of the demand and its relationship to professional knowledge. It might be thought that the 'obvious' procedure would be to construct a two by two matrix and to see how much data it could accommodate. One would get:

Social worker capacity to redefine the presenting problem would depend upon the location of any demand upon this matrix. We recognize that a more complex matrix would have to be constructed to handle limits other than client satisfaction, or further dimensions of client demands. We remain solely with the two dimensions for the purposes of exposition. What we have to say now applies equally to any more complex matrix which could be constructed.

On reflection, the matrix approach is inadequate because it fails to reach the level of action. It is not features of action which are treated by such an account of negotiation and redefinition but abstracted features of the demand. It is not, however, the problem presented which negotiates, or limits redefinition, but social actors.

A determination to locate the process of negotiation in participants' social action necessitates a consideration of the relationship of clients' problems to their general social action. Whether or not our own analysis begins with the presentation of a problem, that is clearly not the case from the clients' point of view. Problems have biographies which pre-date social worker/client interaction. By the time of presentation the problem has already been the object of attention and reflection, and in so attending clients routinely identify the problem and routinely go further in constructing explanations of its cause and formulating strategies for its resolution. No spurious uniformity need be imputed and neither need the client be seen as necessarily reflective. Such identification and explanation doubtless exhibits variance, being more or less complete, exhaustive and successful from the clients' standpoint. For some clients the problem may not even be a problem in the usual sense of the word, being more akin to an act of fate. None the less we can see that the problem presented will at a minimum be embedded in a set of more or less explicit ideas, notions, typifications, experiences and beliefs. To this extent at least, the client 'theorizes' about the issue, and when such theorizing takes the form of supplying explanations it necessitates the utilization of knowledge. The nature and extent of explanatory theorizing depends in a general sense on the particular knowledge and interpretive schemes available to the actor. For clients, cultural knowledge is all that is to hand and the construction of explanations is consequently restricted. Such knowledge can however be supplemented and for a client who, for instance, recognized that he was in a bargaining situation vis-à-vis the social worker, he would be using knowledge less than freely available and his capacity to construct explanations would itself be strengthened. That position mentioned earlier which located client consciousness as the key to understanding the limits to redefinition thus constitutes a special case of the general position presented here.

We can now reintroduce the social worker into the analysis to complete our reformulation of the redefinition issue.

As we have said, the capacity to theorize is the capacity to identify and to provide explanation as it relates to a particular problem. In a negotiation setting, actors' ability to resist or impose definitions, in respect of another actor, of whatever is at issue, depends on his having a stable and resilient definition and a coherent explanation, unless he is willing to withdraw. Social workers' demonstrated capacity to redefine client problems whilst maintaining contact is to be understood, therefore, as relating to the range and sophistication of the explanations available for use by the invocation of professional knowledge. Such has an independent coherence, is used routinely to provide interpretive schemes as a matter of ongoing activity, and, relatively, allows a great stability and consistency in problem identification and explanation.

It must be noted that the analysis does not entail a view of the social worker as intent upon redefinition. Redefinition is only a conscious adjustment of the problem presented by virtue of observer comparison. The process is not one of social-worker distortion of client wants, but social-worker understanding of client needs. Neither does the analysis depend upon an 'Honest John' conception of social workers. Social workers can be, and indeed are in some cases, as Machiavellian as the next man, retaining their analysis for personal and organizational use to avoid upsetting the client or disrupting the treatment plan. But for social workers to maintain contact with the client, and to provide a rational basis for their own action, their participation in the negotiation requires a public explanation of activities as they relate to the presenting problem.

Understanding the negotiation process at this level should not be construed as indicating that the 'limits' earlier identified are not real limits. What is at issue is their status as an account of the situation. Resting content with that account leaves unexplicated the features of participants' action which are the empirical referent of those limits. The key to an understanding of problem negotiation is to be found in the differential availability and stability of explanations which actors bring to the setting. Locating the account at this level, the level of action, transcends other accounts and provides for a grounding in activities themselves.

It will be useful to pause briefly before comparing the foregoing with conventional accounts in order to see what has been achieved. First we now have a very basic idea of the social processes constitutive of 'redefinition'. Secondly, we are not constrained to divorce redefinition cases from those in which redefinition appears not to occur. We understand the setting itself and can subsequently see how the course of interaction generates a conclusion which we may want to depict as a redefinition of the original presenting problem. The setting retains coherence across its range of instances and is not fragmented by the enforced application of notions of obscure empirical referent or the abstraction of certain cases according to problematic criteria for our own sociological purposes. Thirdly, we can pursue with greater confidence the issues of why certain cases, certain social workers or certain departments are characterized by varying incidence of redefinition and we can do so with an appropriate methodology and firmly committed to analysis at the level of action. Such analysis would be framed with reference to actual explanations in different departmental settings and in respect of different presenting problems.

Fourthly, and this is most important, the 'availability of explanations' prepares the ground for an understanding of how generic law, legal categories and legal propositions enter the social worker/client setting. To strive for such understanding without first grasping how a problem obtains a status as treatable would clearly be premature. Are cases accounted in terms of law; with reference to law; in ignorance of law; in defiance of law; or what? What variance if any remains to be described between cases; between social workers, between departments; between welfare workers generally or between countries? These questions are not to be treated as ones concerning mere rates overtly indexed by the researchers own counting procedures, but they are to be treated as cognizant of the properties of social workers' social action. That is, how law enters into case work is a basis, and a necessary basis, for questions concerning how often has law so entered. In other words we need to know what social workers rely on to define problems and handle problems and in what manner law enters such routine work procedures.

We have yet to compare our own with conventional accounts of redefinition. We shall now do so with reference to the notion of power, locating the comparison in a discussion of concept formation and use.

We will first analyse what is involved in the utilization of a concept of power. Of necessity we have to deal with this schematically and might be accused of assuming that all conventional sociology handles the concept of power in the same and simplistic terms. We emphasize, however, that we are concerned to portray the implications of the use of this and similar concepts whatever the degree of sophistication employed in establishing them. For our purposes two features of the conventional conceptualization of power are particularly problematic. First, power is generally defined outside the research situation, and secondly, the concept is frequently utilized as if it stood in relation to the situation as cause to effect.

Establishing a concept outside the research situation can take one of two forms, both of which impose an order on the subject matter of inquiry but to differing degrees. In the first instance we would not only define power but would also establish its relation to other concepts such as authority, manipulation and control, and, thereby, provide a detailed framework for the analysis of particular 'power' situations. This approach necessarily imposes an order on the subject, the nature of the order imposed stemming from the propositions utilized to establish the concept. As far as most attempts to define power are concerned, the ontological status of these propositions is open to question. It is not apparent whether or not they derive from sociology or from some other system of relevances. Alternatively, the concept may be drawn broadly (for instance in a definition of power as the ability to make other men do what they would otherwise not choose to do), in which case the research situation itself provides the necessary refinements to the concept. If this strategy is employed then presumably the research situation must have something to offer in terms of the validity of the categories developed. If, however, our concepts have to be refined in the light of empirical situations, then this makes problematic the rationale for defining concepts in the first place and opens up the alternative of being radically empirical, dispensing entirely with concepts established in this manner. The second problematic feature of the conventional conceptualization of power concerns its use as explanation. We suggest that to the extent that conventional sociology develops concepts as descriptive categories and then utilizes such concepts as part of an explanation, it is engaging in tautology. That features of the situation are abstracted into a pre-existing category to be reintroduced as an explanation of that situation serves to expand and to camouflage the tautology.

The account given of the social worker/client setting in terms of availability of explanation constitutes an alternative which avoids both problematic features of conceptualization. This alternative constitutes the provision of accounts of situations, the concept then presenting itself as a shorthand statement of the account. The existence of the concept cannot pre-date the analysis. The account generated would include within it a full description of the concept. Concepts so derived would not stand in the situation as cause to effect, but as shorthand statements which organize our knowledge in a known relationship to the situation in which it was generated.

The 'concept' of availability of explanation has no status separate from an account given of observable activities. The existence is contingent upon the empirical world rather than sociological usage. The concept would not be applicable to other situations, in a sense of a determination to view other situations in its terms. It *may* present itself in a variety of settings, allowing a post-analytic understanding of superficially dissimilar settings in similar terms, but no sociological justification exists for an *a priori* assumption of this possibility.

Many sociologists will see little difference between this and their own understanding of the nature of concept formation. They also may see concepts as a form of shorthand. The fundamental difference, however, lies in the method by which the concept is generated and the use to which it is put. The wider concern that can be given to methodology and the refusal to accept the division between contexts of discovery and contexts of verification, enables the generation of accounts with a demonstrable and non-problematic relation to activity through their embodiment in accounts given at the level of action. It is insufficient to recognise that social action is interpretive. Sociology must use that level of analysis which translates the axiom into a methodological stance.

MEDIATION OF LEGISLATION

'Availability of explanation' allows an understanding of problem diagnosis at the level of social action. This level comes as a matter of course once 'problems' are not taken for granted. 'Availability of explanation', however, goes further than problem diagnosis by preparing a schema for looking at how law enters into problem diagnosis and strategies for case-work action. We cannot afford to take an unproblematic view of the 'problems' to which social workers may bring law. But neither is it possible to regard law as an unproblematic category of analysis. To do so is to be confronted with the paradox that, whilst other legal agents may be thought to apply law in a very direct fashion, social workers in their routine activity are agents of law and are shrouded in legal duties, but without any massive or immediate legal presence. There are, for instance, statutes relating to child care, and there are social workers routinely implementing such statutes. Knowledge of the one, however, does not provide an understanding of the other.

That we are here starting to overlap considerably with matters of enduring interest to other investigators of law should be apparent by reflecting on the emphasis to be found amongst both jurists and sociologists of law upon the distinction between 'law in books' and 'law in action'. Several formulations of the distinction are available but all rest on the appreciation that to read statutes and formal enunciations of the principles of common law is insufficient to obtain understanding of what law looks like in its actual operation at the point of encounter with that which it is enacted to regulate. Law in operation is held to require study directed along one or another line of sociological or social-psychological investigation.

It would be idiosyncratic to contest the disjuncture displayed by the two levels of existence of law. We would not wish to disagree that a new statute looks quite different from, say, a policeman arresting someone, or a child being taken into care. Similarly it may be easier to predict judicial outcomes if factors apart from the actual letter of the law are given pre-eminence in analysis. Such observations in themselves, however, fail to illuminate the relation between the two levels of law. The issue has to be broadened a little from the outset to inquire as to the imagined nature of such a disjuncture and the conceived relationship of the law in books to law in action.

What needs to be considered are the social processes by which statutes and judicial principles become transformed prior to their entry into settings of application. For present purposes attention has to be directed at the organizational handling of legislation which makes it available for use in problem diagnosis and case careers at the social-worker level. Such handling is best seen in terms of a congeries of practices and routine activities on the part of members at varying levels of the organizational hierarchy which collectively can be depicted as a *mediation of legislation* by social-services departments. At this stage no claim has to be made concerning how mediation takes place; the levels at which important decisions regarding legislative transformation are located; the possibly varying treatments experienced by a range of statutes; the distinctions between law for which the organization is responsible and that law which can intrude without commensurate responsibility; and so on. These are all issues of legitimate concern to be revealed by substantive research. We need only note their compatibility with the central notion of mediation. Emphasis upon the process of mediation orients attention to questions which can be missed by a reliance on the mere recognition of a law in books/law in action disjuncture and the subsequent election to concentrate exclusively on the 'real' level at which law operates. The act of implementation is more than an encapsulable activity located at the point of contact of agent and recipient of law: we cannot afford to take for granted the processes which pre-date an occasion of use of law.

In the sociology of law it is of the utmost importance that the 'mundane', empirical issues which underly the act of implementation and the process of implementation receive due attention.

Within the sub-discipline a whole genre of study has developed which attempts to compare legislative intent with the subsequent distortion of that intent by legal agents.[30] These intent-distortion studies possess the virtue that the statute is not taken at face value but is viewed as the outcome of purposive activity. Further, such studies retain in view the levels of both promulgation and implementation. But they none the less fail to address the social processes at work with regard to the implementation of law. Agent interpretation and activity is seen not so much as a social activity in its own terms but rather as right, wrong, good or bad—the validity of the assessment presumably relying on some notion of observer competence. Such studies usually miss entirely the way in which law is made available for routine action via the routine activities of actors in an organizational setting. To be sure, some of the more sophisticated practitioners have raised this issue, but a recognition that law has an organizational context is never developed into a discussion as to *how* law is mediated and made available in that setting, and the importance this has for an understanding of the empirical properties of law in action.

A competing interpretive account need not simply try and fill in the gap between intent and distortion, nor claim an ability to discern the 'real' intent or the 'real' meaning of an act of application of law on the basis of a more sophisticated methodology. Instead the issue of mediation can be treated as a topic in its own right with attention being paid to the routine activities giving rise to passage of legislation through the organization. If study is undertaken with reference to the form which law takes at the point of contact with agents then analysis can be directed at the social processes giving rise to this form of appearance. Hopefully the organization need be no longer regarded as an arcane black box in which law is mysteriously transformed by some alchemy beyond the ken of the sociology of law.

If the organization is to receive our undivided attention, then, given law's status as a species of social rule, perhaps the available discussions of rules in organizations can provide an identifiable starting point for analysis.[31] In particular that framework for organizational analysis centred on formal and informal rules would seem to have a heuristic value, for, although analysis directed under such a rubric looks to rules pertaining to the organization itself rather than rules treated by the organization, the level of analysis does address the routine activity of members as of importance in understanding organizational behaviour.

The view of organizations as settings for interplay between formal rules and participants' practices had its genesis in the *ex post facto* accounts given by Mayo[32] and his colleagues of the unanticipated results of the study at the Hawthorne electric plant. The view was presented as in contrast to Weber's contentions about efficient bureaucracy by pointing to certain observer-defined need categories of organizational personnel. Such needs were seen as creating a discrepancy between prescribed and actual behaviour. In this way departure from a formal body of rules could be explained by seeing behaviour as constructed consistently via informal rules. The existence of, and participants' knowledge of, informal rules prevented the anarchy of non-regulated activity. Informal rules provided merely a shorthand description of what participants actually did. The defects of such studies are widely known and need not be listed here, save to say that the problem in this particular context can be succinctly depicted. Mayo and his associates sought to understand the discrepancy between formal and informal rules without having first understood either. If they had done so, they would have realized that they were addressing a discrepancy which could not exist separate from their own problematic conceptualization of empirical reality. By pointing to a fictional disjuncture, the manner in which participants construct practical behaviour expressing formal schemes became a question closed to their scrutiny. But the manner in which participants (for instance social workers) construct activity expressing legislation (one particular formal scheme) is, as has been argued, of central importance.

The emphasis upon the construction of practical activity underscores that we are trying to open up to scrutiny the boundaries and operative categories with which social-welfare officers work within the area conventionally designated as one of discretion. We can accept that social workers are not somehow automatically constrained by formal legal rules and that certain formal legal rules allow explicitly, for 'discretion'—for decisions to be made on the basis of the social workers' (or social-services departments) conception of the correct course of action. We do, however, have to investigate how social workers' discretion to invoke legal rules is linked to these rules.

We can begin by noting and emphasizing the obvious. Social workers encounter law routinely as embodied in forms, procedures and policies as these are available at the social-worker level. To the extent that activity is constructed in terms of such features of the social-work setting then we see how the outcome of the mediation process bears directly as a limit on practical activity. If practical activity is seen to be expressive of formal schemes, then we can consider the possible relatedness of the limits of practical activity by social workers to the character of the formal schemes. In other words we can attempt to relate the outcome of the mediation process (forms, procedures, etc.) to features of the legislation transformed. Two features of legislation stand out as dimensions according to which mediation outcomes would seem to vary.

(a) *Specificity of Legislation:* Legislation can be usefully classified according to the degree of specificity or generality which it displays. To the extent that it is highly specific in regard to the events, situations, objects or people to which it refers and highly directive as to the nature of the services to be provided, then the mediation of such statutes could be held to be a relatively simple matter of embodying provisions into working documentation. That documentation would be characterized by unproblematic exposition of legislative terms, with forms and procedures both regularized and exhaustive as to information required for a decision, and constructed with a view to efficient organizational processing of cases. On the other hand, legislation which is general with regard to its provisions, objects of reference and service to be given, would seem to offer the possibility not only of multiple interpretation but is also likely to give rise to procedures and policies with a more permissive orientation. In that the organization retains discretion as to the manner and extent of implementation, then efficient processing may take a secondary place to the deployment of resources according to less explicit merit criteria.

(b) *Requiring Professional Knowledge for Implementation:* We can recognize that two pieces of legislation of equivalent specificity with regard to the recipients and nature of service may yet stand differentiated in that an occasion of use of law requires or does not require the use of specialized professional knowledge which social workers are allowed the discretion to introduce. Where the referent of statute concerns some matter for which a professional evaluation is held necessary, then mediation might be thought likely to take a form cognisant of the need for such extraneous evaluation. Provisions regarding the chronically sick and disabled and those relating to assistance to families likely to reduce the incidence of children in the care of the local authority can be usefully compared here. Although the operationalization of the first—which provides for practical assistance to a fairly discrete client group—need not be unproblematic in that, for instance, the amount of resources available may lead to competing criteria of eligibility, it stands none the less distinguished in terms of reliance on a professional social-work assessment from, say, predictions as to the influence of practical assistance in reducing the incidence of children in care.

In terms of the outcome of mediation as permitting or necessitating varying degrees of discretion at the social-worker level, and the subsequent permissibility of the introduction of legal categories in problem diagnosis or case strategies, it would be possible to construct a predictive matrix parallelling that given earlier with respect to the redefinition of client problems. The result might look something like that given opposite:

Requiring professional knowledge
    High   Low

High

         Extent of Social worker
         discretion

Degree of generality of
legislation

Low

The parallel between the two matrices is not merely fortuitous. As with 'presenting problem' and subsequent redefinition we have a situation in which organizational actors are required to conceptualize something given to them in terms which allow for its treatment. Almost by definition an issue not conceived so as to make it amenable to social-work treatment cannot be handled by a social-services department. This is not to undermine the possibility of competing conceptions of treatable issues. It is simply to appreciate that competent social work and acceptable social-work strategies are recognizable by the actors involved, and that the deployment of social-work time and resources is predicated upon accountable conceptions that a task in hand is appropriate in a social services context. Similarly, either in written policy statements or by the ad hoc application of criteria on occasions of use, some operational meaning has to be given to legislative provisions. In a somewhat perverted sense of the word, the organization has to 'redefine' legislation so as to be able to proceed at all.

As with the earlier matrix, the approach fails, because it is divorced from social action. To paraphrase the 'redefinition' argument; it is not features of legislation which mediate law, but social actors. The analysis seems to work as it stands by relying on commonsense understandings that (a) the language of legislation can be of such specificity as to make unproblematic its interpretation and implementation, and (b) legislation displays a character having a demonstrable relation to professional knowledge.

Both understandings are in a sense true. The problem comes when we adopt those commonsense understandings and embody them into a scheme endowed with predictive, explanatory or classificatory potential. That adoption deflects our own inquiry from ever penetrating the dimensions of the matrix. Allowing the two dimensions to adjudicate empirical data establishes the limits of inquiry short of the dimensions themselves. By putting them to work on our own behalf they become part of the inquiry rather than that which is to be inquired of. We employ them and forego our right to ask about their backgrounds. In the present context we make it difficult to ask questions concerning, for instance, the nature of the professional knowledge cited and how its competent employment is achieved, recognized and sustained. We became the victim of our own taken-for-granted analysis.

It is necessary to analyse what happens to legal propositions, after enactment and before entry into case-work, with attention focused firmly at the action level. We can start to illuminate the process of mediation at an action level by considering certain routine processes which can be seen to occur within social-service-type organizations after passage of a statute empowering or placing duties upon local authorities with respect to matters of social services. It is of course the case that many legislative provisions operated by the social-services department are in a sense already available for social workers as processed legislation dating from earlier eras. Further, the line of approach adopted does not relate to law which is of importance in cases but which the department itself does not administer. But by focusing attention at the point of encounter between existing organization and new legislative provisions we can explicate certain features of the mediation process and learn from this what should constitute the operating categories for research into the process at an action level.

If we reflect upon the passage of a piece of legislation to do with social service, we can note immediately that it will be implemented either by an already existing organization or by an organization established in that statute for the specific purpose of implementation. Legislation impacts upon an organizational nexus in which personnel are organized according to a formal structure—which is not to slip into a reification of that structure but just to recognize that actors are differentially located with respect to their competence in making decisions, reviewing other members' work and so on. Actors are organized in levels of personnel and into sub-departments and divisions. Further, communication between members is conducted along more or less specified arteries between levels and divisions of personnel.

Responsibility for treating new legislation lies with higher levels of personnel, and legislative provisions enter the organizational arena

through a multiplicity of informal channels and through government
circulars, and from publications of local-authority associations and
local-government magazines. From this point on the passage of legislation through the department is best characterized by the terms
distillation and integration—this for simplicity and without wishing
to undermine the coherence of that passage.

Distillation: Legislation is not unilinearly transformed according to a
single set of criteria. As was seen earlier, variance obtains in legislative character with regard to specificity, detail, relationship to
professional knowledge, permissivity and so on. Further, statutes can
and frequently do concern a wide range of related matters of unequal
relevance to a social-services department. Senior organizational
members need to concern themselves only with certain provisions.
A piece of legislation may contain items regulating juvenile-court
procedures and rules for the conduct of child-care cases, whilst at
the same time empowering the department with respect to the
establishment of experimental programmes of residential care. The
organization must sift such provisions and once sifted, allocate responsibility within the organization for the new tasks both between
divisions and levels of personnel. An initial organizational classification is overlaid on the statute according to criteria of relevance to
organizational activities. Appropriate provisions are distilled out
for a peculiarly organizational treatment. That treatment we
term integration.

Integration: If, through being directed to new task areas, the organization is required to accommodate to law, then the legislation also has
to be made to come to terms with organization. No matter how
detailed, legislation does not necessarily provide the conditions of its
own operationalization, nor is such operationalization likely to be
exhausted by any guidance given in government circulars, etc. For
instance, the manner of obtaining consent for voluntary reception of a
child into care may be specified in terms of the information to be
given to a parent and a requirement of a parental signature. Alternatively, a department may be directed to supply services to the
chronic sick without exhaustive supplementation in the form of a
working definition of the chronic sick; the exact level of service to be
provided; the relevant hierarchy level for adjudicating the delivery of
service; and so on.

In the context of processing statutes for routine use, an initial requirement is to simplify legal language. The technicality and style of legal discourse militates against allocating portions of a statute at will throughout the organization. At the same time, such provisions are embodied in organizational policies, procedures and forms. During this process law is progressively 'held up' within the organization in the sense in which lower-level members encounter only organizational versions of legislation. Policies may be idiosyncratic vis-à-vis other departments, more or less liberal, explicit and resourced, but they constitute the prime referent for routine social-work activity. Such an observation is not of course denied by the ability of social workers to avail themselves of competing versions—the organizational version simply provides the working documentation of routine social work.

Clients similarly are unlikely to experience directly the new statute in their encounters with the department. Although information on their legal position may be made available to them, they are more likely to experience only organizational forms, headed perhaps by the name of the relevant statute. The client would not necessarily be aware that legislation was operating nor that his case may have been required to meet criteria laid down by the organization. Law which does reach the client is not necessarily made available for the purpose of communicating rights and duties. Such communication may simply be for organizational purposes of information retrieval or may be required by virtue of the legislation itself or for organizational criteria of implementation—hidden from the client's view.

The process of integration, then, has two facets. First is the facet in which law is integrated into the organizational structure—responsibility for provisions is distributed amongst personnel at varying levels of the hierarchy. The second facet is the integration of law into organizational activity in terms of working documentation for members who actually deal with cases.

From this brief description we can specify the level of analysis required to understand mediation in an action framework. Throughout the proceedings we have been giving an account of the routine activities of organizational members in regard to a new statute. In no sense have we wanted to give the impression that some reified entity, the 'organization', needs to distil and to integrate law. The discussion simply refers to what is done by higher members of social-services organizations pursuant to the mediation of legislation.

LAW AND SOCIAL WORK

So far, we have provided the levels of analysis of 'availability of explanations' and 'mediation of legislation'. These levels are in themselves an understanding of the social processes at work in the encounter between law and social work, but that understanding remains general in character and can be filled out and deepened in more substantive analyses. In a sense, they constitute a framework for locating events, actions and social processes as these are seen to occur in the social-work setting, but that framework is not imported eclectically. Nor will the framework or its elements 'explain' actions and events in the form of 'An actor did X *because* he was mediating legislation.' Rather, action X is seen as constitutive of the process of mediation. Mediation is simply the name we have given to congeries of such actions as a means of communicating the essential features of law-related activity within the organization. The notion presents itself as useful in grasping, classifying and categorizing the events and actions engaged in by organizational members with regard to law in making law available for social workers. In turn, the notion sensitizes work to features of the social-work setting. And we say here 'sensitizes' rather than 'directs', since the character of the notion is such that orientation to features of action is what is achieved, and action is allowed to retain the ability to talk back and contradict.

The two levels of explanation have in fact been utilized in substantive research concerning law and social work, and in part grew out of the focused attention which research dictates. As we turn to consider the general relations of law and social work, we will be relying more heavily on this substantive work to carry the argument.

As a preliminary, consider how the relations of law and social work might be characterized under the contemporary rubric of the sociology of law. We suggest that what would be offered, were it to be explained, would be an account of law in social work as social control. On the one hand we already have numerous statements that social work in general is an exercise in social control, that social workers are either agents of the abstracted process itself, or of the state. Further, prevailing wisdoms attribute to law also the status of social control,[33] with law seen either *as* social control or a mechanism for its enforcement. Law in social work, then, might well be seen as one of the mechanisms used by social workers to enforce social control. *Prima facie*, social-worker activity in regard to law would seem an ideal setting for investigation—by, for instance, Black[34] into the relation between law (as government social control) and 'other forms of social control'. The difficulties with such an approach we have discussed previously. Put simply, they relate, first, to the source of the notion, social control, and, secondly, to its excessive ordering character. Is the notion autonomously constructed; does it flow from one or another social theory; is it comprehensible to, say, social workers, to talk of their activity in these terms; who, quite, is doing the controlling; society, the state, the ruling class or what? The genesis is unwarrantably clouded. Similarily, how do we justify granting to the concept of 'social control' primacy in adjudicating the data? At one level, that of its source, the concept is divorced from the empirical world; at another, that of its application, it obscures and distorts by being over forceful, when it should facilitate. If, however, we reflect a little on a depiction of law/social-worker relations as 'law as social control', we can see that even as it stands it contains the seeds of a radical reorienting of analysis. Accept for the moment that social workers are agents of social control. Accept further that law is a form of social control, and that both law and social control can be taken for granted. Now, if our frame of reference is the *client*, analysis will be susceptible to a depiction of law in social work as social control, with particular attention being given to the consequences for the client. For instance, does the client get his rights; is such control of the client justifiable; and so on? But if the frame of reference is *social-worker activity*, then we have to note that we have an agent of social control in the presence of a form of social control, and we can consider how at an action level the agent *uses* that form of social control. We can look not to the 'objective' consequences of the employment of law, but the nature of that employment itself. What we might get out is that law stands as resource for the agent in the activity of social control.

In the substantive research mentioned earlier, attention was given to the basis on which social workers constructed their available explanations of client problems, and the grounds on which treatment plans and case strategies were generated. Those grounds were seen in the main to be aspects of social-work knowledge, an operating combination of social-work theory and knowledge possessed by virtue of a position as a social-work operative. Law was not an operating category for defining and conceptualizing client problems, but stood as a tool to be used in solving client problems. At this level, law was seen to be *problem solving*. In terms of the organization, the status of law was seen to be somewhat different. Here law was recognized to be *problem orienting*. Law oriented higher members of the organization to areas of deprivation requiring attention; provided the ground rules of organizational activity; and much of their activity was seen to be directed to the fulfilment of legal enactments, with law setting the priorities and adjudicating resource allocation. Whilst social workers were generally guided by conceptions of social-work practice rather than legally set priorities, for organizational activity law was of importance in orienting attention and providing a referent for the construction of policies and procedures and resource allocation.

Whilst the relation of law to social workers was seen to vary according to the level of the organization (remembering that social workers are organizational members, albeit at a lower level), variance was also exhibited in relation to the type of law, the important dimension being the degree of discretion permitted to organizational actors. General law[35] (law referring to welfare legislation for which social-services departments have no formal responsibility) provides the greatest discretion, for the organization can if it wishes simply ignore it. General law need only enter the social-worker arena to the extent that social workers consider it to be of importance in the cases they deal with, according to criteria supplied either by them or by organizational policies. However, within professional law (that law for which the organization is formally responsible) variance also occurs along the dimension of the discretion permitted. To some extent this variance is expressed in the distinction between 'powers' and 'duties', and this distinction largely parallels the amount of social-work content of legislation. Since professional law is generally created with reference to social-services departments it is unsurprising that when issues are signified by *social-work* diagnosis the legislation talks of powers, and where implementation is less a matter of social work than administration, of 'duties'. But the important dimension is that of discretion permitted. In situations of high discretion, law is more available to stand as problem solving; in those of low discretion problem orientation is a more correct characterization.

If we take these two features (organizational level and the degree of discretion), the matrix approach can again be employed.

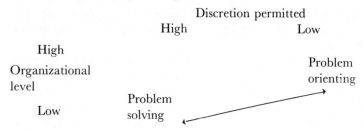

Again, however, we have to reject the matrix at inception, for we find ourselves failing to reach the level of action. The referent of the matrix is not action, but the client problem. The question 'When and where is law likely to be used to solve client problems, or to orient attention to client problems?' can be answered after a fashion, but analysis is still not grounded sufficiently at the action level. We need to consider the relationship of law to social work, not in terms of client problems, but in terms of social-work activity itself.

To achieve a reorientation of analysis, the distinction has to be made between client problems and action 'problems'. The social worker's action problems, for instance, are clearly not the same as those experienced by the client.

There is however, a relationship between the two. The social worker's main action 'problem' is to solve clients' problems. And whilst the relation of law to social work at the level of the social worker and with regard to client problems is one of problem solving, law is a resource *for the social workers* in solving client problems. For social workers, law stands as a resource.

A similar transformation of analysis can be as readily achieved for the organization. First of all, we need to recognize that, as carriers of the organizational purpose, an important relevance for higher organizational members in their activity is to address areas of deprivation, and law is a resource in authorizing or facilitating lines of action to realize that purpose. More particularly, however, research has indicated that more specific relevances can be identified. Organizational defence was seen to be an operating relevance for higher levels of the organization, effort being made to minimize the risk of public disapproval, for instance with regard to child-battering cases. In constructing suitable strategies of defence, officers of the department again used law as a resource in generating policies of procedures thought likely to minimize the risk of spectacular failures. In terms of their own action problems, law was seen to stand as a resource.

Law as resource constitutes a depiction of law to social work at a fairly high level of generality. But generality here does not involve wanton abstraction or divorce from empirical activity. There is a direct, specified and verifiable linkage between the depiction and the data, one which, although simplified for the present exposition, retains contact with the subject-matter of social action. Whilst, say, law as social control has a certain intangibility, the mark of a clouded genesis, we can never escape the fact that 'law as resource' is law as a resource *for social action.*

CONCLUSION

Sociological Inquiry and Legal Phenomena: The Pursuit of Permissive Purity

It would take a surfeit of sociological arrogance to imagine that the exposition given above is sufficient to found the transformation of the existing relationship between sociological inquiry and legal phenomena. We have made a number of claims regarding the sociological study of law and supported these by both argument and demonstration. It would require further empirical work, however, to realize their potential and establish their orthodoxy and limitations. None the less, we have been able to go further than mere speculation concerning the form a reconstructed sociology of law might take. A sociology of law can exist without reliance on the 'obvious facticity' of law and unhampered by the straitjacket of normative conceptions. Our conception of law, by suspending belief in the status of law in everyday life, that is by retaining as a sociological problem how social action relates to the 'obvious' facticity of law, embodies a legitimate sociological purpose and is able to withstand the vagaries of research situations.

Having demonstrated the utility of our conception of law as far as the present context allows, the programmatic purpose of this book is to that extent, complete. A number of issues remain to be explicated and to offer a conclusion as such would, therefore, be anomalous. All that can be done is to codify and make explicit certain principles underlying our own work by which we believe the sociology of law—and indeed any sociological sub-disciple—can best proceed.

We can begin by stating the nature of the relationship between the styles of work offered in this chapter and those sociological approaches reviewed in Chapter V. It will be obvious that we hold no brief for positivism within sociology. At the macro-level of functionalism, meaning is excluded because of theory; at the micro-level of behaviourism, meaning is excluded because of methodology. Neither exclusion is in our view justified. It is the interpretive sociologies that have informed our own work. But despite our having separated out various of the analytic styles available within the interpretive school we have no wish to be more specific concerning the sociological approach giving rise to the notion of law as a categorization of experience and the ensuing analysis of law in the social-work setting. We accept that important differences exist between those styles as reflected in the alternative topics of inquiry and research strategies offered, and in no sense do we wish to forge any false alliance. The point is simply that there is room for more than one series of topics and research strategies as long as those chosen retain a basic commitment to interpretive tenets. We claim only, and not originally, that meaning is constitutive of social life and that any sociology that ignores this provides the conditions for its own failure.

This permissive attitude to competing methodological styles has a parallel in the nature of the reconstruction that we seek for the sociology of law. Whilst we have spelt out in some detail the differences both within and between normative and interpretive approaches, it will be clear from our earlier review of the literature that we regard much work within the sociology of law to be theoretically and methodologically eclectic. Where eclectism has been such as to promote analysis consistent with the meaningful character of social action the work may have value which it is important to retain. Although work may be justifiably castigated for being positivist in tenor, we must be circumspect in its total rejection. To take one example only, we would not wish to lose the narrative value of the American Jury projects, for all the positivism displayed in their presentation. This observation we would extend to many of the studies of legislation, legal actors and indeed those more overarching works discussed in Chapter III. We seek to reconstruct the sub-discipline, and this includes the existing work, not to suggest that no work of value has yet been undertaken.

Following on from this, we do not regard participant observation as exhausting the methodological possibilities of sociology. If interpretation of social behaviour is the touchstone of a valid sociology, then participant observation has a legitimate pre-eminence, but none-the-less our methodological priorities can and must allow for research topics not limited to present-day accessible action settings. If sociology refuses to address historical material, not only will it sever the link with observers such as Weber, but it will do so without any methodological rationale. The utility of participant observation as a research strategy is not to be confused with the methodological commitment from which its utility is derived. Historical sociology does not require the notions of cause or system; nor need it proceed under the aegis of deductive logic. It requires only the possibility of retrospective understanding and interpretation, a project far removed from the establishment of historical laws but valid for all that.

The assessment and utilization of existing studies should not, in our view, rest solely upon their classification as belonging to one or another style or type of sociological work. It should depend on the extent to which a particular study succeeds in grasping the social construction of lines of action, past or present. Similarly with regard to work being undertaken, the rule of thumb to be employed is the ability to conduct analysis at the level of mundane meaning. This rule of thumb does not exist independently of particular research situations as an idealized prescription and cannot therefore be given as an abstract principle. It is possible however, to indicate the means by which its abrogation can be avoided. We state these means in terms of five temptations to be avoided, temptations which, if succumbed to, will act less as short cuts than as short circuits.

The first temptation is to use existing sociological theory and methods unquestioningly. Questioning must relate to the ordering impositions inhering within particular theories and research methods. In terms of substantive theory, Blumer[36] has documented its inability to maintain contact with the empirical world and we argued at length above that deductive theory leads only to understanding by fiat. Similarly, methodologists, so called, must take note of the reasons underlying the rejections of theoretical systems both in constructing the ideas which they subject to empirical test and in formulating the procedures by which empirical investigation can legitimately be undertaken. Cicourel[37] and others have argued persuasively that the methodologist's concern with measurement identifies the characteristics of social phenonema by imposing an order on the social world rather than by the more deliberate empirical task of seeking out such order as does exist.

Related to the above is a temptation to use pre-existing sociological concepts in an uncritical fashion. Lack of critical awareness can take at least two forms. First, existing concepts are frequently used as if they were optically precise spectacles for obtaining a revolutionary view of a segment of social life. Secondly, their employment as *explanations* of social phenomena not only distorts the relation between the concept and the reality it purports to describe, but also serves to buttress the claims of cause and effect within sociological discourse.

The third temptation is to view *any* type of knowledge about a phenomenon as sociological knowledge. Sociology is a developing discipline which addresses itself to the human world. But it can only address itself to certain features, those concerning the nature of social action. Sociology seeks to understand the human world by investigating social action, by investigating the ability of people to comprehend and theorize about the world sufficient for them to construct their own practical activities, conduct their own affairs and provide that sense of order which sociologists have for so long both described and explained in terms of social structure. Sociology can then only claim responsibility for its own concerns. There may be many things we feel we can say about phenomena without regard to the methodological strictures of sociology (i.e. without having regard to or addressing social action), and we may provide criteria against which such statements can be verified. But this will not make those statements in any way sociological. Flowing from this, we must not presume nor be tempted into thinking that sociology can necessarily provide a satisfactory account of phenomena for the purpose of endeavours other than those peculiar to itself. Even if a sociological statement can be generated, it is not generated for the purposes of those who view the phenomena for another purpose or from another perspective.

The fourth temptation is to see the purpose of a sociology of law as being the academic implementation of a definition of law. Not only do we have to guard against establishing the substantive character of law prior to investigation: we must also avoid the pursuit of a theory which somehow would be able to define law for us. The only task prior to analysis is to make contact with the phenomenon in a manner which does not distort its nature of being in the world. We can only do this by engaging in analysis at the level of social action. The purpose of the sociology of law is nothing more nor less than the study of how actors achieve in concerted social action those activities which pertain to law. Law in the context of social action is the proper object of attention, not law generically defined and identifiable independently of routine social activity.

Finally, we must avoid the temptation of allowing immediate purposes to blur the central attempt to achieve an understanding of legal phenomena as social phenomena. Sociologists' purposes as members of a discipline competing with legal science have generated problems flowing from the academic market place rather than from the sociological enterprise. Our purposes as men-in-society can be just as persuasive, if not more so. The question is not whether these purposes are correct, in some sense, but whether they are allowed to mediate between our subject-matter and our endeavour to understand it.

The consequences of succumbing to any of these temptations is to distort both the subject of study and the status of that study. The purpose of study can stem only from an understanding of the sociological enterprise, such an understanding depending on a grasp of what the subject-matter of sociology is and what the relation of the sub-disciplines to the mother discipline consists of. Problems, methods, theories and questions addressed must all derive from the purpose of sociology so established. It is insufficient to recognize that social action is interpretive; sociology must use that level of analysis which translates the axiom into a methodological stance.

References

Chapter I: Discovering the Sociology of Law

1. R. POUND, 'The Need of Sociological Jurisprudence' in R. J. SIMON (ed.), *The Sociology of Law* (1968), Chandler, San Francisco, p. 9.
2. N. TIMASHEFF, 'What is Sociology of Law?', in R. J. SIMON (ed.), op. cit., p. 56.
3. G. GUREVITCH, *The Sociology of Law* (1947), Routledge & Kegan Paul, London, p. 1.
4. R. SCHWARZ, 'Introduction' to 'Law and Society' supplement to *Social Problems*, Vol. 13 (Summer 1965) p. 1.
5. P. MORRIS, 'A sociological Approach to Research in Legal Services', in P. MORRIS et al., *Social Needs and Legal Action* (1973), Martin Robertson, London, p. 49.
6. See for instance, E. SCHUR, *Law and Society* (1968), Random House, New York, p. 5.
7. M. WEBER, *On Law in Economy and Society* (1967), Simon and Schuster, New York; and see pp. 61–79 below.
8. E. DURKHEIM, *Les Règles de la méthode sociologique* (1894), English trans. *The Rules of Sociological Method* (1938), Free Press, New York; *De la Division du travail social* (1893), English trans. *The Division of Labour in Society* (1933), Free Press, New York; and pp. 45–61 below.
9. The most influential implementation of the Marxist programme in relation to law has been K. RENNER, *The Institutions of Private Law* (1949), Routledge & Kegan Paul, London, see pp. 93–101 below.
10. See for instance E. SCHUR, op. cit.; P. SELZNICK, 'The Sociology of Law' in R. J. SIMON (ed.), op. cit.; A. PODGORECKI, *Law and Society* (1974), Routledge & Kegan Paul, London; and R. TREVES, 'Introduction' to R. TREVES and G. VAN LOON, *Norms and Action* (1968), Martinus Nijhoff, The Hague.
11. A. PODGORECKI, op. cit.
12. ibid., p. 8.
13. E. SCHUR, op. cit., p. 4.
14. ibid.
15. ibid., p. 15.
16. P. SELZNICK, op. cit.
17. P. MORRIS, op. cit.
18. See for instance, E. SCHUR, op. cit., P. MORRIS, 'Introduction' to P. MORRIS et. al., op. cit.; R. TREVES, op. cit.; and D. FARRIER, 'False Perspectives', paper presented to the Socio-legal Group Conference, Manchester (1973).
19. K. ZWINGMANN, 'The Sociology of Law in the Federal Republic of Germany', in R. TREVES and G. VAN LOON, op. cit., p. 262.
20. ibid., p. 279.
21. D. REISMAN, 'Law and Sociology: Recruitment, Training and Colleagueship', in W. EVAN, *Law and Sociology* (1962), Free Press, New York.
22. E. SCHUR, op. cit., p. 6.
23. V. AUBERT, 'Introduction' to V. AUBERT (ed.), *The Sociology of Law* (1969), Penguin Books, London.
24. H. BREDEMEIER, 'Law as an Integrative Mechanism', in V. AUBERT (ed.), op. cit., p. 52.
25. T. PARSONS, 'The Law and Social Control', in W. EVAN, *Law and Sociology* (1962), Free Press, New York; D. BLACK, 'The Boundaries of Legal Sociology', in D. BLACK and M. MILESKI (eds.), *The Social Organization of Law* (1973), Seminar Press, New York.

26. D. BLACK, op. cit., p. 42.
27. E. SCHUR, op. cit., p. 4.
28. J. SKOLNICK, 'The Sociology of Law in America', in R. TREVES and G. VAN LOON, op. cit., p. 199.
29. E. SCHUR, op. cit., pp. 72–73.
30. J. GIBBS, 'The Sociology of Law and Normative Phenomena', *American Sociological Review*, Vol. 31 (1966), pp. 315–325.
31. W. EVAN, 'Introduction' to W. EVAN (ed.), op. cit., p. 9; E. SCHUR, op. cit., p. 8.
32. See pp. 61–79 below.
33. N. TIMASHEFF, op. cit.
34. D. BLACK, op. cit.
35. ibid., p. 42.
36. D. SILVERMAN, *The Theory of Organizations* (1970), Heinemann, London.
37. A. PODGORECKI, op. cit., pp. 3–47.
38. D. BLACK, op. cit., p. 53.
39. The following discussion is based in part on T. WILSON 'Normative and Interpretive Paradigms in Sociology', in J. DOUGLAS (ed.), *Understanding Everyday Life* (1973), Routledge & Kegan Paul, London.
40. T. WILSON, op. cit., p. 60.
41. R. CLOWARD and L. OHLIN, *Delinquency and Opportunity* (1960), Free Press, New York.
42. T. WILSON, op. cit., p. 66.
43. L. TAYLOR, 'The Contribution of the Labelling and Social Interactionist School to Criminological Thought', Paper presented to the Fourth National Conference on Research and Teaching in Criminology, Cambridge, July 1970, p. 6.
44. A. SCHUTZ, 'Concept and Theory Formation in the Social Sciences' in D. EMMETT and A. MACINTYRE (eds.), *Sociological Theory and Philosophical Analysis* (1972), Macmillan, London, p. 11.
45. ibid.
46. ibid., pp. 4–5.
47. P. WINCH, *The Idea of a Social Science* (1967), Routledge & Kegan Paul, London.
48. A. MACINTYRE, 'The Idea of a Social Science' in A. RYAN (ed.), *The Philosophy of Social Explanation* (1973), Oxford University Press, London.
49. P. WINCH, op. cit., pp. 83–84.
50. ibid., p. 127.
51. ibid., pp. 127–128.
52. ibid.
53. P. COHEN, *Modern Social Theory* (1969), Heinemann, London, pp. 2–3.
54. ibid., p. 9.
55. G. HOMANS, 'Contemporary Theory in Sociology', in N. DENZIN (ed.) (1970), *Sociological Methods*, Butterworth, London, p. 52.
56. ibid., p. 52.
57. ibid.
58. K. POPPER, *Logik der Forschung*, English trans. *The Logic of Scientific Discovery* (1959), Hutchinson, London, p. 59.
59. P. FILMER, et al., *New Directions in Sociological Theory* (1972), Collier Macmillan, London, p. 84.
60. ibid., p. 87.
61. A. RYAN, op. cit.
62. ibid., p. 79.
63. See pp. 45–61 below.
64. É. DURKHEIM, *The Rules of Sociological Method*, op. cit., p. 3.
65. J. GOLDTHORPE, 'A Revolution in Sociology?', *Sociology*, Vol. 7, No. 3 (1973).
66. H. BLUMER, *Symbolic Interactionism* (1969), Prentice-Hall, Englewood Cliffs, N.J., p. 19.

Chapter II: Déjà Vu: Émile Durkheim
1. É. DURKHEIM, *De la Division du travail social* (1893), English trans. *The Division of Labor in Society* (1933), Free Press, New York, p. 32.
2. ibid., p. 64.
3. É. DURKHEIM, *Les Règles de la méthode sociologique* (1894), English trans. *The Rules of Sociological Method* (1938), Free Press, New York, p. xxvii.
4. ibid., p. 32.
5. ibid., p. 4.
6. ibid., p. 13.
7. É. DURKHEIM (1933), op. cit., pp. 65–66.
8. ibid., p. 65.
9. É. DURKHEIM (1938), op. cit., p. 45.
10. ibid., p. liii.
11. ibid., pp. 53–54.
12. ibid., p. xlv.
13. ibid., p. lvii.
14. J. REX, *Key Problems of Sociological Theory* (1961), Routledge & Kegan Paul, London, p. 44.
15. É. DURKHEIM (1938), op. cit., p. 47.
16. ibid., p. 49.
17. ibid., p. 55.
18. ibid., p. 70.
19. ibid., p. 72.
20. ibid., p. 81.
21. É. DURKHEIM (1933), op. cit., p. 31.
22. ibid., p. 38.
23. ibid., p. 65.
24. ibid., p. 60.
25. ibid., p. 60.
26. ibid., p. 68.
27. ibid., p. 68.
28. ibid., p. 69.
29. ibid., p. 73.
30. ibid., pp. 74–75.
31. ibid., p. 76.
32. ibid., p. 77.
33. ibid., p. 96.
34. ibid., p. 77.
35. ibid., p. 106.
36. ibid., p. 109.
37. ibid., p. 114.
38. ibid., p. 114.
39. ibid., p. 117.
40. ibid., p. 122.
41. ibid., p. 123.
42. ibid., p. 125.
43. R. MERTON, 'Durkheim's Division of Labour in Society' in R. NISBET (ed.), *Émile Durkheim* (1965), Prentice-Hall, Englewood Cliffs, N.J., p. 109.
44. R. SCHWARTZ and J. MILLER, 'Legal Evolution and Societal Complexity', *American Journal of Sociology* (1964).
45. U. BAXI, 'Comment—Durkheim and Legal Evolution: some problems of disproof', *Law and Society Review* (Summer 1974).
46. É. DURKHEIM (1933), op. cit., p. 74.
47. ibid., p. 76.
48. ibid., p. 77.

Max Weber

1. M. RHEINSTEIN (ed.), Introduction to M. WEBER, *On Law in Economy and Society* (1967), Simon and Schuster, New York, p. xviii.
2. ibid., p. xxvii.
3. Quoted in D. ATKINSON, *Orthodox Consensus and Radical Alternative* (1971), Heinemann, London, p. 76.
4. T. PARSONS (ed.), M. WEBER, *The Theory of Social and Economic Organization* (1947), Free Press, New York, p. 88.
5. ibid.
6. ibid.
7. ibid., p. 89.
8. J. FREUND, *The Sociology of Max Weber* (1972), Penguin Books, London, pp. 40–41.
9. A. GIDDENS, *Capitalism and Modern Social Theory* (1921), Cambridge University Press, London, p. 139.
10. T. PARSONS (ed.), Introduction to M. WEBER, *The Theory of Social and Economic Organization*, op. cit., p. 11.
11. See the comparison set out by A. GIDDENS, op. cit., pp. 141 et seq.
12. J. FREUND, op. cit., pp. 59 et seq.
13. M. WEBER, *The Theory of Social and Economic Organization*, op. cit., p. 99.
14. Quoted in A. GIDDENS, op. cit., p. 148.
15. M. WEBER, *The Theory of Social and Economic Organization*, op. cit., p. 99.
16. ibid., pp. 99–100.
17. ibid., p. 100.
18. J. FREUND, op. cit., p. 99.
19. A. GIDDENS, op. cit., p. 141.
20. M. WEBER, *On Law in Economy and Society*, op. cit., p. 11.
21. ibid., p. 13.
22. M. RHEINSTEIN, op. cit., p. lix.
23. Quoted in JULIEN FREUND, op. cit., pp. 257–258.
24. M. WEBER, *On Law in Economy and Society*, op. cit., p. 63.
25. ibid.
26. ibid.
27. M. RHEINSTEIN, op. cit., p. lii.
28. ibid., pp. lii–liii.
29. ibid., p. liii.
30. M. WEBER, *On Law in Economy and Society*, pp. 98–99.
31. ibid., p. 122.
32. ibid., Ch. VI.
33. See pp. 214–215 below.
34. T. PARSONS, op. cit., p. 20.

Introduction to Part Two

1. J. SKOLNICK, 'Social Research on Legality', *Law and Society Review* (1966).
2. P. SELZNICK, 'Sociology and Natural Law', in D. BLACK and M. MILESKI (eds.), *The Social Organization of Law* (1973), Seminar Press, New York.

Chapter III: Law and Society

1. T. PARSONS, *The Structure of Social Action* (1961), Free Press, New York, p. 25.
2. D. ATKINSON, *Orthodox Consensus and Radical Alternative* (1971), Heinemann, London, p. 9.
3. T. PARSONS (ed.), Introduction to M. WEBER, *The Theory of Social and Economic Organization* (1947), Free Press, New York, p. 20.

4. T. PARSONS, *The Structure of Social Action*, op. cit., p. 740.
5. L. SKLAIR, 'Functionalism and Deviance', Paper presented to the British Sociological Association Annual Conference, 1971, p. 2.
6. T. PARSONS, 'The Law and Social Control', in W. EVAN (ed.), *Law and Sociology* (1962), Free Press, New York.
7. ibid., p. 57.
8. ibid., p. 56.
9. ibid., p. 57.
10. ibid., p. 57.
11. ibid., p. 58.
12. ibid., p. 63.
13. ibid., p. 65.
14. H. BREDEMEIER, 'Law as an Integrative Mechanism', in V. AUBERT (ed.), *Sociology of Law* (1969), Penguin Books, London.
15. ibid., p. 55.
16. ibid., p. 57.
17. ibid., p. 60.
18. K. RENNER, *The Institutions of Private Law* (1949), Routledge & Kegan Paul, London.
19. Preface to K. MARX, *Critique of Political Economies* (1904), London, quoted in K. RENNER, op. cit., at p. 55.
20. K. MARX, *Neue Zeit*, p. 744, quoted in K. RENNER, op. cit., at p. 56.
21. K. RENNER, op. cit., p. 56.
22. K. MARX, *Neue Zeit*, p. 779, quoted in K. RENNER, op. cit., at p. 57.
23. K. RENNER, op. cit., p. 52.
24. ibid., p. 52.
25. ibid., p. 45.
26. ibid., p. 48.
27. ibid., p. 48.
28. ibid., p. 51.
29. ibid., p. 51.
30. ibid., p. 51.
31. ibid., p. 54.
32. ibid., p. 55.
33. ibid., p. 55.
34. ibid., p. 56.
35. ibid., p. 58.
36. ibid., pp. 69–70.
37. ibid., p. 76.
38. ibid., p. 76.
39. ibid., p. 77.
40. ibid., p. 84.
41. ibid., p. 86.
42. ibid., p. 196.
43. W. CHAMBLISS and R. SEIDMAN, *Law, Order and Power* (1971), Addison-Wesley, Reading, Mass.
44. ibid., pp. 6–9.
45. ibid., p. 53.
46. ibid., p. 4.
47. ibid., p. 25.
48. ibid., p. 73.
49. ibid., p. 33.
50. ibid., p. 113.
51. ibid., p. 113.
52. ibid., p. 151.

53. ibid., p. 181.
54. ibid., p. 73.
55. P. SELZNICK, 'The Sociology of Law' in R. J. SIMON (ed.), *The Sociology of Law*, Chandler, San Francisco, pp. 190–200.
56. ibid., p. 191.
57. ibid., p. 195.
58. ibid., p. 192.
59. ibid., p. 193.
60. ibid., p. 197.
61. P. SELZNICK, 'Sociology and Natural Law', in D. BLACK and M. MILESKI (eds.) (1973), *The Social Organizaion of Law*, Seminar Press, New York, p. 27.
62. ibid., p. 31.
63. ibid., p. 25.

Chapter IV: Law in Society

1. E. SCHUR, *Law and Society* (1968), Random House, New York.
2. ibid., pp. 14–15.
3. R. TREVES and G. VAN LOON (eds.), *Norms and Actions* (1968), Martinus Nijhoff, The Hague.
4. ibid., p. 2.
5. W. G. SUMNER, *Folkways* (1906), Ginn & Co., Boston, Mass.
6. See J. GROSSMAN and H. GROSSMAN, *Law and Change in Modern America* (1971), Goodyear Publishing, California.
7. E. SCHUR, op. cit., p. 127.
8. ibid., p. 122.
9. W. EVAN, 'Law as an Instrument of Social Change', in A. GOULDNER and S. MILLER (eds.), *Applied Sociology* (1965), Free Press, New York.
10. E. SCHUR, op. cit., p. 128.
11. L. MAYHEW, 'Law and Equal Opportunity: Anti-Discrimination Law in Boston' (1963), Ph.D. dissertation, Harvard University. Quoted by J. SKOLNICK in his article in R. TREVES and G. VAN LOON (eds.), op. cit.
12. J. GUSFIELD, *Symbolic Crusade* (1963), University of Illinois Press, Urbana.
13. E. SCHUR, op. cit., p. 92.
14. ibid., p. 95.
15. R. MACIVER, *Power Transformed* (1964), Macmillan, New York, p. 207.
16. J. SKOLNICK, 'The Sociology of Law in America', in R. TREVES and G. VAN LOON (eds.), op. cit., p. 169.
17. R. DAHRENDORF, 'Law Faculties and the German Upper Class', in V. AUBERT (ed.), *Sociology of Law* (1969), Penguin Books, London.
18. ibid., p. 306.
19. ibid., p. 306.
20. K. RENNER, *The Institutions of Private Law* (1949), Routledge & Kegan Paul, London.
21. W. CHAMBLISS and R. SEIDMAN, *Law, Order and Power* (1970), Addison-Wesley, Reading, Mass.
22. Z. BANKOWSKI and G. MUNGHAM, *Images of Law* (1976), Routledge & Kegan Paul, London.
23. B. ABEL-SMITH and R. STEVENS, *Lawyers and the Courts* (1967), Heinemann, London.
24. W. G. CARSON, 'Symbolic and Instrumental Dimensions of Early Factory Legislation', in R. HOOD (ed.), *Crime, Criminology and Public Policy* (1974), Heinemann, London; and W. G. CARSON, 'Some Sociological Aspects of Strict Liability and the Enforcement of Factory Legislation', *Modern Law Review* (1970), v. 33, p. 346.
25. V. AUBERT, 'Some Social Functions of Legislation' in V. AUBERT (ed.), op. cit.

26. T. DUSTER, *The Legislation of Morality* (1970), Free Press, New York; H. BECKER, *Outsiders* (1967), Free Press, New York.
27. W. CHAMBLISS, 'A Sociological Analysis of the Law of Vagrancy', *Social Problems* (1964), V. 12.
28. J. GUSFIELD, op. cit.
29. W. G. CARSON, 'The Sociology of Crime and the Emergence of Criminal Laws' in P. ROCK and M. MACINTOSH (eds.), *Deviance and Social Control* (1974), Tavistock, London, p. 66.
30. W. CHAMBLISS, *Crime and the Legal Process* (1969), McGraw-Hill, New York.
31. W. G. CARSON, in P. ROCK and M. MACINTOSH (eds.), op. cit.
32. J. GUSFIELD, op. cit., p. 67.
33. See T. DUSTER, op. cit., pp. 9–23.
34. M. RHEINSTEIN (ed.), M. WEBER, *On Law and Economy in Society* (1967), Simon and Schuster, New York, p. 338.
35. J. GORECKI, 'Divorce in Poland—a socio-legal study', in V. AUBERT (ed.), op. cit.
36. V. AUBERT (ed.), op. cit.
37. W. G. CARSON, in R. HOOD (ed.), op. cit.; and W. G. CARSON (1970), op. cit.
38. S. LUKES, *Power—A Radical View* (1974), Macmillan, London.
39. V. AUBERT, op. cit., p. 116.
40. ibid., p. 117.
41. W. G. SUMNER, op. cit.
42. V. AUBERT, op. cit., p. 117.
43. ibid., p. 121.
44. ibid., p. 125.
45. W. G. CARSON (1970), op. cit.
46. M. SMITH and A. PEARSON, 'The Value of Strict Liability', *Criminal Law Review* (1969), pp. 5–16.
47. W. G. CARSON (1970), op. cit., p. 398.
48. ibid., p. 401.
49. ibid., p. 405.
50. ibid., p. 405.
51. ibid., p. 399.
52. W. GUSFIELD, op. cit.
53. W. G. CARSON, in R. HOOD (ed.), op. cit., p. 113.
54. ibid., p. 113.
55. ibid., p. 122.
56. ibid., p. 123.
57. ibid., pp. 136–138.
58. C. WRIGHT MILLS, *The Power Elite* (1956), Oxford University Press, New York.
59. D. REISMAN, *Thorsten Veblen: A Critical Interpretation* (1975), Seabury Press, New York.
60. N. POLSKY, *Community Power and Political Theory* (1965), Yale University Press, New Haven.
61. R. DAHL, 'A critique of the Ruling-Elite Model', *American Political Science Review* (1958), V. 52, pp. 463–469.
62. P. BACHROCK and M. BARATZ, 'The Two Faces of Power', *American Political Science Review* (1962), V. 56, pp. 947–952.
63. S. LUKES, op. cit., p. 22.
64. ibid., p. 41.
65. T. JOHNSON, *Professions and Power* (1973), Macmillan, London. Major trait theorists include: G. MILLERSON, *The Qualifying Associations: A study in Professionalisation* (1964), Routledge & Kegan Paul, London and E. GREENWOOD, 'Attributes of a Profession', *Social Work* (1957), V. 2, pp. 44–55.
66. T. PARSONS, *Essays in Sociological Theory* (1954), Free Press, New York.
67. D. RUESCHMEYER, 'Lawyers and Doctors: A comparison of two professions', in V. AUBERT (ed.), op. cit., pp. 267–278.

68. See also the discussion in Z. BANKOWSKI and G. MUNGHAM, op. cit.
69. T. JOHNSON, op. cit.
70. Z. BANKOWSKI and G. MUNGHAM, op. cit.
71. T. JOHNSON, op. cit., p. 54.
72. ibid., p. 59.
73. Z. BANKOWSKI and G. MUNGHAM, op. cit., p. 54.
74. J. CARLIN, *Lawyers on their Own* (1962), Rutger's University Press, New Jersey; and E. SMIGEL, *The Wall Street Lawyer* (1964), Free Press, New York.
75. J. SKOLNICK, op. cit.
76. J. LADINSKY, 'Careers of Lawyers, Law Practice and Legal Institutions', in R. SIMON (ed.), *The Sociology of Law* (1968), Chandler, California, p. 218.
77. D. RUESCHMEYER, op. cit.
78. P. NANET· and J. CARLIN, 'The Legal Profession', quoted in J. SKOLNICK, op. cit.
79. A brief account of which can be found in J. SKOLNICK, op. cit.
80. L. FULLER, 'An Afterword: Science and the Judicial Process', *Harvard Law Review* (1966), v. 79, p. 1612.
81. See, for instance, the studies in S. NAGEL, *The Legal Process from a Behavioral Perspective* (1969), Dorsey Press, Illinois.
82. e.g. those in S. NAGEL, op. cit.
83. L. FULLER, op. cit., p. 1607.
84. H. BLUMER, *Symbolic Interactionism* (1969), Prentice-Hall, Englewood Cliffs, N.J.
85. J. VAN HOUTTE and O. VINKE, 'Attitudes Governing the Acceptance of Legislation among various Social Groups', in A. PODGORECKI, et al., *Knowledge and Opinion of Law* (1973), Martin Robertson, London.
86. J. SKOLNICK, op. cit., p. 165.
87. H. KALVEN JR. and H. ZEISEL, 'Disagreement between Judge and Jury', in V. AUBERT (ed.), op. cit.
88. ibid., p. 243.
89. ibid., p. 243.
90. ibid., p. 244.
91. ibid., p. 252.
92. ibid., p. 253.
93. ibid., p. 251.
94. D. BROEDER, 'Plaintiff's Family Status as affecting Juror Behaviour: some tentative insights', in R. SIMON (ed.), op. cit.
95. ibid., p. 351.
96. J. SKOLNICK, op. cit., p. 167.
97. On this, and for an alternative to knowledge and opinion studies generally, see F. BURTON, 'The Irish Republican Army and its Community; a struggle for legitimacy', in P. CARLEN (ed.), *The Sociology of Law* (1976), Sociological Review Monograph, Keele.
98. Z. BANKOWSKI and G. MUNGHAM, op. cit.
99. S. MACAULAY, 'Non-contractual relations in Business: A Preliminary Study', American Sociological Review (1963), v. 28, pp. 55–67.
100. H. GARFINKEL 'Some Rules for Correct Decision-Making Observed by Jurors', in H. GARFINKEL, *Studies in Ethnomethodology* (1967), Prentice-Hall, Englewood Cliffs, N.J.; and H. GARFINKEL, 'The Origins of the Term "Ethnomethodology"', in R. TURNER (ed.), *Ethnomethodology*, Penguin Books, London, p. 16.
101. D. MCBARNETT, 'Pre-Trial Procedures and Construction of Conviction', in P. CARLEN (ed.), op. cit.
102. P. CARLEN, 'Remedial Routines for the Maintenance of Control in Magistrates' Courts', *British Journal of Law and Society* (1974), v. 1, p. 107.
103. F. BURTON, op. cit.
104. J. CARLIN and J. HOWARD, 'Legal Representation and Class Justice', *University of California at Los Angeles Law Review* (1965), v. 12, pp. 381–431.

105. ibid.
106. L. MAYHEW and A. REISS, JR., 'The Social Organization of Legal Contacts', *American Sociological Review* (1969), v. 34, pp. 309–318.
107. P. MORRIS, et al., 'Public Attitudes to Problem Definition and Problem Solving: A Pilot Study', *British Journal of Social Work*, v. 3, No. 3.
108. P. LEWIS, 'Unmet Legal Needs', in P. MORRIS et al., *Social Needs and Legal Action* (1973), Martin Robertson, London.
109. C. REICH, 'The New Property', in *Yale Law Journal* (1963), v. 73.
110. P. MORRIS, et al. (1973), op. cit.
111. Z. BANKOWSKI and G. MUNGHAM, op. cit.
112. P. MORRIS, et al. (1973), op. cit.
113. Z. BANKOWSKI and G. MUNGHAM, op. cit., p. 73.
114. ibid.
115. ibid., p. xii.
116. See S. NAGEL, op. cit.
117. In H. KALVEN JR. and H. ZEISEL, op. cit.
118. See V. AUBERT, op. cit., at various junctures in the exposition.

Chapter V: Sociology in the Presence of Law

Positivism and Functionalism

1. P. FILMER, et al., *New Directions in Sociological Theory* (1972), Collier Macmillan, London, p. 16.
2. P. COHEN, *Modern Social Theory* (1968), Heinemann, London, p. 37.
3. ibid., p. 35.
4. ibid., p. 37.
5. T. WILSON, 'Normative and Interpretive Paradigms in Sociology', in J. DOUGLAS (ed.), *Understanding Everyday Life* (1974), Routledge & Kegan Paul, London.
6. T. KUHN, *The Structure of Scientific Revolution* (1970), University of Chicago Press, U.S.A.
7. T. WILSON, op. cit., p. 61.
8. A. DAWE, 'The Two Sociologies' in J. TUNSTALL and K. THOMPSON (eds.), *Sociological Perspectives* (1971), Penguin, London.
9. ibid.
10. K. DAVIS, 'The Myth of Functional Analysis as a Special Method in Sociology and Anthropology', *American Sociological Review*, v. 24 (1959), pp. 757–773.
11. See, for instance, A. HACKER, 'Sociology and Ideology', in M. BLACK (ed.), *The Social Theories of Talcott Parsons* (1961), Prentice-Hall, Englewood Cliffs, N.J.
12. G. HOMANS, 'Bringing Men Back In', *American Sociological Review*, v. 29 (1964), pp. 809–818.
13. E. SCHUR, *Law in Society* (1968), Random House, New York, p. 82.
14. ibid., p. 82.
15. ibid., p. 83.
16. L. SKLAIR, 'Functionalism and Deviance', Paper presented to the British Sociological Association Annual Conference, 1971, p. 10.
17. ibid., p. 11.
18. P. COHEN, op. cit., p. 57.
19. ibid., p. 57.
20. ibid., p. 57.
21. ibid., p. 58.
22. ibid., pp. 57–58.
23. ibid., p. 58.
24. E. DEVEREUX JR., 'Parsons's Sociological Theory' in M. BLACK (ed.), op. cit., p. 20.
25. T. PARSONS, 'The Point of View of the Author', in M. BLACK (ed.), op. cit., p. 324.

26. ibid., p. 324.
27. H. BLUMER, *Symbolic Interactionism* (1969), Prentice-Hall, Englewood Cliffs, N.J., p. 143.
28. ibid., p. 141.
29. ibid., p. 142.
30. ibid., p. 142.
31. É. DURKHEIM, *Les Règles de la méthode sociologique* (1894), English trans. *The Rules of Sociological Method* (1938), Free Press, New York, p. 46.
32. A. GIDDENS (ed.), *Positivism and Sociology* (1974), Heinemann, London, pp. 3–4.
33. ibid., p. 3.
34. D. BLACK, 'The Boundaries of Legal Sociology', in D. BLACK and M. MILESKI (eds.), *The Social Organization of Law* (1973), Seminar Press, New York, p. 48.
35. A. GOULDNER, 'Anti-Minotaur: The Myth of a Value-Free Sociology', *Social Problems*, v. 9 (1962), pp. 199–213. See also H. BECKER, 'Whose Side are we on?', *Social Problems*, v. 14 (1967), pp. 239–247.
36. In P. FILMER, et al., op. cit.
37. A. GIDDENS, op. cit.
38. D. BLACK, op. cit., p. 53.
39. A. SCHUTZ, 'Concept and Theory Formation in the Social Sciences' in D. EMMETT and A. MACINTYRE (eds.), *Sociological Theory and Philosophical Analysis* (1972), Macmillan, London, p. 6.
40. S. NAGEL, *The Legal Process from a Behavioral Perspective* (1969), Dorsey, Illinois, p. 2.
41. A. SCHUTZ, op. cit., p. 11.
42. ibid., p. 11.
43. A. CICOUREL, *Method and Measurement in Sociology* (1964), Free Press, New York, p. 13.
44. S. NAGEL, op. cit., p. 13.
45. ibid., p. 14.
46. ibid., p. 15.
47. H. BLUMER, op. cit., p. 128.
48. ibid., p. 136.

Interpretive Sociology

1. See G. ALLPORT, *Becoming* (1955), Yale University Press, New Haven.
2. ibid., p. 8.
3. ibid., p. 12.
4. ibid., p. 19.
5. See G. H. MEAD, *Mind, Self and Society* (1934), Chicago University Press, Chicago.
6. See H. BLUMER, *Symbolic Interactionism* (1969), Prentice-Hall, Englewood Cliffs, N.J., especially pp. 1–60.
7. ibid., p. 3.
8. ibid., p. 4.
9. ibid., p. 80.
10. ibid., p. 27.
11. ibid., pp. 27–29.
12. ibid., p. 49.
13. See M. PHILLIPSON, 'Phenomenological Philosophy and Sociology', in P. FILMER, et al., *New Directions in Sociological Theory* (1972), Collier Macmillan, London; A. SCHUTZ, *The Phenomenology of the Social World* (1972), Heinemann, London.
14. For a good account of this 'imperàtive'.undertaken from a non-phenomenological standpoint, see D. MATZA, *Becoming Deviant* (1969), Prentice-Hall, Englewood Cliffs, N.J.
15. 'Rules' appear in inverted commas because of the particular status they enjoy in phenomenological sociology.

References 303

16. w. i. THOMAS, *The Child in America* (1928), Knopf, New York; and see w. i. THOMAS, 'The Behaviour Pattern and the Situation', in E. BURGESS (ed.), *Personality and the Social Group* (1929), University of Chicago Press, Chicago.
17. M. ATKINSON, 'Order in Court', Paper presented to the International Sociological Association Research Group on the Sociology of Law: Conference on the Sociology of Law and Legal Sciences, Balatonszeplak, Hungary, September, 1976, p. 18.
18. ibid., p. 19.
19. D. WALSH, 'Sociology and the Social World', in P. FILMER, et al., op. cit., p. 19.
20. ibid.
21. ibid., p. 21.
22. D. SUDNOW, *Passing On* (1968), Prentice-Hall, Englewood Cliffs, N.J.
23. ibid., p. 8.
24. ibid.
25. ibid.
26. ibid., p. 61.
27. ibid., p. 10.
28. See D. ZIMMERMAN, 'Fact as a Practical Accomplishment', in R. TURNER (ed.), *Ethnomethodology* (1974), Penguin Books, London; and D. ZIMMERMAN, 'The Practicalities of Rule Use', in J. DOUGLAS (ed.), *Understanding Everyday Life* (1974), Routledge & Kegan Paul, London.
29. D. ZIMMERMAN, 'The Practicalities of Rule Use', op. cit., p. 222.
30. ibid., p. 222.
31. ibid., p. 224.
32. ibid., p. 224.
33. ibid., p. 225.
34. D. ZIMMERMAN, 'Fact as a Practical Accomplishment', op. cit., p. 128.
35. ibid., p. 128.
36. ibid., p. 132.
37. ibid., p. 133.
38. ibid., p. 135.
39. w. G. CARSON, 'Some Sociological Aspects of Strict Liability and the Enforcement of Factory Legislation', *Modern Law Review* (1970), Vol. 33; and w. G. CARSON, 'Symbolic and Instrumental Dimensions of Early Factory Legislation' in R. HOOD (ed.), *Crime, Criminology and Public Policy* (1974), Heinemann, London.
40. M. SMITH and A. PEARSON, 'The Value of Strict Liability', *Criminal Law Review* (1969), pp. 5–16.
42. M. PHILLIPSON, 'Theory, Methodology and Conceptualization' in P. FILMER, et al., op. cit.
43. ibid., p. 103.
44. H. BLUMER, op. cit., p. 197.

Chapter VI: Law in the Presence of Sociology

1. See Chapter II, supra.
2. T. PARSONS (ed.), Introduction to M. WEBER, *The Theory of Social and Economic Organization* (1947), The Free Press, New York, p. 12.
3. See Chapter II, supra.
4. See Chapter II, supra.
5. K. RENNER, *The Institutions of Private Law* (1949), Routledge & Kegan Paul, London, p. 45.
6. See Chapter III, supra.
7. See Chapter III, supra.
8. See R. TURNER, 'Role-Taking Process versus Conformity', in A. ROSE (ed.), *Human Behaviour and Social Process* (1962), Routledge & Kegan Paul, London; and T. SHIBUTANI, 'Reference Groups and Social Control', in ibid.

304 *Sociological Inquiry and Legal Phenomena*

9. A favourite of Tony Crowle, Fellow of Linacre College, Oxford.
10. T. WILSON, 'Normative and Interpretive Paradigms in Sociology', in J. DOUGLAS (ed.), *Understanding Everyday Life* (1974), Routledge & Kegan Paul, London, p. 68.
11. J. GOLDTHORPE, 'A Revolution in Sociology?', *Sociology*, Vol. 7, No. 3, p. 449; and see the present author's reply, 'Reforms as Revolutions', *Sociology*, Vol. 9, No. 3.
12. J. GOLDTHORPE, op. cit., pp. 456–457.
13. ibid., p. 456.
14. Herbert Blumer noted that the processes of social interaction subtending the concept of norms and rules were 'necessary not only for their change but equally well for their retention in a fixed form', H. BLUMER, *Symbolic Interactionism* (1969), Prentice-Hall, Englewood Cliffs, p. 19. Similarly, we are also concerned not with the fact that 'norms' may change, but with the manner of existence of norms, whether changing or stable.
15. See J. L. AUSTIN, *Philosophical Papers* (1961), Oxford University Press, London; and R. TURNER, 'Words, Utterances and Activities', in R. TURNER (ed.), *Ethnomethodology* (1974), Penguin Books, London.
16. A. CICOUREL, *Cognitive Sociology*, op. cit., p. 102.
17. ibid., pp. 102–112; and see A. CICOUREL, *The Social Organization of Juvenile Justice* (1968), John Wiley, New York.
18. A. CICOUREL, *Cognitive Sociology*, op. cit., p. 102.
19. ibid., p. 31; and see generally pp. 11–41.
20. H. DREITZEL, Introduction to H. DREITZEL (ed.), *Recent Sociology* (1970), Collier Macmillan, London, p. xvii.
21. A. CICOUREL, *Cognitive Sociology*, op. cit., p. 31 (our emphasis).
22. H. BLUMER, *Symbolic Interactionism*, op. cit., p. 19.
23. J. BRUNER, *A Study of Thinking* (1965), Wiley, New York, discussed in D. L. WIDER 'On Meaning by Rule', in J. DOUGLAS (ed.), op. cit., p. 117.
24. ibid., p. 12.
25. R. BROWN, *Words and Things* (1958), Free Press, Illinois, p. 230.
26. See also pp. 262–264 below.
27. See, for example, D. ZIMMERMAN and M. POLLNER, 'The Everyday World as a Phenomenon', in J. DOUGLAS (ed.), op. cit.
28. P. MORRIS, 'Sociological Approach to Research on Legal Services', in P. MORRIS, et al., *Social Needs and Legal Action* (1973), Martin Robertson, London, p. 53.
29. S. REES, 'No more than Contact: An outcome of Social Work', *British Journal of Social Work*, vol. 4, No. 3 (1974).
30. See pp. 280–283 below.
31. For an illuminating discussion of organizations generally, see D. SILVERMAN, *The Theory of Organizations* (1970), Heinemann, London, and see P. SELZNICK, 'Foundation of the Theory of Organizations', *American Sociological Review*, Vol. 13, pp. 25–35.
32. E. MAYO, *The Social Problems of an Industrial Civilization* (1945), Harvard University Press, Boston.
33. See for instance D. BLACK, 'The Boundaries of Legal Sociology' in D. BLACK and M. MILESKI (eds.), *The Social Organization of Law* (1973), Seminar Press, New York.
34. D. BLACK, op. cit.
35. Central Council for Training and Education in Social Work, *Legal Studies in Social Work Education* (1974), London.
36. H. BLUMER, op. cit., especially pp. 140–152.
37. A. CICOUREL, *Method and Measurement in Sociology* (1964), Free Press, New York, especially pp. 39–72 and 189–224.

Recommended Reading

Chapter I: Discovering the Sociology of Law

General Texts:

v. AUBERT (ed.), *Sociology of Law* (1969), Penguin Books, London.

D. BLACK and M. MILESKI (eds.), *The Social Organization of Law* (1973), Seminar Press, New York.

w. EVAN (ed.), *Law and Sociology* (1962), Free Press, New York.

R. SCHWARZ and J. SKOLNICK (eds.), *Society and the Legal Order* (1971), Basic Books, New York.

R. J. SIMON (ed.), *Sociology of Law* (1968), Chandler, San Francisco.

The Debates:

J. DOUGLAS (ed.), *Understanding Everyday Life* (1971), Routledge & Kegan Paul, London.

D. EMMET and A. MACINTYRE (eds.), *Sociological Theory and Philosophical Analysis* (1972), Macmillan, London.

J. GOLDTHORPE, 'A Revolution in Sociology?', *Sociology*, Vol. 7, No. 3 (1973).

c. GRACE and P. WILKINSON, 'Reforms as Revolutions', *Sociology*, Vol. 9, No. 3 (1975).

A. RYAN (ed.), *The Philosophy of Social Explanation* (1973), Oxford University Press, London.

P. WINCH, *The Idea of a Social Science* (1967), Routledge and Kegan Paul, London.

Journals:

British Journal of Law and Society.
Law and Society Review.

Chapter II: Déjà Vu

Émile Durkheim:

É. DURKHEIM, *The Rules of Sociological Method* (English trans. 1938), Free Press, New York.

É. DURKHEIM, *The Division of Labour in Society* (English trans. 1933), Free Press, New York.

s. LUKES, *Émile Durkheim: His Life and Work* (1973), Allen Lane, London.

R. NESBIT, *The Sociology of Emile Durkheim* (1975), Heinemann, London.

Max Weber:

M. ALBROW, 'Legal Positivism and Bourgeois Materialism: Max Weber's View of the Sociology of Law', *British Journal of Law and Society*, Vol. 2, No. 1 (1975).

R. BENDIX, *Max Weber, An Intellectual Portrait* (1962), Doubleday, New York.

J. FREUND, *The Sociology of Max Weber* (1972), Penguin Books, London.

P. WALTON, 'Max Weber's Sociology of Law', in P. CARLEN (ed.), *The Sociology of Law* (1976), Sociological Review Monograph 23, University of Keele.

D. ATKINSON, *Orthodox Consensus and Radical Alternative* (1971), Heinemann, London.

A. GIDDENS, *Capitalism and Modern Social Theory* (1971), Cambridge University Press, London.

Chapter III: Law and Society

D. ATKINSON, *Orthodox Consensus and Radical Alternative* (1971), Heinemann, London.

M. BLACK, *The Social Theories of Talcott Parsons* (1961), Prentice-Hall, Englewood Cliffs, N.J.

T. BOTTOMORE and M. RUEBEL (eds.), *Karl Marx: Selected Readings in Sociology and Social Philosophy* (1961), Penguin Books, London.

W. CHAMBLISS (ed.), *Sociological Readings in the Conflict Perspective* (1975), Addison-Wesley, Reading, Mass.

W. CHAMBLISS and R. SEIDMAN, *Law, Order and Power* (1971), Addison-Wesley, Reading, Mass.

A. GOULDNER, *The Coming Crisis of Western Sociology* (1971), Heinemann, London.

T. PARSONS, *The Structure of Social Action* (1937), Free Press, New York.

K. RENNER, *The Institutions of Private Law* (1949), Routledge & Kegan Paul, London.

J. RAWLS, *A Theory of Justice* (1973), Oxford University Press, London.

P. SELZNICK, *T.V.A. and the Grass Roots* (1949), University of California Press, Berkeley.

Chapter IV: Law in Society

Z. BANKOWSKI and G. MUNGHAM, *Images of Law* (1976), Routledge and Kegan Paul, London.

J. CARLIN, *Lawyers on their Own* (1962), Rutgers University Press, New Jersey.

W. CHAMBLISS and R. SEIDMAN, *Law, Order and Power* (1971), Addison-Wesley, Reading, Mass.

J. GUSFIELD, *Symbolic Crusade* (1963), University of Illinois, Urbana.

T. JOHNSON, *Professions and Power* (1973), Macmillan, London.

S. LUKES, *Power* (1974), Macmillan, London.

See also the general texts cited for Chapter I.

Chapter V: Sociology in the Presence of Law

H. BLUMER, *Symbolic Interactionism* (1969), Prentice-Hall, Englewood Cliffs, N.J.

A. CICOUREL, *Method and Measurement in Sociology* (1964), Free Press, New York.

P. COHEN, *Modern Social Theory* (1968), Heinemann, London.

P. FILMER et al., *New Directions in Sociological Theory* (1972), Collier Macmillan London.

A. GIDDENS, *Positivism and Sociology* (1974), Heinemann, London.

D. MATZA, *Becoming Deviant* (1969), Prentice-Hall, Englewood Cliffs, N.J.

R. MERTON, *On Theoretical Sociology* (1949), Free Press, New York.

A. SCHUTZ, *The Phenomenology of the Social World* (1967), North-Western University Press, Chicago.

Chapter VI: Law in the Presence of Sociology

J. AUSTIN, *How To Do Things with Words* (1968), Oxford University Press, London.

R. BRAITHWAITE, *Scientific Explanation* (1968), Cambridge University Press, London.

A. CICOUREL, 'Basic and Normative Rules in the Negotiation of Status and Role', in A. CICOUREL, *Cognitive Sociology* (1973), Penguin Books, London.

H. GARFINKEL, *Studies in Ethnomethodology* (1967), Prentice-Hall, Englewood Cliffs, New Jersey.

C. GRACE and P. WILKINSON, *Negotiating the Law* (1978), Routledge & Kegan Paul, London.

K. POPPER, *Objective Knowledge* (1972), Oxford University Press, London.

R. TURNER, 'Words, Utterances and Activities', in J. DOUGLAS (ed.), *Understanding Everyday Life* (1971), Routledge & Kegan Paul, London.

A. SCHUTZ, 'Concept and Theory Formation in the Social Sciences', in D. EMMET and A. MACINTYRE (eds.), *Sociological Theory and Philosophical Analysis* (1972), Macmillan, London.

D. SUDNOW, *Passing On* (1968), Prentice-Hall, New Jersey.

R. RORTY (ed.), *The Linguistic Turn* (1970), University of Chicago Press, Chicago.

D. L. WIEDER, 'On Meaning by Rule', in J. DOUGLAS (ed.), *Understanding Everyday Life* (1971), Routledge & Kegan Paul, London.

D. ZIMMERMAN, 'Fact as a Practical Accomplishment', in R. TURNER (ed.), *Ethnomethodology* (1974), Penguin Books, London.